TAXING TO PREVENT INFLATION

TAXING TO PREVENT INFLATION

✦

Techniques for Estimating Revenue Requirements

By CARL SHOUP
MILTON FRIEDMAN
And RUTH P. MACK

New York : Morningside Heights
COLUMBIA UNIVERSITY PRESS
1943

COLUMBIA UNIVERSITY PRESS, NEW YORK

Foreign agents: OXFORD UNIVERSITY PRESS, Humphrey Milford, Amen House, London, E.C. 4, England, AND B. I. Building, Nicol Road, Bombay, India

MANUFACTURED IN THE UNITED STATES OF AMERICA

FOREWORD

THIS RESEARCH PROJECT and the publication of its findings were made possible by funds granted by the Carnegie Corporation of New York to the Institute of Public Administration. That Corporation is not, however, the author, publisher, or proprietor of this publication, and is not to be understood as approving by virtue of its grant any of the statements made or views expressed herein.

The work was accomplished under the auspices of a joint advisory committee of the Carnegie Corporation and the Institute of Public Administration, consisting of Henry Bruère, W. Randolph Burgess, Richard S. Childs, Luther Gulick, Roswell Magill, and Elihu Root, Jr. (Chairman). The committee held several meetings during the past year and a half, starting in May, 1941, at which the progress of the work was reported on and constructive suggestions were offered by the members. However, no responsibility for the statements made or views expressed in this volume is to be attributed to the members of the advisory committee, the Institute of Public Administration, or, as explained above, the Carnegie Corporation.

Active work was started in June, 1941, with the appointment of Milton Friedman and Ruth P. Mack as associate directors of the project. Harlan Bramble and George E. Lent performed valuable work as research assistants, and Dorothy Harmon, as secretarial assistant. A preliminary 51-page mimeographed report, "Amount of Taxes Needed in June, 1942, to Avert Inflation" was completed October 15, 1941. Copies were distributed within the United States Treasury and to those in other government departments who were working on the same problem. A series of conferences among technicians in the Treasury and these other departments was held during November and December, 1941, at which the mimeographed report was discussed and helpful suggestions made concerning the method of presentation and the basic data on defense expenditures, national income, and so on. This preliminary report is not reproduced in the present volume, since practically everything that was in it appears, in expanded form, in Parts I and II. Copies of the mimeographed report may be obtained, however, on request.

In forming an opinion on the availability of the income tax as a check to inflation, it was necessary to ascertain the extent to which collection at the source would be practicable. George E. Lent was assigned this topic, and his findings are presented in the *Journal of Political Economy* for October, 1942, pp. 719–37, "Collection of the Personal Income Tax at the Source."

We are deeply indebted to many individuals, but especially to Professor Luther Gulick; for it was through his interest in some preliminary exploration in this field undertaken by the present writer in the winter of 1940–41 and out of his subsequent discussions with the Carnegie Corporation that the present study developed. To the members of the advisory committee, also, for their helpful suggestions and encouragement, special thanks are due.

For the valuable suggestions and important factual material that they have so generously supplied, grateful acknowledgment is made to James W. Angell, Chester I. Barnard, V. Lewis Bassie, E. M. Bernstein, Roy Blough, Richard Breithut, Arthur F. Burns, Arthur R. Burns, John M. Clark, V. Frank Coe, Gerhard Colm, Morris A. Copeland, Lauchlin Currie, Mordecai Ezekiel, Oscar Gass, Murray Geisler, Milton Gilbert, Richard Gilbert, Raymond Goldsmith, George C. Haas, Robert Murray Haig, Seymour E. Harris, Albert Gailord Hart, George Jaszi, Hildegarde Kneeland, Martin Krost, Victor Perlo, Lawrence H. Seltzer, Harold D. Smith, Walter Salant, William Salant, Henry H. Villard, and H. D. White.

Special acknowledgment is due to those who pioneered in the task of estimating the timing and the size of a prospective inflationary rise in prices; their contributions are described in Part III by Milton Friedman. The necessarily critical analysis to which all such pioneering efforts need to be subjected and the areas of disagreement or differing interpretation that emerge (as indicated in Part III) do not obscure the invaluable service that these studies have rendered in facilitating further inquiry. Without them as a point of departure, the present research project, for instance, would have been severely handicapped both in estimating the amount of inflationary pressure and in the further task, not undertaken by these studies, of estimating the amount of additional taxation needed to eliminate that pressure.

The outlines of the approach that is taken in Part I were developed first by Milton Friedman; factual details were then assembled and the technique elaborated in successive conferences of the staff, so that there is a joint responsibility for the conclusions reached in this part of the volume. Some of the material in the section headed "Simplified Illustrations" in Part I has been taken from the note on the "Inflationary Gap" by Milton Friedman that appeared in the *American Economic Review* (June, 1942, pp. 314–20). We are indebted to the *American Economic Review* for permission to use this material. Ruth P. Mack undertook the task of exploring the possibilities of a month-to-month analysis that, unlike Part I, would include the effects of a general rise in prices, even though the deficiencies in the available data and the size of the task involved in moving from month to month over an extended period (which Part I does not attempt) indicated that a final estimate of tax needs could not be reached under this approach within the time and resource limitations of the present project. The resulting study is offered as a technique to be explored further with the aid of a much larger research staff. The remaining section, Part II, is an attempt by the present writer to analyze the chief considerations governing the choice among alternative taxes or sets of taxes. The last section of Part II, explaining the methods used to estimate the tax base, is the work of Milton Friedman and George E. Lent. While responsibility for the methods used and the conclusions reached in each of Parts II, III, and IV attaches to the respective writers, each section of course embodies suggestions made in the course of joint discussions.

The amount of taxation needed to avert inflation (or, more precisely, the amount of taxation consistent with an unchanged general level of prices under given assumptions concerning rationing, direct price control, and so on) is not capable of close determination; but the view taken in the present volume is that the problem must, after all, be recognized as a quantitative one, and that a more nearly correct estimate will be obtained if the necessary steps by which it is to be reached are made as explicit as possible instead of being hidden, or perhaps in large part not taken at all. It was the lack of any such detailed statement in the spring of 1941 that prompted the present study.

CARL SHOUP

Columbia University
New York City
December 1, 1942

CONTENTS

TABLES

CHARTS

TAXING TO PREVENT INFLATION

Part I

A TECHNIQUE FOR ESTIMATING THE AMOUNT OF TAXATION NECESSARY TO AVERT INFLATION

RISE IN PRICES AND "INFLATION"

IN A war economy, a general rise in prices may be initiated by any one of several forces. The nature of the stimulating factor determines whether or not the threatened rise can be averted by additional taxation.

Prices may be about to rise because production and transportation have become more difficult, so that each unit of finished product requires more man-hours of effort than before. Although time rates of wages remain unaltered, there is a rise in labor cost per unit, and possibly in other unit costs also. Under these circumstances it is unlikely that taxation can keep prices down; taking away purchasing power from consumers by taxation will not alter the fact that costs, per unit of finished output, will have risen. Prices must rise with costs unless the government provides subsidies. Taxation could put prices back to the original level if the consequent decrease in consumer demand brought about a sufficient reduction in the time-rate of wages, but this result appears highly unlikely. The only other possibility is that, at a lower level of production enforced by added taxation, unit costs would be lower even with no decrease in time-rates of wages, interest rate, and so on.

Similarly, if costs rise because the agents of production arbitrarily raise the price of their services by concerted action, taxation is no cure. The business world in general might refuse contracts unless promised a higher rate of money profits; labor might insist on higher rates of money wages. Whether the result were an increased money flow supported by an expansible credit system, or a decreased volume of production, or both, would depend in part on the tax policy that was adopted; but the rise in prices would be present in any case, in the absence of subsidies combined with rationing.

The kind of price rise that taxation can check is the one that is touched off by something other than a rise in money costs. Consumers, for whatever reason, increase their spendings, or the supply of goods and services available declines, or there is a combination of both. As a result, dealers find that they can raise their selling prices without having goods pile up on their shelves. Even under these circumstances, prices will not rise if the increase in consumer spendings is met by an increase in output without an increase in cost, or by a drawing down of inventories, or if goods and services are rationed. To the extent, however, that these preventives are not employed, taxation of consumers can be used to dampen their spending proclivities so that the threatened rise in prices is averted. Even in this case taxation may not be very effective if the new consumer spending is directed chiefly against goods the output of which cannot be increased, while that of many other kinds of goods can be increased; consumers may meet the tax merely by diminishing their consumption of the latter type. Unless the prices of these commodities fall, the general price level must rise. This situation implies an inability to transfer manpower, materials, and plant from the production of goods that are in ample supply to the production of the kind of goods that have risen in price. For short periods in the early stages of a defense program, taxation may in large measure be found powerless to control the general price level in a highly segmented, rigid-wage economy; but soon the scarcities become more general and the passage of time allows mobility of the factors of production to develop, while consumers resign themselves to diminished purchasing of very scarce goods. The present study assumed that this second stage would be closely approached, if not reached, in June, 1942.

In wartime, both of the price-raising forces noted in the preceding paragraph are likely to be present. Consumers are increasing their spendings, usually because their money income is increasing through new jobs, longer hours, or greater effort on old jobs, and through more intensive use of property that leads to higher net rents and profits. At the same time, the absolute amount of goods and services that can be offered for sale is diminishing, as government diverts manpower, plant, and materials to the production of tanks, ammunition, airplanes, and battleships that are not for sale. In the first stage of a defense program, to be sure, the absolute amount of consumer goods and services may increase as idle resources are utilized both for defense and to increase the output of consumer goods and services demanded by those employed in defense (and by those now employed to increase the output of consumer goods and services). Even in this stage there will be danger of a price rise if the rate of increase in output for consumers falls behind the rate of increase in their spendings. Soon, a second stage is reached: the output of consumer goods and services levels off, while total output (national income) and hence total money incomes continue to grow; the entire increase in production is for war use. At a third stage, total output and total money incomes stabilize, because the continually growing war effort can be fed only by drawing men and plant from civilian production, not by increasing total production. But a rise in prices is still possible, owing to the decline in consumer goods as more production is devoted to war.

If, in any of these stages, prices are allowed to rise, money incomes of course rise correspondingly (but not necessarily proportionately). Such a rise does not, obviously, reflect an increase in activity. Rather, it produces windfall profits, at least in the first instance. In these respects it differs from the price rise caused by increased difficulty of production (except that windfall profits may accrue in so far as the higher prices apply to some part of the output that is not affected by the new difficulties); and it resembles the rise that results from a concerted, arbitrary lifting of reward to the agents of production. In this study, "inflation" will be used to designate the kind of rise where "money income is expanding more than in proportion to income-earning activity." [1]

The present study will be concerned exclusively with the kind of inflation that threatens to arise from the discrepancy between consumer incomes and the volume of goods and services available. It may develop in any of the three stages of a defense or war program as described above. To distinguish it from the type of inflation that results from a concerted, arbitrary lifting of wages or profits, it might be called "atomistic inflation," or whatever term would best

[1] A. C. Pigou, "Types of War Inflation," *Economic Journal*, Dec., 1941, p. 439.

indicate the essential fact that it does not depend on concerted action by one or more groups of the agents of production. "Deficit-induced inflation"[2] is probably a better term for most purposes. In some circumstances the rise in prices can be averted only by increasing tax revenue faster than expenditures are increasing, thus diminishing the size of the annual deficit. When the third stage is reached, where the war effort can be expanded only by drawing man-power and plant away from the production of civilian goods, the resulting necessary decline in consumer spending can probably be obtained only by adding taxation in an amount somewhat larger than that decline. The added taxation is therefore somewhat larger than the increase in government expenditures, since the latter is about the same in dollar terms as the necessary decline in consumer spendings.

SIMPLIFIED ILLUSTRATIONS

The point can be clarified by a simple illustration (in which business taxes and net capital formation may be ignored). Let us assume that in Period I the war output is 40 units and consumer goods output 60 units, while consumer income is 100 units, of which 60 is spent, 15 saved, and 25 paid in personal taxes; if in Period II the war output is increased 10 units by cutting down consumer output 10 units, then the consumers may need to be taxed not 10 units more, but 15 units more to induce them to cut their purchases from 60 to 50; and the government's rate of deficit will have decreased by 5 units.

Moreover, the need for increased taxation to avert inflation may arise in Period II even though the government's total expenditure and even its deficit are unchanged from Period I. The consumers may have altered their ideas concerning the amount they are willing to save. Possibly some of the savings in the first period were only savings in transit, destined from the start to be spent, after a lag of a year or so. Perhaps the savings of the first period, added to the accumulations of preceding years, have made consumers feel so well protected that in Period II they decide to save a smaller part of their

[2] *Ibid.*, pp. 442 ff.

(unchanged) incomes. If they do so, prices will rise, and, incidentally, money incomes will then not remain at the level of the first period.

The possibility of this species of "deficit-induced" or "atomistic" inflation can be illustrated by reducing the illustrative data to tabular form.

Period I

A *Income received by consumers*	*Units*	B *Disposal of income by consumers*	*Units*
1. From government, chiefly for producing war goods and services	40	1. For purchase of consumer goods and services	60
2. From business, for producing consumer goods and services	60	2. For personal taxes	25
		3. Saved	15
Total	100	Total	100

Column A shows who pays the salaries, wages, interest, rent, and profit [3] that individuals count as their income. Column B shows how the individuals, en masse, dispose of their income. The 60 units paid out by business in Column A is payment for the production of the goods and services that are listed in Column B as sold to consumers. In a more realistic example, part of the amount paid out by business would be for the production of capital equipment, plant, and so on, over and above the amount needed for replacement purposes (this replacement amount is covered in the aggregate purchase price of consumer goods).

The total in Column A (income received) balances with the total in Column B (disposal of income), as indeed it must. But this bookkeeping, two-sides-of-the-coin kind of balance does not imply that the economic system is in balance in the sense that it contains no germs of disruption. It does not even show whether prices have been stable during the period it covers. If prices and incomes did rise month by month through that period, consumers may not have im-

[3] Distributed profit only; retained profits are ignored in this simplified example.

mediately raised their expenditures to the new high levels that might be expected eventually. Or a type of income, say, profits, of which a large part is saved may have been higher that it can remain in the face of competition from other income recipients. In order to determine whether the Period I data represent an equilibrium situation, it is necessary to go behind the books to the underlying forces, to engage in economic analysis, not simply in bookkeeping.

Suppose that in the next period, Period II, both the total volume of resources and the volume of resources employed by the government remain the same as in Period I. In that case, if prices remain the same, Column A of the books, income paid to consumers, must be the same for Period II as for Period I; and item B-1, amount spent on consumer goods and services, must be the same (since this item is simply A-2, resources employed by business, in another guise). This statement is based on (1) predictions about certain facts for the next period—the volume of resources and their use; and (2) specification of a goal—price stability. If the prediction is correct, and if the goal is attained, then the three items just noted (A-1, A-2, and B-1) must assume values that can be derived from the data for Period I, the predictions, and the goal.

There remain to be determined items B-2 and B-3, the amount paid by consumers in personal taxes and the amount saved. What values of these items are consistent with the predetermined values of the other items? In other words, what amount of taxes must be imposed so that consumers would, out of an income of 100 units in Period II, spend exactly 60? Given sufficient knowledge about the behavior of consumers, the distribution of income, and the effect of taxes, a table could be set up as shown on page 9.

The factors that would have to be considered in filling in the last two columns of such a table, the saving and spending columns, are varied and numerous. Among them are the relative prices in Period II (the general level of prices is given by the goal of price stability), the distribution of income, consumer expectations about future prices and future availability of goods, changes in the incomes of individual members of the community, the general sentiment toward saving and spending (for example, the extent to which consumers may think it

Illustrative Table of Income Disposition

If		So that disposable income was	Then consumers would	
Consumer income were	And taxes were		Save	Spend on consumer goods
100	0	100	27	73
100	5	95	23	72
100	10	90	19	71
100	15	85	15	70
100	20	80	12	68
100	25	75	9	66
100	30	70	7	63
* 100	35	65	5	60
100	40	60	4	56

patriotic to save or to spend), and the stock of consumer goods individuals have on hand. Another very important factor is the kind of tax levied. A progressive tax on income is likely to be associated with a larger volume of total spending out of a given aggregate disposable income than is a regressive tax on income; a tax on income is likely to be associated with a larger volume of spending than a tax of the same amount from the same people but based on amount spent instead of on amount received. The particular figures given in the table imply that saving in Period II is proceeding at a slower rate than in Period I; taxes of 25 out of an income of 100 go with savings of 9, not with savings of 15.

The line of the table marked with an asterisk is the only one that is consistent with the predictions for Period II and the goal of price stability. If taxes of the type assumed in drawing up the table were levied to yield 35 out of an income of 100, then, this table says, consumers would spend 60 and save 5; and 60 is the amount that must be spent if prices are to remain stable, since business will be using only 60 units' worth of resources to produce consumer goods and services. The internally consistent picture for Period II is therefore:

Period II

(*Unchanged Prices*)

A: *Income received by consumers*	*Units*	B: *Disposal of income by consumers*	*Units*
1. From government, chiefly for producing war goods and services	40	1. For purchase of consumer goods and services	60
2. From business, for producing consumer goods and services	60	2. For personal taxes	35
		3. Saved	5
Total	100	Total	100

This process of arriving at the answer that taxes must withdraw 35 units out of an income of 100 in order to achieve price stability is in many ways the reverse of the process whereby prices are actually determined. Consumers decide upon the proportions in which their incomes shall be distributed between saving and spending only after considering the taxes they must pay. Their decisions are felt in the market in the flow of purchasing power offered for goods; there results an upward or downward pressure on prices, as the flow of consumer goods is too small or too large to satisfy the demand at preexisting prices. This in turn is reflected in incomes received and through them in the volume of spending. The whole process is one of the mutual determination of incomes, prices, and output.

Suppose that, in Period II, tax rates are not raised enough to extract 35 out of an income of 100 but are left at a level that would extract only 25 out of an income of 100. At the preëxisting price levels and with incomes of 100, consumers would, if the table on p. 9 is correct, want to spend not 60 but 66. The value of goods available for sale, at preëxisting prices, is, however, only 60. The picture is, therefore, inconsistent. There are many ways in which the inconsistency can be resolved.

1. Prices may rise. With consumers trying to spend 66 units, while only 60 units of goods are available for purchase at preëxisting prices,

there is clearly an upward pressure on prices. But a rise in prices, with no other changes in the table, will not by itself lead to a consistent picture. A 10 percent price rise would raise the value of consumer goods to 66. But if this were to happen, aggregate income would no longer be 100. If, for the moment, other things are assumed unchanged, government would be spending 40, consumers would be spending 66, and aggregate income would be 106. The increase in the price of consumer goods means an increase in payments to some persons: in other words, an increase in the price of the resources—labor, for instance—that they are selling. If government, to compete, should have to raise the price paid to comparable persons (resources), total income paid would rise even more—at this stage, to 110. But under a higher price level, and with a higher total income, consumers will want to spend more than 66. In short, if consumers were to insist on spending 66 percent of income, and the government were to insist on employing 40 percent of the resources, the immovable object would be meeting the irresistible force.

The answer to this dilemma is, of course, that a price change does not involve merely a revaluation of goods and of incomes. Because of frictions and lags, price changes lead to a redistribution of incomes and to a change in spending-saving relationships. The initial increase in income from a rise in prices is likely to be concentrated in the hands of recipients of profits, a group that tends to receive fluctuating incomes and that is accordingly predisposed to save a disproportionately large part of any increase in income. Moreover, the receipt and spending of incomes are not simultaneous. All along the line, it takes time for recipients of higher incomes to readjust their spending patterns; it also takes time to make competitive readjustments of resource prices. While employing, in some sense, 40 percent of the real resources, government may not be disbursing 40 percent of the money income. Under conditions like the present, of course, this adjustment of resource prices is likely to be concealed. The initiating impulse arises from the government, not from the private sector. Government, in bidding away resources from the private sector, is raising prices, not lowering them, except to some extent in conscription and possibly in renegotiation of contracts. The share of money income disbursed by the government may well be larger than the share of resources employed by it.[4] The point is that the secondary changes in the private sector make this difference smaller than it would otherwise be. Finally, part of the increase in incomes will be taken away automatically by the existing tax system.

A price rise will lead to a consistent picture, therefore, by increasing the ratio of saving to spending, or the ratio of tax revenue to spending, or both, and by changing the ratio of the value of goods available for sale to the total value of goods produced. At the end of the period, the balanced books will show a percentage of income saved or devoted to taxes exactly equal to the percentage of income disbursed in the production of goods not available for sale. In the simplified example above, if government throughout disburses 40 percent of the income, the balanced books will show that individuals have saved and paid in taxes 40 percent of their income.

How large a price rise will be required depends on the speed with which readjustments take place. If, for example, when profits rise, labor is quick in demanding and successful in obtaining higher wages and consumers are quick in interpreting rising prices as a forerunner of further price rises and hence are as quick to increase their expenditures, a very large price rise may be required. Much will also depend on the nature of the tax system. With higher incomes, taxes will also be higher. If they are quickly responsive to a change in income and are progressive, they may take a higher percentage of aggregate income, and thereby contribute to a reduction in the percentage of income spent. Conversely, if slow to respond or regressive, the taxes may become a less important part of total income and make the adjustment more difficult.

2. Consumers may be forced to increase savings. The inconsistent picture sketched above would be resolved in a second way if sellers of consumer goods simply refused to raise prices despite the high level of demand (or were forbidden to do so), permitting their shelves to become empty. "Bare-shelves rationing" would then replace rationing through the price system and consumers would be forced to save 6 units more than they wanted to.

3. Consumers may decide to increase savings. Still another possi-

[4] These are inexact statements, touching on the extremely troublesome problem of defining the volume of real resources in other than monetary terms.

bility is that, aside from the increase in savings as a result of the redistribution of income, savings might increase because of a "buyers' strike"; unable to obtain the desired goods at accustomed prices, buyers might simply refuse to purchase at the higher prices.

These are the only ways in which, under the simplified assumptions used here, the inconsistency can be resolved. In the real world, of course, there are still other ways. A price rise might mean a larger output than the 100 assumed in this example, and hence more goods available for sale; it might mean a smaller proportion of resources going to government, and hence a larger proportion of the output available for sale; and goods can be made available for sale not only from current production but also by drawing on the stock of capital. Under the last method, the increase in goods sold does not increase incomes; it merely substitutes one form of asset for another—money for goods.

However the inconsistency is resolved, the books for Period II will necessarily be consistent at the end of the period. They might, for example, look somewhat as follows:

Period II

(*Higher Prices*)

A *Income received by consumers*	*Units*	B *Disposal of income by consumers*	*Units*
1. From government	60	1. For purchase of consumer goods and services	90
2. From business	90	2. For personal taxes	35
		3. Saved	25
Total	150	Total	150

These illustrative figures imply a 50 percent higher price level and a higher percentage of disposable income saved than is the case in a solution with constant prices. They also imply a tax system that, either because it is regressive, or because there is a lag between the increase in income and the increase in taxes, takes a smaller percentage of income in Period II than in Period I (25 percent in Period I, 23½ percent in Period II).

The amount of taxes actually collected, according to these illustrative figures, is the same as the amount that would be needed to keep prices constant. There is the important difference, however, that to keep prices constant at the Period I level required a tax system that would yield 35 out of 100 units of income; whereas the tax system implied above for Period II would raise only 25 out of 100 units of income. Taxes reach 35 only because of a 50 percent rise in income.

The examples above could be refined by adding assumptions concerning capital formation (additional to whatever replacement capital formation is implied in the figures on production of consumer goods and services), the part of business net income that is retained instead of being disbursed to consumers, increase in total output, and business taxes. Consideration of these matters is, however, postponed to the main body of analysis that follows.

DETAILED ANALYSIS OF CHANGE FROM OCTOBER, 1941 (ACTUAL) TO JUNE, 1942 (ESTIMATED)

The analysis made in the fall and winter of 1941 and presented to the Treasury Department in the preliminary memorandum referred to in the Foreword attempted to ascertain the relevant facts for October, 1941, and then to construct the situation for June, 1942, as it would be if prices were substantially unchanged from the October, 1941, level. The problem therefore became one of finding what amount of taxation, of a given kind, would make possible an unchanged price level, when accompanied by the other important variables (extent of direct price control and rationing, rate of government spending, and so on) in their given forms and amounts. No attempt was made to measure the extent of the price rise that would occur if the amount of taxation in June, 1942, were something short of what would be required to make possible an unchanged price level.

The analysis is in terms of changes in annual rates. In many stages of the computation this procedure makes unnecessary the determination of total amounts. At one stage of the analysis, for example, the national income is assumed to be flowing at an annual rate that is

$6.7 billion higher in June, 1942, than in October, 1941. The annual rate prevailing in October, 1941, did not therefore play a direct part in the computation, although it was, of course, useful in forming a judgment on the size of the prospective increase.

In the first set of computations, made in September, 1941, the initial date selected was June, 1941, the latest date for which information on most of the important items was available; but in computations made later it was possible to move the base to October, 1941. June, 1942, was selected as the terminal point in the first set of computations, because it was the nearest date that could be used without involving adjustments for seasonal factors. It was, however, retained, when the base month was changed to October, to permit comparison of the revised estimates with the original ones. The word "date" is used here instead of "period," although both the initial and terminal data are for a month; the data were regarded as reflecting the annual rate that was experienced (or forecast) on the average for the month.

The only reason for publishing the results of the study at this time, when the data have become obsolete, is to illustrate the possibilities and limitations of casting the analysis of an important problem in fiscal theory in terms that make use of available quantitative records or estimates. With this aim in view, the sources of the data used and the steps taken in adapting the data to the problem will be presented in considerable, though not exhaustive, detail. One of the methodological standards followed was to break the problem down into parts small enough so that a quantitative record or estimate could be obtained from specialists who had been concentrating their attention in each particular field. The aim was to minimize the amount of over-all estimating. If the work were to be redone now, still finer breakdowns with more accurate estimates could be employed, so swift has been the advance in compiling and publishing data on retail sales, inventories, and similar series. The data are presented here as they appeared at the time the computations were made in 1941; no attempt has been made to revise them in the light of the more precise and extensive information that has since become available.

PRELIMINARY ANALYSIS: JUNE, 1941, COMPARED WITH JUNE, 1942

A comparison of October, 1941, with the prospective June, 1942, in October dollars, indicated that the government would be spending at a substantially increased rate under the defense program. Employees (private and government), management, renters, security holders, and others to whom the government would be paying the money under this program would have correspondingly more to spend.

The problem would have been simplified if it could have been assumed that the total output of goods and services, measured in terms of October, 1941, prices, would increase by June, 1942, by about the same amount as the estimated increase in the government's defense demands. In fact, there seemed to be a fairly close approach to equality between these two amounts—increase in total output and increase in defense output—under the first set of computations, where June, 1941, was compared with June, 1942. Although this equality vanished under the October-to-June computations, it is instructive to notice how the first stages of the analysis develop when the two amounts are equal. The next four paragraphs will therefore proceed on this assumption, using June-to-June changes; the analysis will then return to the October-to-June framework, where it was found that the increase in defense needs was sure to be substantially greater than the increase in total production.

Under this assumption, that the increase in the output of goods and services would be equal to the increase in demands of defense, nothing would be produced to satisfy those increased civilian demands stimulated by the increased payments to employees and others by the government. Individuals would receive more money in June, 1942, than in June, 1941, because they would then be producing more goods and services; but these additional goods and services would not be available for civilian purchase. With more money to spend and no more civilian goods to spend it on, the income receivers of the country would, of course, be apt to bid up prices until the weaker or less willing civilian purchasers dropped out of the market.

Under these first crude assumptions concerning defense spending and total output, what amount of taxation in June, 1942, would be consistent with a price level unchanged from June, 1941? If by June, 1942, the government were taking away from the income recipients, in taxation, just as much more as it was giving out to them in increased expenditure for defense, then their total disposable income—income net after taxes, disposable for spending or saving—would be running merely at the same rate, in June, 1942, as it had been in June, 1941. And since the total output of civilian goods would be running at the same rate, there would be a *prima facie* case for believing an unchanged price level possible.

To illustrate, let it be assumed that both defense spending and defense production rose to an annual rate of $14 billion above the June, 1941, level. Under these circumstances, an approximate solution to the problem of how much taxation would be required to avert inflation could be obtained by assuming that civilian spending would be unchanged if civilian disposable income could be kept unchanged. The disposable income could be kept unchanged by taking away an additional $14 billion in taxes (annual rate) in June, 1942, compared with June, 1941. With one hand the government would be giving the civilian sector $14 billion a year more to spend in June, 1942, than in June, 1941, and with the other hand it would be taking back the $14 billion a year in added taxation. Consequently—so would run the simplified argument in its first stages—the civilian sector, spending the same number of dollars as a year before, for the same physical amount of goods and services as before, could expect about the same price level as before.

Where would the extra $14 billion in taxation come from? The tax system as of June, 1941, would be yielding some $6 billion more by June, 1942, for by that time the recently enacted Revenue Act of 1941 would be almost fully effective, and its higher rates and new taxes would be drawing on the greatly increased national income. Hence the requisite $14 billion increase in taxation, June, 1942, over June, 1941, could be obtained by passing another Revenue Act designed to bring in $8 billion more (annual rate) by June, 1942.

Virtually all of the assumptions made in this initial approach are so crude that there is an embarrassment of options in determining where the refining process should begin. A start will be made with the data on increase in defense spending and increase in total output.

INCREASE IN ANNUAL RATE OF TOTAL OUTPUT AND DEFENSE EXPENDITURES, OCTOBER, 1941, TO JUNE, 1942

The probable increase in total output (using "total output" as identical with national income in constant prices) was based primarily on the rate of increase that had been achieved in the preceding twelve months or so. The number of unemployed as of October, 1941, was considered only as a limiting factor (its limiting power qualified moreover by the existence of a labor reserve that is not revealed in the usual unemployment estimates), and not as itself a measure of the amount by which output could be increased within a short period. Recent experience suggested that, no matter how large the number of unemployed, the annual rate of output could be increased by no more than about $10 billion in a twelve-month period, at the price levels of October, 1941. In the twelve months ending June, 1941, total output (in constant prices) had increased about $12 billion. This had been accomplished by increasing civil, nonagricultural employment by some three and a half million, and average hours per week in manufacturing industries by about 10 percent.[5] But the task of increasing the annual rate of output would be harder in the 1941–42 period. The additional man-hours would be worked primarily by the less skilled, since they were the ones who in October, 1941, were unemployed or working short hours. Scarcity of materials and limitations in plant space and equipment were appearing at an increasing number of points. The necessity of using substitute materials was tending to increase the real cost per unit of finished product. And some empirical evidence was given by the slackening rate at which the Federal Reserve Board index of production (see Table I) had been increasing in May–August, 1941. Moreover, monthly data on income payments, converted to a national-income basis and deflated by the Bureau of Labor Statistics cost-of-living index, indicated that the annual rate of real output increased during the four-month period by only $2.2 billion (October, 1941, prices), implying an increase in the annual

[5] *Survey of Current Business,* Aug., 1941, pp. S–7, S–9, and Sept., 1941, p. S–9. In October, 1941, the average hours worked per week in manufacturing were virtually unchanged from June, 1941. Civil nonagricultural employment, unadjusted, was one million higher. *Ibid.,* Jan., 1942, pp. S–7, S–9.

rate during an eight-month period (October to June) of only $4.4 billion.

In view of these considerations, the increase in total output (national income) from October, 1941, to June, 1942, was set at a maximum of $6.7 billion, equivalent to an increase of $10 billion over a year, and a minimum of $3.0 billion ($4.5 billion over a year). Two intermediate estimates, $4.4 billion and $5.3 billion, were made. Just where the figure would fall in practice would depend not only on the given technical possibilities of increasing various types of production —defense goods and services, consumer durables, consumer nondurables, and so on—but also, of course, on the force of the new currents of demand set in motion by the change to a defense economy. To give but one illustration: If the kind of goods and services needed for defense could be obtained for the most part not from the pool of idle resources but only from resources already active in civilian production; and if the civilian buyers, dispossessed of some of their usual goods and services by this incursion of the military, found no very attractive substitutes in whatever the idle-resources pool could turn out, then a low figure for increase in national output would have to be assumed. More explanation of these variations is given on pp. 23–31 below in the section on "diversion." The point to emphasize here is that at least four sets of computations, four answers to the question, "how much taxation?" were thus implied at the outset.

The rate at which defense spending would be running in June, 1942, was based chiefly on official forecasts and on the known rate of expenditure in recent months.[6] "Defense expenditures" included those so designated in the budget, plus expenditures by government-owned corporations for defense, plus purchases for war purposes by belligerents. The total was estimated to have been at an annual rate of $11.8 billion in June, 1941, and $21.2 billion only four months later, in October. For June, 1942, it appeared likely that purchases by belligerents would decline to $0.7 billion, from an estimated $1.7 billion in October, 1941, and that defense expenditures of the government corporations would rise to $2.5 billion, from $1.5 billion in October. Budget expenditures for defense were expected to reach an annual

[6] In addition, use was made of confidential estimates, both for budgetary and nonbudgetary expenditures, in the Treasury and the Bureau of the Budget.

TABLE I

FEDERAL RESERVE BOARD
INDEX OF INDUSTRIAL PRODUCTION

(Physical Volume)
(1935–39 = 100) [a]

	ADJUSTED		UNADJUSTED	
1940	*Index*	*Increment*	*Index*	*Increment*
January	122		117	
February	116	–6	113	–4
March	113	–3	112	–1
April	112	–1	112	0
May	116	4	117	5
June	122	6	121	4
July	122	0	120	–1
August	124	2	124	4
September	127	3	132	8
October	130	3	135	3
November	134	4	136	1
December	139	5	136	0
1941				
January	140	1	135	–1
February	144	4	140	5
March	147	3	144	4
April	144	–3	144	0
May	154	10	155	11
June	159	5	160	5
July	160	1	159	–1
August	161	1	162	3
September	161	0	167	5
October	164	3	168	1
November	166	2	166	–2

[a] *Federal Reserve Bulletin,* Dec., 1941, p. 1263.

rate of $27 billion to $28 billion in June, 1942. Total defense spending was therefore estimated at approximately $30 billion to $31 billion, or $9 billion to $10 billion above the October, 1941, rate. These estimates apparently were based on an assumption of little or no rise in prices, and so could be fitted, without adjustment on this score, into the framework of the present analysis. The $10-billion figure was used in three of the four series based upon the four estimates of increase in production given on p. 19 above. The $9-billion figure was used in the fourth series in combination with a particular estimate on the amount of diversion of resources from civilian production to defense production, in a manner to be explained below.[7]

CHANGES IN CIVILIAN SPENDING

With the increase in total output and the increase in defense expenditures given, it was convenient to turn next to refining the assumption, already noted, that the volume of civilian spending would remain unchanged if the volume of consumer disposable income remained unchanged (with the price level unchanged). This assumption, together with the assumption of an unchanged volume of consumer disposable income, had been selected from among many possibilities because it fitted the initial postulate that the increase in defense spending would equal the increase in total output. When, under examination, this equality vanished, it seemed best to investigate first the assumption that civilian spending would be unchanged if disposable income were unchanged. The other assumption, that disposable income would be unchanged, was retained for the time being because it was not clear that any other supposition concerning disposable income would be both more nearly correct and more convenient for subsequent steps in the analysis.

The assumption of unchanged spending (if disposable income were unchanged) was soon discovered to be untenable for a number of reasons. In the first place, an important part of "civilian spending," as that term is used here, is carried on by state and local governments; and federal nondefense spending is another part. Variations in these spendings need have no relation to variations in total consumer disposable income. Secondly, another important part of civilian spending is spending by business in increasing its capital equipment (including inventories), or negative spending, through permitting its capital equipment to be used up. (The spending that it needs to do if it is to keep its plant, equipment, and inventories up to their initial level while filling orders is reflected in the computation of consumer

[7] See pp. 23–24.

spendings.) The rate of this investment spending—or, when capital equipment decreases, negative spending—does not necessarily remain stable just because total consumer disposable income remains stable. Indeed, a leveling-off of consumer disposable income after a period of increase is apt to induce a decline in the rate of investment spending. In the third place, the consumers—families, single individuals, and institutions—may be inclined to alter the amount of their spending even if their own disposable income remains stable.

Governmental nondefense spending.—The item of federal nondefense spending was dismissed, after being considered independently, for it seemed fairly certain that the total amount of such spending would not be appreciably different in June, 1942, from what it had been in October, 1941, provided the price level did not rise. State and local spendings were omitted, not so much because they might not change as because it seemed likely that any significant change would be matched, roughly, by a corresponding change in tax revenue and other current receipts. This conclusion rested partly on recent experience that showed very little change in state and local debt outstanding.[8] A minor change in public works expenditures is, however, allowed for (p. 48).

Investment spending, or disinvestment, by business had to be estimated separately, in a manner to be described on pp. 40–51.

Consumer spending.—Consumer spending could be expected to change, although consumer disposable income stayed the same (increased income with correspondingly increased personal taxes) for two general classes of reasons: The distribution of disposable income among individuals would be different in June, 1942, from what it had been a year earlier, and therefore specific individuals would have different disposable incomes at the two dates; and any given person who did have the same amount of disposable income at both dates might change his attitude toward spending, owing to changes in his attitude toward prospective shortages of consumer goods, changes in his access to installment credit, and so on.

It was more convenient to study first the reasons why consumer

[8] U.S. Dept. of Commerce, *State and Local Government Debt: 1940* (Special Study No. 13, April, 1941), Table 2, p. 9, showing a total state and local gross debt less sinking funds of $17.7 billion in 1932, $17.6 billion in 1937, and $18.2 billion in 1940.

spending might change even if every individual's disposable income were the same in June, 1942, as in October, 1941. The first reason considered is the check to spending caused by the unavailability of certain consumer goods and services owing to the diversion of resources to defense.

1. Diversion of resources to defense. A defense program of a given size may be accomplished either by utilizing idle resources or by drawing away resources that have been occupied in civilian production. To the extent that the second option must be exercised, and manpower, plant, and materials must be diverted from the production of certain kinds of civilian goods and services to defense, consumers must change their buying habits (ignoring for the moment possible changes in net investment). They must substitute goods and services of a kind that can be produced by drawing on the pool of unemployed resources (unless the war program moves so fast that it absorbs all of that pool), or they must expend their purchasing power in rising prices, or they must save more. If, for instance, the war program calls for 100 units; if the pool of unemployed manpower and unutilized plant can produce 200 units in all, but only 60 units of the kind the war program must use; then consumers must give up 40 specific units. The question then arises how many units they will purchase by calling on the remaining pool of idle resources. Presumably they will not buy a full 40 units; the chances are that the idle pool either cannot produce quite the same kind of units the consumers used to buy, or can do so only at a higher cost. The 40 units given up by the consumers to the war program is a measure of what is here called "diversion"; and the difference between the 40 units and what consumers will purchase from the pool of idle resources measures the decrease in consumer spending due to diversion.

The maximum possible increase in the annual rate of total production, October, 1941, to June, 1942, was estimated at \$6.7 billion as explained on p. 19. Defense spending, it was estimated, would increase by \$9 billion at the least. Under these assumptions, the smallest possible diversion of active civilian resources would be \$9 billion minus \$6.7 billion, or \$2.3 billion. The diversion could be this small only if the government increased its defense spending by methods that absorbed directly all the unemployed and the idle plant capacity that could be absorbed in any case within the period in question, and hence had to divert from the civilian sector only the remaining $2.3 billion. At the other extreme the diversion could be as high as $10 billion: The government might increase defense expenditures by $10 billion, and, in doing so, might find no use at all for any of the idle men and capital from which the maximum $6.7 billion increase in total output could come. These idle resources would all go into the production of civilian goods, so far as they proved usable at all, under these assumptions; and the government would spend its $10 billion on men and capital drawn out of active use in civilian industry. Still another, wider concept of diversion is feasible: The government might find that it had to discard some of the labor and capital it was using on the basic date, and draw from the active civilian sector for replacements. Under the circumstances as they appeared in the fall of 1941, however, such a shuffling of resources seemed unlikely.

The possibility, in fact the probability, of a diversion greater than the minimum is important with respect to possible changes in the amount of money that consumers want to spend. They can, to some extent, draw on unemployed labor and capital for substitutes, and if the substitutes are close, there will be correspondingly little effect on the volume of consumer spending. This point is illustrated by the substitution of glass for tin and steel in the production of beer containers. Active tin-making and steel-making agents are drawn into defense; hitherto idle glass-making agents are drawn into civilian production; the two sets of agents are so closely substitutes for one another that the effect on consumer spending of the diversion of tin-making and steel-making agents to defense is not noticeable. But where the diverted civilian agents have no close substitutes among the idle agents, some estimate of the effect on consumer spending is needed. Conceivably, consumers might refuse to spend on anything else at all, but this seems improbable.

The agents drawn from the idle pool may be able to operate with a degree of efficiency that does not imply an appreciable rise in prices of the substitute commodities and services from their hitherto prevailing levels. On the other hand, they may be so inefficient as to be usable only at a higher price for each unit of finished product (the time-wages, the rate of interest, etc., remaining unchanged); in this case, the consumers' resort to substitutes tends to raise the price level.

The finished product that the consumer gets from the hitherto idle agents may be exactly the same as that produced by the agents now taken over by the government. This result, too, probably implies that the civilian sector pays higher prices. The government may divert the efficient textile mills to defense use, forcing the consumers to call on hitherto submarginal plants and labor for their textiles.

To the extent that consumers do not purchase from the pool of idle resources as much as they have been stopped from purchasing by diversion, there is a corresponding shrinkage in the volume of total production, as compared with the maximum levels tentatively assumed at first. The consumers' refusal to shift to new spending channels tends to leave more unemployed labor and capital at the terminal date than was provisionally assumed. This result was taken into account by selecting three likely levels of diversion and associating the largest amount of diversion with the smallest amount of increase in total output (Assumption D), the next largest with the next smallest (Assumption B), and the third, the smallest figure on diversion, with the two top figures on increase in output (Assumptions A and C). And, by methods to be described below, a smaller amount of consumer spending (out of an unchanged disposable civilian income) was associated with a higher level of diversion, and hence with a lower level of output.

The estimates of increase in diversion were necessarily rough. They were based chiefly on two sources: unpublished estimates made by the Office of Price Administration and certain other government agencies of prospective gross curtailment of various categories of producer and consumer goods; and unpublished estimates by the Bureau of Labor Statistics that total employment in defense industries would be 3 million higher in June, 1942, than in June, 1941, and that half of this increase would represent diversion of workers from civilian employment, the civilian industries to draw in, meanwhile, about half a million new workers in the same period. The increase in diversion was estimated to range from $4 billion to $8 billion if defense spending increased $10 billion, and to be $4 billion if defense spending increased only $9 billion. The four sets of estimates for the three items described thus far are summarized in Table II.

TABLE II

ASSUMED INCREASES IN TOTAL OUTPUT (NATIONAL INCOME) AND DEFENSE SPENDING, AND DIVERSION, JUNE, 1942, OVER OCTOBER, 1941

Annual Rates, in Billions of Dollars

	ALTERNATIVE SETS OF ASSUMPTIONS			
	A	*B*	*C*	*D*
1. Assumed increase in total output	5.3	4.4	6.7	3.0
2. Assumed increase in defense spending	9.0	10.0	10.0	10.0
3. Assumed diversion to defense	4.0	7.0	4.0	8.0

The final step in arriving at the influence of diversion on consumer spending was to split the diversion between diversion from consumer spending and diversion from net capital formation (that is, net investment spending by business). Consumer spending is so much larger in total than net capital formation, even when services and perishable goods are excluded, that the larger part of the total diversion might appear necessarily to come from consumption. But the estimates by the Office of Price Administration and others on curtailment suggested that net capital formation would bear the larger share of diversion. A compromise was employed whereby consumption bore the larger share under Assumptions A, B, and C (see Table II), and net capital formation the larger share under Assumption D, where the increase in total output was assumed to be only $3 billion and diversion was assumed to be at its highest level, $8 billion. The result is shown in Table III.

The gross amount of goods and services that consumers would have to forego in June, 1942, compared with October, 1941, was therefore estimated to range from $2.5 billion to $4.0 billion (annual rate). How much of this would consumers try to replace by spending on other things? It seemed likely that in so far as they would have been spending money borrowed specifically for the spending, they would

TABLE III

ALLOCATION OF DIVERSION BETWEEN CONSUMPTION AND NET CAPITAL FORMATION

Annual Rates, in Billions of Dollars

	ALTERNATIVE SETS OF ASSUMPTIONS CONCERNING INCREASE IN OUTPUT AND DEFENSE SPENDING, AND DIVERSION (SEE TABLE II)			
	A	*B*	*C*	*D*
3. Assumed diversion to defense	4.0	7.0	4.0	8.0
a. From consumption	2.5	4.0	2.5	3.0
b. From net capital formation	1.5	3.0	1.5	5.0

not, when blocked by the unavailability of the article, borrow anyway to spend on something else. A consumer who contemplates borrowing in order to buy some expensive consumer durable, like an automobile, and who finds that it cannot be bought is unlikely to borrow anyway to buy nondurables. Moreover, it seemed likely that whatever decrease in installment credit might be shown in June, 1942, below that of October, 1941, would be accounted for almost entirely by the unavailability of durable goods. The restrictions on the granting of installment credit that had been introduced by the Federal Reserve Board on August 21, 1941, were mild compared with the force that was evidently going to be exerted by direct action through allocations and priorities.[9] Therefore, if the amount of the decrease in consumer appeal to installment credit could be estimated and subtracted from the gross decrease in consumer spending represented by diversion, the remainder could be treated separately as cash purchases of goods that must be foregone because of diversion; and no doubt a significant proportion of those cash purchases, in contrast to the installment-credit-financed purchases, would be replaced by spending on other things.

The answer sought, on installment credit, was not the difference in the amount of such credit outstanding on the two dates; it was instead the difference in the amount by which the outstanding credit was increasing. For example, the amount of credit outstanding on June

[9] *Federal Reserve Bulletin,* Sept., 1941, pp. 839 ff., "Regulation W."

30, 1942, might be \$8 billion—or \$3 billion—compared with, say, \$6 billion outstanding on October 31, 1941, but neither figure would tell anything of the pressure on prices in either month. If the amount outstanding were \$8 billion on June 1, 1942, and remained so every day during June, the net spending attributed to installment credit during June, 1942, would be zero. Some persons would have been spending, to be sure, but others would have been saving an equal amount (evidenced by payments on their installment debts). But if the amount outstanding were \$7 billion on June 1 and rose regularly to \$8 billion on June 30, consumer spending of installment credit would be counted at \$1 billion for that month, or at an annual rate of \$12 billion. This kind of spending, it will be recalled, is not out of the consumer's income: it is the spending of borrowed money. The amount of such spending by the consumer is likely, however, to bear some relation to the size of his income; and the spending of course creates income for those who make and sell the objects bought on this credit.

The question may be raised whether it is not necessary to ascertain also the extent to which the rate of increase in the initial and terminal months is composed of a gross increase on the part of those who are purchasing. A given net result may reflect either a large or a small volume of purchases. If the installment credit outstanding were \$5 billion on October 1 and \$6 billion on October 31, it might be that purchases on the installment plan during October were, say, \$3½ billion, which would imply repayments of \$2½ billion on contracts outstanding October 1 (\$6 billion minus \$3½ billion new purchases leaves \$2½ billion old contracts outstanding October 31, indicating repayment of the other \$2½ billion). Or it might be that purchases were only \$2 billion, and repayments \$1 billion. If the kind of durable goods purchased were to be completely unavailable in the second period, would it not make a difference, in estimating total consumer spending in the second period, whether the purchases had been running at a rate of \$3½ billion or \$2 billion in the earlier month? If they had been \$3½ billion, a correspondingly larger absolute decrease would be registered in such loan-financed purchases in the second period (June, 1942)—an important consideration in view of the likelihood that this kind of purchase is not, when blocked by unavailability of goods, likely to turn to other fields.

Logically, it would indeed be necessary to study separately the amount of purchases. This would involve separating into two parts the difference between the rates at which installment credit outstanding was changing in the two months (the increase during June, 1942, minus the increase during October, 1941): (1) The difference between purchases financed by installment credit in the two months, and (2) the difference between repayments in the two months. Both items affect consumer spending, and the two together give the net effect on consumer spending of changes in installment credit. But the first item is the only one directly relevant to diversion; it gives the reduction in installment-financed expenditures for goods made unavailable. The second item, the difference between repayments, would logically be taken account of elsewhere in the analysis.

So refined an analysis was not justified, however, in view of the sparseness of the data on installment credit. Consequently, the entire installment credit item was treated at this point as a reflection of diversion. This treatment implicitly assumes that the difference in repayments would be negligible relatively to the difference in purchases—an assumption that did not seem entirely without foundation in view of the earlier assumptions that the unavailability of goods would be the major factor affecting the use of installment credit.[10]

The total amount of consumer installment credit outstanding at the end of October was about $6 billion.[11] Of this total, consumer durables likely to be affected severely by priorities and allocations—chiefly automobiles and household appliances—probably accounted for more than one half, or $3 billion.[12] From what is generally known about the terms of the credit outstanding, it appeared that if no further installment credit at all were granted for automobiles and appli-

[10] See p. 27.

[11] *Survey of Current Business*, Sept., 1941, p. 9, says the amount outstanding at the end of June, 1941, was approximately $5.8 billion; and the *Survey* for Feb., 1942, p. 32, that it reached a record peak of $6.1 billion at the end of August, 1941, and declined to about $5.6 billion by the end of the year.

[12] *Survey of Current Business*, Sept., 1941, pp. 9 ff. See Duncan M. Holthausen, in collaboration with Malcolm L. Merriam and Rolf Nugent, *The Volume of Consumer Installment Credit, 1929–38*, pp. 45, 98.

ances, about three-quarters of the consumer debt outstanding on their account would be retired within a year.[13] Thus, at the maximum, the annual rate of absolute decrease in the amount of credit outstanding on automobiles and appliances would be $2.25 billion, during the year October, 1941 to October, 1942, and hence during June, 1942. The total amount outstanding, which had been increasing at a rate of about $1.3 billion a year during the period July, 1940–June, 1941, was by October apparently changing little. Consequently, if a decrease of $2.25 billion (annual rate) were attributed to June, 1942, by coupling with the assumption above a further assumption of no change in credit outstanding during June on items other than automobiles and appliances, then the net change in the rate of change in total credit outstanding would also be minus $2.25 billion. But this figure, although not strictly the maximum possible, represented assumptions that seemed too drastic on the side of net curtailment of credit outstanding. The various stages by which this first rough estimate was corrected will not be given here, but the final result was a net change in rate of change of minus $1.2 billion, raised slightly for two of the sets of assumptions, as indicated in Table IV.

From the total diversion of consumer goods and services to defense, there was subtracted the decline in the rate at which consumers would be spending installment credit; the remainder was cash spendings halted by diversion. Some of these cash spendings were down payments on purchases made chiefly on installment credit; some had no connection with it. Credit sales like those made on open account with department stores were counted here as cash sales, owing to the short term of the credit.

It was assumed that by far the larger part of the money blocked from cash purchases in June, 1942, by diversion would be spent by the consumer, without appreciable delay, for other things, if he could get them at no rise in prices over October, 1941. The effect of diversion on consumer spending, under each of the four sets of assumptions concerning increases in output and defense spending, and diversion, are summarized in Table IV. The net result was that consumers, even

[13] Holthausen, Merriam, and Nugent, *op. cit.*, p. 46; Gottfried Haberler, *Consumer Installment Credit and Economic Fluctuations*, chart on p. 93.

with an unchanged disposable income distributed in the same way in both periods, would be spending from $1.4 billion to $2.1 billion less (annual rate) in June, 1942, than in October, 1941.

TABLE IV

EFFECT OF DIVERSION ON CONSUMER SPENDING, JUNE, 1942, COMPARED WITH OCTOBER, 1941

Annual Rates, in Billions of Dollars

	ALTERNATIVE SETS OF ASSUMPTIONS CONCERNING INCREASE IN OUTPUT AND DEFENSE SPENDING, AND DIVERSION (SEE TABLE II)			
	A	*B*	*C*	*D*
3. a. Change in consumer spending representing diversion, consumer goods to defense	–2.5	–4.0	–2.5	–3.0
(i) Change in net spending of installment-credit money (i. e. change in rate of change of installment credit outstanding)	–1.2	–1.5	–1.2	–1.3
(ii) Change in spending of cash (i. e. the negative items represent gross blockage of cash spending resulting from diversion)	–1.3	–2.5	–1.3	–1.7
4. Consumer spending (cash) on other goods, induced by gross blockage of cash spending on usual goods (item 3(a) (ii))	1.1	1.9	1.1	1.5
5. Net change in consumer spending caused by diversion of consumer goods (or the agents producing them) to defense (item 3(a) minus item 4)	–1.4	–2.1	–1.4	–1.5

2. Consumer buying in anticipation of shortages. In any given period, consumers may spend an abnormally large proportion of their current income, for fear that diversion will become worse, that priorities and allocations will make still more goods unavailable.

Conversely, they may spend an abnormally small proportion of their current income because they are recuperating financially from such a period. Recent experience has indicated that this kind of fluctuation in consumer spending takes place over fairly short intervals of time. A burst of anticipatory buying seems to have occurred in July and August of 1941, followed by normal or even subnormal spending in September and October, 1941.

The buying to which "anticipatory" here refers is all "cash" buying, that is, buying other than on the installment plan; the estimates above on change in the spending of installment-credit money—Table IV, 3a (i)—are intended to embrace all influences playing on installment credit.

"Normal," in relation to this discussion of anticipatory buying, refers to the ratio of consumer spending to disposable income that might have been expected, first, on the basis of historical data, assuming the disposable-income level had been in effect several months at least, and secondly, with an adjustment downward because the disposable-income level had in fact been rising in the months immediately prior to October, 1941, and consumers might not yet have adapted their spending to the unfamiliar level of income.[14] If the level of cash spending differed from this (adjusted) normal level, the cause was to be sought in anticipatory buying arising from fear of shortages, or, secondarily, in the defense-bond campaign.[15]

Little statistical basis exists for estimating the extent of anticipatory buying thus defined; the chief reason for considering it at all was to be certain that no obvious, unmistakable indication was being overlooked. This attempt was probably justified, for it called to attention the fact that September and October, 1941, were months of abnormally low pressure on prices, that is, abnormally low consumer spending, considering the current volume of consumer income, even after allowing for the fact that much of the increase had been recent. Unless there could be found some reason for expecting the same abnormality the following June, that month would have to be considered, with respect to this particular point, one in which consumers would be spending more than in October, 1941, even assuming an un-

[14] See p. 34.
[15] See p. 35.

changed consumer disposable income. No such reason was found. The September–October slackening in buying appeared to be a reaction from heavy anticipatory buying in the July–August period. A similar reaction for June, 1942, would imply a wave of abnormally high consumer spending in the early months of 1942. The study, to be complete, would have had to compare October, 1941, with every month following it, not merely with June, 1942; and the net result over the period might then have been found to be about the same whether June, 1942, was assumed to be close to normal, following months themselves close to normal, or whether it was assumed to be abnormally low, following months abnormally high. ("High" and "low" refer to percentage of consumer disposable income spent.) Consequently the level of spending in June, 1942, was, on the whole, assumed to be about normal in relation to the unchanged disposable income assumed for that period. But this "normal" was adjusted downward to take account of the decline to be anticipated because of diversion actually in operation, as given in Table IV, item 5—"actually in operation" to be distinguished from diversion anticipated, which is the underlying cause of anticipatory buying. And the estimate was then marked up slightly for the two high-diversion sets of assumptions (B and D) to allow for some positive anticipatory buying in those cases.

The low level of consumer spending in October, 1941, is indicated by the two series of data on retail sales in Table V. Part of the reason for this was doubtless the tendency for cash spending to lag a bit until consumers' spending habits could catch up with their new high level of incomes; this factor is accounted for separately below. But most of it seems to have been a reaction from the anticipatory buying of the preceding months.

Apparently, despite an increase of some $5 billion (annual rate) in consumer disposable income, consumer outlay in October, on a seasonally adjusted basis, was about the same as, or $1 or $2 billion lower than in June,[16] whereas it might have been expected to be at

[16] R. B. Bangs, "The Changing Relation of Consumer Income and Expenditure," *Survey of Current Business*, April, 1942, p. 8, gives seasonally adjusted annual rates of disposable income of $89.1 billion in June, 1941, and $93.0 billion in October, 1941, and of consumption expenditure of $73.7 billion in June and $72.6 billion in October. (These data were not available when the computations for the present study were made.)

TABLE V

RETAIL SALES, JUNE–OCTOBER, 1941 [a]

	DEPARTMENT OF COMMERCE SALES OF ALL RETAIL STORES			FEDERAL RESERVE DEPARTMENT STORE SALES	
	Index		*Total Sales*	*Index*	
	Adjusted	Unadjusted	(millions of dollars)	Adjusted	Unadjusted
June	138.0	145.1	4,576	104	100
July	142.4	134.6	4,441	115	79
August	149.0	139.7	4,596	134	106
September	136.2	140.6	4,472	116	125
October	131.0		4,650	104	111

[a] These are the figures that were available at the time the study was made. They have since been revised.

least a billion dollars higher, after allowing for some lag in spending under a rising income.

The net result was an assumption that consumer spending would be higher, in June, 1942, if prices were unchanged, by $2.2 billion under assumptions A and C, by $2.3 billion under D, and $2.4 billion under B, than in October, 1941, assuming unchanged disposable consumer income. These changes were attributable to the anticipatory element alone; [17] they were to be added (algebraically) to the changes estimated to result from actual diversion as given above, and to changes from other causes, to be discussed below.

3. Elimination of lag in adjustment to changing income. Consumers' disposable incomes had been increasing rapidly in the months before October, 1941; but in the months preceding June, 1942, they would not have been increasing at all, under the basic assumption used in these computations. If it takes some time (say, a few months) for an increase in disposable income to produce the volume of consumer spending that is normally associated with such an income over

[17] More precisely, to the existence (chiefly) of a reaction in October from earlier anticipatory buying.

a long period (say a year or two), then a different amount would be spent in June, 1942, out of a disposable income that was the same as in October, but to which the recipients had had time to become accustomed. The present computation concerned only cash and charge-account purchases, all the factors affecting installment sales having been considered above.

In other words, part of the savings that were being made out of October incomes were savings in transit, savings that were destined shortly to be spent; in still other words, the picture of October spending had an acceleration factor in it, much as an automobile that may at a given point in time be said to be traveling at a rate of 40 miles an hour can at the same time be in the process of accelerating steadily from 30 up to 50 miles an hour.

The lag was estimated at $1.0 billion; it was assumed that consumers would be spending $1.0 billion more in June, 1942, than in October, 1941, as their spending habits became adjusted to their incomes.

4. Defense savings-bond campaign; other patriotic appeals to reduce consumption. A fourth and final reason why consumer spending might change even if consumer disposable income and the way it was distributed remained unaltered was the growing pressure to save that was being exerted by the Defense Savings Bond campaign and other appeals to reduce consumption. Actually, this kind of adjustment seemed at the time (November, 1941) to be one for the period lying beyond June, 1942. The government was merely asking the public to buy bonds, not to reduce consumption. The amount of bond sales was not large enough to indicate that they represented anything other than purchases out of savings that would have been made anyway, or that had already been accumulated in savings banks and elsewhere. Moreover, the major part of the defense-bond purchases was in the Series F and G, designed for wealthier investors; and two-thirds of the money put into Series E bonds had gone into the larger denominations ($500 and $1,000).[18] There seemed no reason, at the same time, for assuming much change in these factors by the succeeding June. The change in consumer spending on this score

[18] These details cover May and June, 1941. U.S. Treasury Dept., *Annual Report . . . for the Fiscal Year Ended June 30, 1941*, p. 25.

was therefore set at a nominal amount, minus one-tenth of a billion dollars, under all four (A, B, C, D) assumptions.

5. New distribution of disposable income among income groups. If prices in June, 1942, were to be no higher than in October, 1941, the amount of personal taxes taken from consumers would have to be larger in June. This much appeared evident from the beginning of the study, no matter how consumers' or producers' desires to spend might change (within reason), so large would be the additional income created by the government's increased spending on armaments. A combination of increased government spending and increased tax revenue is almost sure to alter the flow of disposable income among income levels. This change in turn is almost sure to alter the proportion of disposable incomes that consumers in the aggregate try to spend. If the persons to whom the government spending goes have in general lower incomes than the persons from whom the added tax revenue comes, the result will tend to be an increase in consumer expenditures.

To estimate the effect of this change, however, it was necessary to assume something about the amount and sources of the added tax revenue; in other words, it was necessary to assume the answer, as a further bit of first-approximation technique. This was done by disregarding this changed-distribution factor for the time being, working through to an answer giving the amount of the tax revenue needed, and then returning to the item of changed distribution to ascertain whether its size was enough to make necessary an adjustment in the answer. The new tax revenue would in part be provided by the expected higher yield of the existing taxes; in part, from the enactment of additional taxes.

The kind of added tax revenue had to be assumed, also; for reasons advanced in Part II of this volume, revenue from an increase in the individual income tax with personal exemptions no lower than $500 and $1,000 was postulated as the chief new source. Although the new tax was assumed to be at a flat rate, the personal exemptions made it progressive; that is, it would be a larger percentage of the higher incomes (computed before exemptions) than of the smaller.[19]

Estimates of the effect on spending of a changed distribution of

[19] On the very highest incomes the added rate might have to be regressive.

disposable income were made in detail only for the June-to-June analysis. In the October-to-June analysis these initial estimates were modified roughly to allow for the change in the assumed extent of redistribution of income. Consequently, to avoid introducing an additional set of estimates, only a qualitative description of the method used will be given.

The assumed increase in real output fixed the increase in national income before taxes. This "new" stream of income would however be reduced by increases in corporate retained reserves other than tax reserves, by additional business taxes,[20] and by additional personal taxes. The increase in corporate retained reserves other than tax reserves (item 23 below) was all attributed to this "new" stream of income rather than to the previously existing income; a more than proportionate share of the additional business taxes was attributed to the "new" stream because of the excess-profits tax, aimed directly at that new income; and a less than proportionate share of the personal taxes, since the distributed part of the new income was likely to go to persons with income in general below those taxed heavily by either the existing personal taxes or the postulated addition. Subtracting these items from the increase in real output gave the increase in disposable income attributable to the "new" stream of income. Since this income was assumed to go primarily to relatively low income groups, a fairly high percentage might be used to increase consumption. On the basis of budget studies, about three-quarters was assumed used in this way.

The rest of the additional taxes would come from the income of October, 1941, serving to reduce this block of disposable income. Since these taxes were to come from relatively high incomes, they would presumably be met in large part by reduced savings rather than reduced consumption. Available data suggested that probably no more than half of the additional business taxes—which are assumed to reduce incomes paid—would be met by reduced consumption. An even smaller percentage of additional personal taxes was assumed to be met by reduced consumption to allow for the tendency of indi-

[20] Additional business taxes may have their incidence on the payments to factors of production, on the price paid by civilians for goods, or on the price paid by government for goods. The first two can both be treated as equivalent and as a reduction in income; the third cannot, since it consists of a payment by government to itself. For present purposes, the third type of incidence was assumed negligible.

viduals to adjust their spendings somewhat to their income before taxes, despite the fact that their disposable income (i. e. after personal taxes) is less.

The difference between the increased spending out of the "new" block of income and the decreased spending out of the previously existing income gave the net change in spending. This net change is attributable, however, not only to an altered distribution of a constant disposable income but also to a change in the amount of disposable income, since the taxes needed plus the increase in retained reserves did not equal the increase in real income. The effect of the changed amount of disposable income must be eliminated since it will be taken into account at a later point in the analysis. At that point, it is assumed that two-thirds of a change in disposable income is spent, one-third saved. The difference between the increased spending out of the "new" block of income and the decreased spending out of the previously existing income was therefore adjusted by adding two-thirds of the decrease in disposable income implicit in the above analysis (or subtracting two-thirds of the increase). The resulting figure is an estimate of the effect of the altered distribution of a constant disposable income.

This analysis, modified to conform to the October estimates, indicated that the altered distribution of disposable income would lead to net increases in spending of $1.7 billion, $1.5 billion, $2.5 billion, and $1.1 billion for the A, B, C, and D sets of assumptions respectively.

6. Increased turnover of employment. Individuals who become temporarily unemployed tend to maintain their standards of living by drawing on savings until they become reëmployed. Consequently, the larger the turnover of employment in the immediately preceding months, the larger will be the proportion of disposable income that consumers will want to be spending at any given time. The available evidence as of November, 1941, indicated that turnover had been increasing and would continue to do so. Moreover, the turnover would be greater, the larger the total amount of diversion. But the absolute amounts of change in consumer spending that would be caused by this change in turnover seemed not to be large; hence rough guesses of $0.3 billion, $0.5 billion, $0.3 billion, and $0.5 billion were made for assumptions A, B, C, and D respectively.

7. Summary. Table VI presents the estimates of change in spending by consumers out of a disposable income assumed unchanged in amount, June, 1942, compared with October, 1941, for all the items considered. The net result was an estimate that if consumers did have

TABLE VI

ESTIMATED CHANGE IN AMOUNT CONSUMERS WOULD WANT TO SPEND, JUNE, 1942, COMPARED WITH OCTOBER, 1941, ASSUMING PRICES AND AMOUNT OF CONSUMER DISPOSABLE INCOME UNCHANGED

Annual Rates, in Billions of Dollars

	ALTERNATIVE SETS OF ASSUMPTIONS CONCERNING INCREASE IN OUTPUT AND DEFENSE SPENDING, AND DIVERSION (SEE TABLE II)			
	A	*B*	*C*	*D*
3 a (i) Change in net spending of installment-credit money (Table IV)	−1.2	−1.5	−1.2	−1.3
3 a (ii) Change in spending of cash (gross blockage owing to diversion) (Table IV)	−1.3	−2.5	−1.3	−1.7
4. Change in cash spending on other goods induced by gross blockage owing to diversion (Table IV)	1.1	1.9	1.1	1.5
6. Change in anticipatory buying due to fear of further priorities and allocations	2.2	2.4	2.2	2.3
7. Elimination of lag in adjusting cash buying to recent upward change in disposable income	1.0	1.0	1.0	1.0
8. Change owing to savings-bond campaign and other patriotic appeals to reduce consumption	−0.1	−0.1	−0.1	−0.1
9. Change owing to altered distribution of disposable income	1.7	1.5	2.5	1.1
10. Change owing to increased turnover of employment	0.3	0.5	0.3	0.5
11. Total change in amount consumers would want to spend out of unchanged disposable income	3.7	3.2	4.5	3.3

the same total amount of disposable income during June, 1942, as they had in October, 1941, and if prices were unchanged, they would be wanting to spend, during that month, at an annual rate some $3 billion to $4 billion higher than in October, 1941. This is not the whole story; what would happen to prices—and money incomes, and thus spendings themselves—in June if this desire to spend more were not checked, is not estimated here. In other words: the assumption that there would exist a desire to spend in June, 1942, $3 billion or $4 billion more out of an unchanged disposable income at unchanged prices itself implies the existence of forces that, unless neutralized, would make impossible the existence of an unchanged disposable money income and an unchanged price level in that month. The picture of the economy as of June, 1942, so far as it has been sketched up to this point, is an inconsistent, impossible picture. Its frame is bulging with forces that will break through. But the inconsistency can be ignored for the moment, as the analysis proceeds to study possible changes in capital formation, and, finally, possible changes in taxation; the latter, at least, can be so postulated as to neutralize the forces referred to above, thus relieving the frame of the pressure that threatens to split it—and relieving the research student from the task of finding out how far and in what direction the contents would spill in that unhappy event.

Producer spending.—The drain on manpower and capital that would be exerted in June, 1942, by an increase in consumer spending could be either intensified or offset by a change in another sector of civilian activity, capital formation. The country's stock of material capital—inventories, buildings, machinery, and equipment—was not merely being maintained but was actually increasing at a substantial rate in October, 1941. In the common terminology of national income, net capital formation was occurring. In June, 1942, this process of accumulation of material capital might be proceeding at an even faster pace, thus putting still greater pressure on the price level than would be accounted for by the increase in consumer spending indicated in the last line of Table VI. Or it might be proceeding more slowly in June than in the preceding October, thus releasing men, materials, and so on, to help produce consumer goods and services, and in so doing it might be relieving the pressure on prices caused by consumers' increased desire to spend. Net capital formation would still be going on, but on a lower level than before. Finally, the accumulation might not merely slacken; it might turn into decumulation. Part of the capital equipment would not be replaced as it was used up. Gross capital formation would still be going on, but at a level so low that it would not to any extent be called net capital formation.

1. Construction of civilian plant and equipment. Among the several items into which capital formation can be divided, plant and equipment gave indications of showing the largest amount of change, June over October, in the rate at which it was being produced. The influences operating to change the rate of this kind of capital formation may be grouped under four headings: change in the rate at which consumer spending had been increasing; change in the composition of that spending; increase in the construction of civilian plant and equipment necessitated by the expanding defense program, but not yet reflected in the government's budget estimates for that program; decrease caused by diversion to defense through priorities, allocations, and other measures (in addition to whatever decrease is implied by the similar allowance in the consumer-spending computation above).[21] The amount of change in capital expenditures on plant and equipment depends on the assumed amount of diversion, but would probably be affected little by differences in the change in total real output. Consequently, only three alternative estimates are needed: one estimate for Assumptions A and C of Table II (concerning increase in output and defense spending), for, as shown in Table III, these assumptions involve the same total amount of diversion ($4.0 billion) and the same distribution of diversion between net capital formation ($1.5 billion) and consumption ($2.5 billion), differing only in change in real output assumed; another estimate for Assumption B, where the total diversion was $7.0 billion and the diversion from capital formation, $3.0 billion; and another for Assumption D, where the total diversion was $8.0 billion and the diversion from capital formation $5.0 billion.

The change in the rate at which consumer spending had been in-

[21] See Table IV, p. 31.

creasing in the few months prior to the month in question (October, or June) would evidently be a negative one, under the first-approximation assumption that consumer disposable income remained unchanged in amount. Consumers would evidently be spending at a greater rate in June than in October; but this is not the issue here. The October rate of spending was a point on a curve that had been rising substantially over the preceding few (say, seven or eight) months. Would the June rate, similarly, be on a curve that had been rising as steeply? Evidently there would be a rising curve, but it would be less steep. Capital formation probably has some tendency to decline if an increase in consumer spending slackens appreciably. Though this result is not to be counted on invariably, it seemed to deserve some consideration in the present analysis. The statistical basis for estimating it was however very weak. Plant and equipment expenditures in October, 1941, were at an annual rate of $11 or $12 billion, of which perhaps $4 or $5 billion could be considered net capital formation.[22] It would be clearly wrong to assume that the slackening in the increase in consumer spending would induce a complete cessation of net capital formation. A minus item of $1.5 billion seemed reasonable to couple with the two highest estimates of consumer spending (Assumptions A and C); and a minus $1.8 billion for the other two levels of consumer spending.

The second influence operating to change the annual rate of creation of plant and equipment is the change in the composition of spending by consumers that would be forced by the diversion of productive resources from the civilian to the military sector. In drawing on the pool of idle resources to help make good this loss, the civilian sector would have to change its pattern of consumption somewhat. This change influences, in two opposing ways, the amount of capital formation in plant and equipment that is associated with a given volume of consumption. On the one hand, there is likely to be a shift in con-

[22] Original estimates based on preliminary confidential estimates made available by Department of Commerce and other government agencies. The figures have since been published in revised form. See Milton Gilbert and Robert Bangs, "National Income and the War Effort—First Half of 1942," *Survey of Current Business*, Aug., 1942, p. 14, for private gross capital formation by quarters, and page 8, Table 4 of the same issue of the *Survey* for a breakdown of construction expenditures by type.

sumption toward those kinds of goods and services that require smaller amounts of capital, that is, where the final sales price reflects costs like salaries and wages and carrying charges on inventories in larger proportion than before, and depreciation and interest on plant and equipment in smaller proportion. The pressure of priorities is heavier on plant and equipment than on the labor force or liquid capital market in the early stages of a defense program. On the other hand, any shift in consumption is likely to require the construction of some new plant and equipment; and the current drain on the economy's resources of manpower and physical capital caused by such construction is of course far greater than the value added by the new plant and equipment to the first year's output of the new consumers' goods. The money cost is spread over a number of years through depreciation and obsolescence accounting, but the cost in terms of using up resources is all felt at once in the year of construction.

The importance of the change in the composition of spending depends not on the amount of diversion from capital formation, but rather on the amount of diversion from consumption. Consequently, the increase in plant and equipment expenditures from this source was taken to be least ($0.8 billion) under Assumptions A and C, which involve diversion of $2.5 billion from consumption; and most ($1.3 billion)under Assumption B, which involves diversion of $4.0 billion from consumption. An intermediate figure of $1.0 billion was used for Assumption D, which involves diversion of $3.0 billion from consumption.

The third influence on the annual rate of creation of civilian plant and equipment is the extent to which it is being built for defense purposes but not, for the time being, counted as a defense expenditure. A power company may decide to undertake certain construction in some month because it foresees a defense demand for power later; it may be merely guessing or it may hold a firm government contract for the power. A warplane company may similarly be expanding its plant and equipment on the basis of government orders. Sometimes the government pays for this kind of construction as it proceeds; but to a substantial degree it reimburses the company at a later date, in the depreciation and obsolescence cost element in the purchase money paid for the warplanes as they are produced. The statistical basis for estimating the amount of defense expenditure appearing as private capital formation was very weak, but the volume of certificates of necessity that had been issued suggested that for October, 1941, the amount in question was not more than $2 billion; and a reasonable estimate for the following June seemed to be not much over $3 billion. Consequently an item of $1.1 billion was entered for the change in this item, October to June. Since there was little reason to expect this item to be much influenced by the amount of diversion, the same figure was used for all assumptions.

A fourth and final influence that was considered with respect to the construction of civilian plant and equipment was the restrictive effects of priorities, allocations, and other direct methods used to divert resources to defense purposes. In a way, there is no need to make such an estimate. The purpose of the present piecemeal approach that analyzes separately plant and equipment, inventories, and so on is to build up a figure of net total change in capital formation from a series of estimates, each of which is more reliable than any over-all guess at the total. But so far as the priorities and allocations factor is concerned, the net total change has already been estimated; it is the figure on diversion from capital formation, shown in Table III, 3b and explained on pp. 25–26. There is no necessity to break this total down among plant and equipment, inventories, residential construction, and so on. Still, it may be useful to do so, both as a check on the reasonableness of the total, and for the by-product it yields in making possible an addition that shows the total change in plant and equipment construction due not only to allocations and priorities but also to the other three influences (altered rate of rise of consumption, change in composition of consumption, and change in private capital formation designed for defense).

Slightly over half of the total diversion from capital formation was attributed to plant and equipment, giving $–0.8 billion under Assumptions A and B, $–1.8 billion under Assumption B, and $–3.0 billion under Assumption D.

The estimates under the four influences on plant and equipment for the three sets of assumptions are brought together in Table VII.

TABLE VII

CHANGE IN RATE OF CONSTRUCTION OF PLANT AND EQUIPMENT, JUNE, 1942, COMPARED WITH OCTOBER, 1941, ASSUMING PRICES AND AMOUNT OF CONSUMER DISPOSABLE INCOME UNCHANGED

Annual Rates, in Billions of Dollars

CAUSE OF CHANGE	ALTERNATIVE SETS OF ASSUMPTIONS CONCERNING INCREASE IN OUTPUT AND DEFENSE SPENDING, AND DIVERSION (SEE TABLE II)		
	A and C	*B*	*D*
12. Altered rate of rise of consumption	–1.5	–1.8	–1.8
13. Change in composition of consumption	0.8	1.3	1.0
14. Private financing of defense	1.1	1.1	1.1
15. Priorities and allocations (diversion to defense)	–0.8	–1.8	–3.0
20. Total	–0.4	–1.2	–2.7

2. Accumulation of inventories. Inventory held by private business was estimated to be increasing in October, 1941, at the rate of about $3 billion a year.[23] The factors that might make this rate significantly different in the succeeding June are the same four that have just been considered in relation to plant and equipment construction, plus a fifth, speculation. In these inventory computations, the amount of diversion that is assumed is of virtually no importance, and the estimates are the same under the A, B, C, and D assumptions, excepting (1) the inventory change caused by changes in consumption pattern, where the A–C estimate differs from the B–D estimate, and (2) the priorities and allocations item, where the problem is merely one of breaking down, not of creating, a basic estimate.

The first factor, the change in the rate at which consumer spending had been increasing, would affect only that part of inventory accounted for by civilian goods; and within this sector, primarily goods

[23] See Gilbert and Bangs, *op. cit.* A considerably larger figure (between $4 billion and $5 billion) is given there than the one that seemed reasonable when this analysis was made in late 1941.

in process. Possibly one-third of the $3 billion increase would be affected. Accumulation on this count seemed unlikely to drop to zero by the succeeding June, since consumers' spendings would have been rising to a new high level (under the assumption of unchanged prices and unchanged disposable income), but it would be accumulation at a slower pace, since the rise in consumers' spendings would have been slower than before October. Consequently the accumulation would be lower by something between zero and $1 billion. The estimate was set at $–0.5 billion, and the same figure was used under all the assumptions, although logically it should vary with the variation in the level of consumer spendings.

The second factor, a shift in the pattern of consumption away from durable consumers' goods toward semidurable and perishable goods and services, would tend to decrease the rate of inventory accumulation. The shift would be smaller, the smaller the diversion from consumption. The decrease was estimated at $–0.3 billion under Assumptions A and C, and $–0.5 billion under B and D.

The third factor, the private financing of defense, would affect that part of the increase in inventories necessitated by the expanding defense program that does not appear, at the time, in the official estimates of defense spending. A warplane company, for example, may be accumulating large stocks of aluminum in October, 1941, for planes that will not be produced and paid for until later; or the value of partly finished planes may be increasing as the output increases. It appeared that this kind of inventory accumulation would be going on at a still faster rate in June, 1942. Estimates of recent increases in inventories, set against the recorded increase in defense expenditures, suggested that the estimated defense expenditures in the coming period would be accompanied by a rise of something less than $0.5 billion increase in rate of inventory accumulation on this score. A figure of $0.3 billion was adopted for all four assumptions, A, B, C, and D.

As noted above, the fourth factor—priorities and allocations (diversion)—raises merely a question of how to break down the already estimated total for all types of capital formation. Under A and C $–0.2 billion was assigned to inventories; under B, $–0.3 billion; and under D, $–0.5 billion.

There seemed likely to be an increased tendency, by June, 1942, to stock up on inventory for speculative purposes, in anticipation of price increases in certain lines if not in all, and in anticipation of increasing shortages. Doubtless speculation for a fall in price would be occurring in some lines (temporary understocking), but the net result would probably be on the positive side. Chiefly as a matter of keeping this factor in mind, a figure of $0.2 billion was entered under all four assumptions.

A recapitulation of the inventory estimates is given in Table VIII.

TABLE VIII

CHANGE IN RATE OF NET ADDITION TO INVENTORY, JUNE, 1942, COMPARED WITH OCTOBER, 1941, ASSUMING PRICES AND AMOUNT OF CONSUMER DISPOSABLE INCOME UNCHANGED

Annual Rates, in Billions of Dollars

CAUSE OF CHANGE	ALTERNATIVE SETS OF ASSUMPTIONS CONCERNING INCREASE IN OUTPUT AND DEFENSE SPENDING, AND DIVERSION (SEE TABLE II)		
	A and C	*B*	*D*
12. Altered rate of rise of consumption	–0.5	–0.5	–0.5
13. Change in composition of consumption	–0.3	–0.5	–0.5
14. Private financing of defense	0.3	0.3	0.3
15. Priorities and allocations (diversion to defense)	–0.2	–0.3	–0.5
16. Speculation	0.2	0.2	0.2
20. Total	–0.5	–0.8	–1.0

3. Residential construction. As the defense program proceeded, many workers would evidently have to move, to be near the newly erected defense plants. Under the assumption of a small diversion of existing plant, equipment, and materials from civilian to military uses, the number of newly erected defense plants would be greater, and the movement into new homes would therefore be greater. Hence the amount of new dwelling construction attributable to such changes

in the location of the population would vary inversely with the degree of diversion assumed. The change in location of population had also been considered in drawing up the estimates of change in inventory accumulation and change in plant and equipment construction, but its influence had appeared negligible, and it was therefore not introduced into the discussion on pp. 41–47.

The new housing for defense workers would not, however, be an addition to an unchanged volume of October, 1941, dwelling construction. It seemed likely instead to be a diversion, a shifting from private construction of a normal type to construction for defense purposes of a kind that was not reflected directly in the defense budget and hence had to be labeled "private." The diversion would be not to defense as ordinarily computed but to "privately financed defense." Data on defense housing suggested that, at the most, defense housing (privately financed) would be running at an annual rate of $0.8 billion more in June, 1942, than in October, 1941. Under the assumptions of larger total diversion, this was scaled down to $0.6 billion (Assumption B) and $0.4 billion (Assumption D). These three figures were entered as the plus items due to change in location of population. Similar negative items (slightly smaller under Assumption D) were then entered under diversion from privately financed nondefense housing.

The priorities and allocation situation, however, seemed to assure some net decrease in dwelling construction. The diversion from capital formation, in general, had already been estimated.[24] Hence it was here, as under plant and equipment and inventories, merely a matter of allocating a part of it to fall in the dwellings category. This was set at $–0.2 billion under Assumptions A and C, $–0.5 billion under B, and $–1.0 billion under D.

4. State and local public works. The shift in the location of the population would require expenditures by the state and local governments on water and sewer systems, streets, school buildings, and other public works. The increase in such expenditures was estimated at $0.2 billion for Assumptions A and C, and $0.1 billion for B and D.

Only $–0.1 billion was allocated from the total of diversion from

[24] See pp. 25–26.

capital formation to federally financed defense. Under "diversion to privately financed defense" an estimate of $-0.3 billion was made, under all four assumptions. This estimate was rather arbitrary, being designed to make the total change in state and local public-works construction add up to about $-0.3 billion, a figure suggested by independent data on probable changes in state and local capital expenditures.

5. Export balance. An excess of exports over imports produces a net flow of money income into the hands of domestic wage earners and others, with no corresponding volume of consumer goods being made available for purchase domestically; instead, an investment is created, in the form of a claim on foreign countries. In October, 1941, a substantial part of the export balance was attributable to British purchases for war. By June, 1942, much of those purchases would be taking place through lend-lease, and counted in the defense spending item. Hence the private capital formation sector would show a similar decrease, in the form of diversion to defense (including lend-lease). The amount thus diverted was estimated at $0.2 billion for Assumptions A and C, $0.3 billion for B, and $0.4 billion for D.

It was evident, even before Pearl Harbor, that exports to Asia and Oceania would drop off; and there was some chance that exports to South America would increase. The course of imports was uncertain. But it seemed likely that one factor that might permit a relatively large increase in total output and a relatively small amount of diversion would be relatively large imports, particularly from South America. Consequently, Assumptions A and C were taken to imply relatively large imports, implying a relatively large decline in the excess of exports over imports. The net result was a decrease of $0.8 billion under Assumptions A and C, but much less under B and D. Declines of $0.2 billion and $0.1 billion were assigned to the last two, respectively.

Table IX summarizes the estimates for change in residential construction, change in state and local public works construction, and change in private export balance.

Table IX

CHANGE IN RATE OF RESIDENTIAL CONSTRUCTION AND STATE AND LOCAL PUBLIC WORKS CONSTRUCTION, AND IN PRIVATE EXPORT BALANCE, JUNE, 1942, COMPARED WITH OCTOBER, 1941, ASSUMING PRICES AND AMOUNT OF CONSUMER DISPOSABLE INCOME UNCHANGED

Annual Rates, in Billions of Dollars

CAUSE OF CHANGE	CHANGE IN RATE OF RESIDENTIAL CONSTRUCTION			CHANGE IN RATE OF STATE AND LOCAL PUBLIC WORKS CONSTRUCTION			CHANGE IN PRIVATE EXPORT BALANCE		
	A and C	*B*	*D*	*A and C*	*B*	*D*	*A and C*	*B*	*D*
15. Diversion to federally financed defense, including lend-lease	–0.2	–0.5	–1.0	–0.1	–0.1	–0.1	–0.2	–0.3	–0.4
17. Change in location of population	0.8	0.6	0.4	0.2	0.1	0.1	....	....	....
18. Diversion to privately financed defense	–0.8	–0.6	–0.2	–0.3	–0.3	–0.3	....	....	....
19. Change in exports other than diversion to lend-lease	....	....	....	....	....	....	–0.8	–0.2	–0.1
20. Total	–0.2	–0.5	–0.8	–0.2	–0.3	–0.3	–1.0	–0.5	–0.5

6. Summary. Table X recapitulates Tables VII, VIII, and IX, showing all the changes in all the elements of gross capital formation. The summary picture was that civilian capital expenditures would be running at a lower level in June, 1942, than in October, 1941. There would still be some net capital formation occurring; the minus items in Table X are not so large as to suggest that the civilian sector would fail to be replacing its capital. But capital formation would be proceeding at an annual rate at least $2 billion less and perhaps as much as $5 billion less in June than in the preceding October (Table X, totals of the three right-hand columns).

Net change in civilian spending.—The totals for the changes in consumer spending (Table VI, item 11) and in producer spending (Table X, item 20) are brought together in Table XI. The last line in Table XI indicates that in June, 1942, net civilian spending would increase slightly from October, 1941, under Assumptions A and C; remain virtually unchanged under Assumption B; and decrease slightly under Assumption D—if consumer disposable income were unchanged in amount (though changed in distribution as indicated on pp. 36–38 above) and if prices were about the same in June as in the preceding October.

These totals were, it will be recalled, obtained by adding separate estimates of the effect of the various factors that might be expected to cause changes in civilian spending. This procedure implies, of course, that the estimates of the different items are entirely independent, which is palpably untrue. For example, the change in consumer outlay as a result of a lead or lag in the adjustment of cash spending to changing incomes will not be independent of, and cannot simply be added to, the change arising from an altered distribution of consumer income. There is no explicit step in the procedure at which account is taken of these interrelationships. Allowance for them is implicit in the separate estimates. In making these estimates, the attempt was made to bear in mind possible dependence on other items and to adjust the estimates accordingly.

Table X

CHANGE IN RATE OF CAPITAL FORMATION, JUNE, 1942, COMPARED WITH OCTOBER, 1941, ASSUMING PRICES AND AMOUNT OF CONSUMER DISPOSABLE INCOME UNCHANGED

Annual Rates, in Billions of Dollars

CAUSE OF CHANGE	RESIDENTIAL CONSTRUCTION			INVENTORIES			PLANT AND EQUIPMENT			STATE AND LOCAL			EXPORT BALANCE			TOTAL		
	A and C	*B*	*D*	*A and C*	*B*	*D*	*A and C*	*B*	*D*	*A and C*	*B*	*D*	*A and C*	*B*	*D*	*A and C*	*B*	*D*
12. Altered rate of rise of consumption				–0.5	–0.5	–0.5	–1.5	–1.8	–1.8							–2.0	–2.3	–2.3
13. Change in composition of consumption				–0.3	–0.5	–0.5	0.8	1.3	1.0							0.5	0.8	0.5
14. Private financing of defense				0.3	0.3	0.3	1.1	1.1	1.1							1.4	1.4	1.4
15. Diversion to federally financed defense	–0.2	–0.5	–1.0	–0.2	–0.3	–0.5	–0.8	–1.8	–3.0	–0.1	–0.1	–0.1	–0.2	–0.3	–0.4	–1.5	–3.0	–5.0
16. Speculation				0.2	0.2	0.2										0.2	0.2	0.2
17. Change in location of population	0.8	0.6	0.4							0.2	0.1	0.1				1.0	0.7	0.5
18. Diversion to privately financed defense	–0.8	–0.6	–0.2							–0.3	–0.3	–0.3				–1.1	–0.9	–0.5
19. Change in export balance													–0.8	–0.2	–0.1	–0.8	–0.2	–0.1
20. Total	–0.2	–0.5	–0.8	–0.5	–0.8	–1.0	–0.4	–1.2	–2.7	–0.2	–0.3	–0.3	–1.0	–0.5	–0.5	–2.3	–3.3	–5.3

TABLE XI

CHANGE IN RATE OF CIVILIAN SPENDING, JUNE, 1942, COMPARED WITH OCTOBER, 1941, ASSUMING PRICES AND AMOUNT OF CONSUMER DISPOSABLE INCOME UNCHANGED

Annual Rates, in Billions of Dollars

	ALTERNATIVE SETS OF ASSUMPTIONS CONCERNING INCREASE IN OUTPUT AND DEFENSE SPENDING, AND DIVERSION (SEE TABLE II)			
	A	*B*	*C*	*D*
11. Total change in consumer spending	3.7	3.2	4.5	3.3
20. Total change in producer spending (change in capital formation)	–2.3	–3.3	–2.3	–5.3
21. Total net change in civilian spending	1.4	–0.1	2.2	–2.0

MAINTAINING CONSUMER DISPOSABLE INCOME UNCHANGED IN AMOUNT

Starting with an actual situation, in October, 1941, the analysis worked out a hypothetical situation for June, 1942. But it turned out to be an impossible hypothetical situation, internally inconsistent. The amounts in the basic categories did not fit together. The computations indicated too great an increase in civilian spending to be consistent with both the postulated increase of national output (national income) and the postulated increase in defense expenditures. This was so, even if enough additional taxes were to be in force by June, 1942, to keep consumer disposable income down to the level of October, 1941. The four basic assumptions were: Increase in annual rate of national income (output) ranging from $3.0 billion to $6.7 billion; increase in defense expenditures of either $9 billion or $10 billion; a consumer disposable income unchanged in total from October, 1941; and no change in general level of prices. But they did not fit together; the increase in defense expenditures would be appreciably greater than the increase in national output, and therefore the civilian sector would be forced to spend appreciably less than in October, 1941. But civilians, so far from curtailing their expenditures, except by a small, inadequate amount under Assumption D, would probably maintain them virtually unchanged (Assumption B) or even increase them (Assumptions A and C). Were either of these indications fulfilled, prices would have to rise, to fill the gap between money expenditures and the volume of goods and services available at October, 1941 prices.

Since the estimates of national income (output) and defense spending could not be altered, the disposable income of consumers would have to be contracted, in order to shrink the civilian desire to spend. The contraction could be accomplished by taxation (or compulsory saving): still more taxation, that is, than that required to keep disposable income unchanged.

Before attempting to compute this extra amount of taxation, however, it was necessary to find how much taxation would be needed merely to keep consumer disposable income unchanged. In other words, it was necessary to describe the last step in filling in the internally inconsistent hypothetical picture of June, 1942, before finding out how to remedy the inconsistency.

There were two forces that, if not counteracted, would tend to cause an increase in consumer disposable income in June, over the preceding October: The increase in spending by the Federal Government, and, under Assumptions A and C, the increased civilian desire to spend out of an unchanged disposable income. Both of these increased flows of expenditure, it must be noted, would arise in the absence of an increase in consumer disposable income. If the flows were not neutralized, dollar for dollar, they would of course in turn cause a rise in consumer disposable income, since they would be income to the recipients. And the part that would be respent would in turn become additional income, to the second rank of recipients, and so on. But these possibilities need not be studied, if, for every dollar in these two original increases in expenditure flow, there is taken away a dollar in additional income tax. The disposable income, the income after taxes, would then be kept unchanged. The national income, of course, would still show an increase, for the new personal taxes would not affect its total.

If, then, as under Assumption A, government spending was to increase by $9.0 billion and civilians were to be wanting to spend $1.4

billion more than in October, out of an unchanged disposable income, an increase in the revenue of income taxes of $10.4 billion would be needed merely to keep total consumer disposable income unchanged. Total net income, total national income, would still be higher than in October, since national income is computed before the deduction of personal taxes.

Actually, the full $10.4 billion increase in revenue would not be needed. Some part of the two flows would be drained off into an idle pool of savings by the business corporations through which they were passing en route from the spenders, and thus would not reach the wage earners, investors, and so on, to become part of their income. At least it would not reach them by June, 1942. This increase in corporate retained income (other than effective tax reserves) was set at $0.6 billion under Assumption A, leaving an added personal income, to be offset by added tax revenue, of $10.4 billion minus $0.6 billion, or $9.8 billion.

Not all of this $9.8 billion would have to be raised by new revenue laws. The existing system would be collecting $5.5 billion more per year in June, 1942, than in October, 1941, owing partly to an increased national income and partly to the fact that the Revenue Act of 1941 was not in full effect, so far as collections were concerned, in October, 1941.

"Collecting" and "collections," as used here, have a somewhat special meaning for corporations. In general, corporations were setting up income-tax reserves in 1941 on the basis of payments that would be due in 1942. Some of them were setting up the reserves purely in a bookkeeping sense, that is, their actual spending or disbursements to investors were not being checked thereby. But the larger part of the corporate income-tax payments due in 1942 were probably being anticipated not only in a formal sense but in the economic sense that the money was being set aside when it otherwise would have been spent or distributed in dividends or interest. To the extent that this self-restraint was being exercised in October, 1941, thus relieving pressure on prices at that time, the proper comparison with the next June was not October collections against next June's collections, but October restraint (effective tax accrual) against June restraint. In the present analysis it was assumed that half the corporate tax was handled on an effective accrual basis, the other half not being effective in influencing corporate action until actually paid to the government. The net result was an increase of $2.0 billion in corporate tax "collections." The increase in collections from other taxes (no accrual assumptions were made here) was $3.5 billion.[25]

Some of this $5.5 billion added revenue from the existing tax system was to come not from personal taxes nor from corporate income taxes, but, as already indicated, from other kinds of taxes collected from business firms, largely excises on gasoline, liquor, and tobacco. To this extent it is not quite exact to speak of the entire $5.5 billion as reducing consumer disposable income. But the effect is the same. A dollar of this additional excise revenue arises either from an increase in the amount of the article sold, or from an increase in the tax rate. If an added dollar's worth of liquor, for instance, is sold, and if the seller must take 40 cents from the dollar and pay it to the government, the production and sale of the added liquor results in only 60 cents of income to wage earners, investors, and so on. The tax does not decrease the liquor consumer's disposable income, but does make it inefficient, so to speak, in creating income to others.[26] In so far as the additional liquor revenue results from an increase in the liquor tax rate, the same analysis applies, except that the price level tends to be higher in June than in the preceding October—at least higher to a greater degree than if the money were coming from an income tax. This effect would be unimportant quantitatively, however, and will be disregarded here.

Of the $10.4 billion of added spending (out of an unchanged consumer disposable income) that threatens, under Assumption A, to add at once $10.4 billion to corporate and individual incomes, $0.6 billion is held back in corporate savings and $5.5 billion is mopped up by the existing tax system. This leaves $4.3 billion in taxes from new revenue legislation that is needed if consumer disposable income is to

[25] Details of these computations were based on confidential, tentative estimates in the Treasury.

[26] The present analysis is, at this stage, concerned with matching with taxes, dollar for dollar, the initial increased flow from government ($9.0 billion) and civilians ($1.4 billion) that will, unless matched, create additional disposable income above the October level. Hence the matching effect of the liquor excise, though formally somewhat different from that of a personal income tax, does quite as well.

be kept unchanged. Table XII presents these figures under Assumption A, and the corresponding sets under Assumptions B, C, and D.

Except for the increase in tax payments or reserves under legislation in force October, 1941, the only new estimate needed for these computations is the change in corporate retained income other than tax reserves. In the absence of still further business taxes—ruled out

TABLE XII

COMPUTATION OF ADDITIONAL TAX REVENUE, JUNE, 1942, OVER OCTOBER, 1941, REQUIRED TO MAINTAIN CONSUMER DISPOSABLE INCOME UNCHANGED

Annual Rates, in Billions of Dollars

	ALTERNATIVE SETS OF ASSUMPTIONS CONCERNING INCREASE IN OUTPUT AND DEFENSE SPENDING, AND DIVERSION (SEE TABLE II)			
	A	*B*	*C*	*D*
2. Assumed increase in defense spending (Table II)	9.0	10.0	10.0	10.0
21. Net increase in civilian spending, if consumer disposable income is unchanged (Table IX)	1.4	−0.1	2.2	−2.0
22. Total initial increase in spending (hence, initial increase in disposable income) if not counterbalanced	10.4	9.9	12.2	8.0
23. Increase in corporate retained income other than tax reserves	0.6	0.5	1.0	0.4
24. Increase in tax payments or reserves under legislation in force October, 1941				
(a) Corporate income and profits taxes	2.0	2.0	2.0	2.0
(b) Other	3.5	3.5	3.5	3.5
25. Tax revenue needed from additional legislation, to maintain consumer disposable income unchanged (item 22 minus items 23 and 24)	4.3	3.9	5.7	2.1

by the assumed type of new taxes to be used—retained income might be expected to increase with an increase in total national income. The final answer on the increase in national income is given by the assumed increase in output (item 1, Table II). This is largest for Assumption C, least for Assumption D, and accordingly the increase in reserves is largest for Assumption C and least for Assumption D. The figures used assume that an increasingly larger part of successive increases in national income would take the form of corporate retained income.

REDUCTION OF CONSUMER SPENDING FROM WHAT IT WOULD BE UNDER UNCHANGED DISPOSABLE INCOME

The tax measures suggested up to this point were enough to guarantee that consumer disposable income would be no higher in June than in the preceding October. But, as already noted, even an unchanged level of consumer disposable income would be incompatible with both unchanged prices and the increased demands of defense, for with that level of income would go a level of spending by consumers and civilian producers that would not be appreciably lower in June than it was in October—indeed, under Assumptions A and C, definitely higher. And that level had to be lower, if the defense demands were to be satisfied, in view of the limitations on the increase in total national output (national income).

A reduction could be forced, by further taxation, in either consumer spending or civilian producer spending. But consumer spending seemed to be the preferable object; the extent to which a dollar in tax would check consumer spending is somewhat less difficult to estimate than its effect on producer spending. At least, the effect on consumer spending is perhaps not altogether impossible to estimate.

The task that a given tax dollar had to accomplish at this point must be distinguished from the task that was assigned to it on pp. 54–55, where it was used to counterbalance a force (increased government and civilian spending) that threatened to create additional consumer income. In that case a dollar of tax was needed to match every dollar of the spending. In the present case, the task in hand, a decreasing of consumer expenditures by a dollar in June, 1942, over what it would be under a disposable income unchanged from the

October, 1941, level, could be accomplished by less than a dollar of added taxation. To be sure, a dollar of tax taken from a consumer would induce that particular consumer to restrict his spending by something less than a dollar, say two-thirds of a dollar, that is, whatever proportion he would not ordinarily save. But this check to his spending would automatically deprive someone else of two-thirds of a dollar in income that he would otherwise have been receiving; and this second income recipient might cut his expenditures by two-thirds of two-thirds of a dollar—and so on. These successive effects did not need to be taken into account in the analysis on pp. 54–55. There, the prospective increase in consumer disposable income was itself reckoned without taking into account its own successive effects. That case could have been made analogous to the present one by first allowing the prospective initial increase in consumer income to work itself out through respending into still more income, still more spending, and so on, until an equilibrium was reached at a new high level of national money income (and prices), and then asking how much taxation would at that point be needed to bring the situation back to the level where consumer disposable income would be unchanged. The amount would be the same as already indicated, for then the successive effects of each dollar of tax could have been allowed for; and each dollar of tax would have reduced income, and spending, too, by more than a dollar. This procedure was not followed because it would have been simply exploration into a difficult jungle followed by backtracking.[27] The present analysis does not aim to count the trees in the jungle of inflation; its concern is to avoid the trip, so far as possible. But it must now enter that jungle. The analysis to this point still leaves inflation. The problem is to produce a deflation, as it were, back to the original price level of October, 1941. In order not to overdo the deflation, account must be taken of the successive spending and respending.

Continuing under Assumption A: Civilian spending in June, 1942,

[27] Implicit in our procedure is, of course, the assumption that the prospective increase in consumer income will have the same "multiplier" effect as the decrease in disposable income achieved through taxation, except for the effect of the altered distribution of disposable income, taken into account explicitly in item 9 of our analysis. While this assumption may not be entirely valid, there seems no reasonable basis for judging even the direction of the error, let alone its magnitude.

out of an unchanged disposable income would have to be reduced by $5.1 billion. The increase in output would be only $5.3 billion, whereas the government's defense spending and the civilian desire to spend would be higher by $9.0 billion plus $1.4 billion, or $10.4 billion. The difference is $5.1 billion.

How much taxation would be needed to reduce consumer spending $5.1 billion? If, on the average, a dollar of individual income tax of the kind contemplated would reduce the taxpayer's spending by two-thirds of a dollar, and if the successive effects were also two-thirds on spendings and one-third on savings, each dollar of tax would cut spendings by two dollars ($\frac{2}{3} + \frac{4}{9} + \frac{8}{27} \ldots\ldots = 2$). Then $2.55 billion more in tax would cut consumer spending by the required $5.1 billion. Producer spending—capital formation—would presumably slacken somewhat as a result of this decline in consumer spending; hence total civilian spending would decrease by more than $5.1 billion. But the amount involved would probably be too small to be worth estimating. Consequently, under such a tax measure, the total decrease in civilian spending was estimated to be $5.1 billion.

Consumer disposable income, incidentally, would be decreased three dollars (not two) by each dollar of tax. The first effect of the tax would be to reduce the taxpayer's own disposable income by $1. His income, but not his disposable income, would remain unchanged. Those whose incomes would be cut by the decrease in his spending would find their incomes and their disposable incomes decreased by the same amount, that is, a total of $2.

The multiplier of 2 was of course nothing but the roughest sort of estimate. Indeed, from the time the present study was initiated, one of the aims kept constantly in mind was to devise a technique that depended as little as possible on the use of an over-all multiplier or successive-effects relationship. This aim is in large part the explanation of why the analysis soon developed into the piece-by-piece building-up of probable consumer and producer spending patterns, described on pp. 22–51. If the amounts by which spending had to be reduced (once disposable income had been maintained unchanged) had been even a few billions greater than the $5 billion it turned out to be (p. 65, Table XIII, item 27), it would have been imperative to work through the steps of pp. 22–51 again, on an assumption of a somewhat reduced consumer disposable income. As it was, the $5 billion seemed small enough to permit use of the rough over-all multiplier technique.

TOTAL TAX REQUIREMENT, ASSUMPTION A

The $2.5 billion in tax designed to reduce consumer spending from what it would be under an unchanged disposable income must be added to the $4.3 billion in tax that was needed merely to keep consumer disposable income unchanged; and in addition there is the $5.5 billion increase postulated to come from the existing revenue system. Thus the analysis under Assumption A ends with the estimate that the general level of prices in June, 1942, could be maintained unchanged—under the given conditions of price control, and so on, and apart from rises in price due to increases in real costs or to a rise in wage rates or profit rates obtained by concerted action—only if the federal tax system were yielding $12.3 billion more revenue (annual rate) in June, 1942, than in October, 1941, of which $6.8 billion would be from new revenue measures (see Table XIII, p. 65).

Similar computations under Assumptions B, C, and D are explained briefly on pp. 66–67.

There may at first sight appear to be some double counting in the two-stage computation of tax requirements, especially with respect to the measures taken to neutralize the $1.4 billion increase (Assumption A data) in the amount that the civilian sector would want to spend, with disposable income unchanged. The neutralizing was done by $1.4 billion of added taxation (pp. 54–55), plus one-half of $1.4 billion (p. 60). It may be asked, is not this an overestimate of the tax requirements? The answer is no, for the increase of $1.4 billion in what consumers would want to spend has two aspects: its income-creating aspect and the fact that it is a drain on resources that need to be released to the government or, alternatively, a pressure on prices. The added disposable income that it creates in the hands of those on whom it is spent can be neutralized by taxation of an equal amount; but the drain on resources or pressure on prices remains. Further taxation is needed to get the resources released for government use without a price rise. For example: In Period I, the government is absorbing $40 and ten consumers are absorbing $60 of a

$100 output; the ten consumers are receiving $100 income, spending $60, saving $30 and paying $10 in taxes; their disposable income is therefore $90. In Period II it appears that the consumers will want to spend, not $60, but $70, if their disposable income remains at $90 and the price level remains unchanged. This spending, with government continuing to spend $40, would produce more than $90 disposable income (it would produce $100, before taking account of successive respendings). Tax measure "A," consisting of $10 of income tax, makes it possible to keep disposable income unchanged. To emphasize the point, let it be assumed that a particular consumer, *C*, is responsible for the increase in spending; he was spending $10 in Period I, but now, with the prospect of an unchanged disposable income, wants to spend $20. In doing so, he draws some men away from government work, by bidding up their wages, for there are no idle resources to draw on; or he pays more to the men who were producing civilian goods, without actually getting more goods. Tax measure "A" takes $10 away from the men who are receiving the extra $10 that *C* is spending, leaving them, and everyone else, with the same disposable income as in Period I, although total consumer spendings have risen from $60 (Period I) to $70. But the government is short some workers, and (or) civilian prices have risen. The government is absorbing less than 40 percent of the real output, although still spending $40; or individuals are paying $70 for goods that formerly cost $60. Government can get back the workers, and (or) eliminate the civilian price rise, by tax measure "B," designed to cut the spending of consumer *C*, the workers, and all other individuals by $10, that is, by enough to reduce total spending to the same amount as previously. The amount of taxation to be raised by "B" will be less than $10 because of successive effects in cutting spending down the line. If, for instance, $5 is taken from *C* in tax in Period II, again in Period III, and so on, and if *C*, in Period III, cuts his spending by $3⅓ because of the $5 tax of Period II, and if the persons whose income is cut in Period III by the $3⅓ that *C* fails to spend, cut their own spending by $2 2/9 in Period IV—and so on—then, after enough periods have elapsed, there will be a level of civilian spending that is $10 lower per period because of an increase in tax of $5 per period, accompanied by no increase in government dollar expenditures. For purposes of the present computations, the successive effects were assumed to take place instantaneously, so that their full effect would be felt in Period II (June, 1942). For the practical application of the results of the computations this means that the tax measure would have to take effect some time before June, 1942. The amount involved seemed not large enough to warrant an attempt at a more precise statement in view of the degree of uncertainty attaching to the larger items in any case.

The example in the preceding paragraph has been distorted to emphasize the point at issue. Actually, the $10 tax would have to come partly or wholly from others than the workers receiving the extra income. And the higher price level brought about by *C*'s bidding for their services should change the underlying data on willingness to spend, and so on. But the practical program would call for imposing the full $15 tax at once, or perhaps imposing the $5 segment first, and not, as in the illustration, allowing *C*'s spending to take place before doing anything. Hence these particular distributions of taxes in the example do not invalidate the conclusions concerning an adequate tax program.

ALTERNATIVE METHOD OF COMPUTING TAX REQUIREMENT

The procedure followed on pp. 53–61, whereby the tax requirement was computed in two stages, one of which involved keeping consumer disposable income unchanged, is merely one of several possible methods of computation. An understanding of the implications and limitations of the answer may be enhanced by using an alternative method. The answer must turn out to be the same, since the alternative method must use the results obtained up to p. 53 and the assumptions concerning the effect of added taxation on spending and saving that are employed on pp. 58–60. The following computation will be in terms of Assumption A.

In June, 1942, there would be need for three blocks of taxation.

The first block would be required to absorb the increase in money incomes that would flow from the increase in production, for none of this production would be for sale, and the money incomes paid for producing it would, in so far as they were spent at all, put pressure on the price level of civilian goods. The increase in production would be $5.3 billion. Some of this, say $0.6 billion, would be absorbed in increased corporation saving, leaving $4.7 billion added tax revenue in this first block.

The second block would be required to make the civilian sector release, in June, $3.7 billion of resources that it had been absorbing in October, for the government's needs would be $9.0 billion higher, only $5.3 billion of which would be met by an increase in production. To make civilians give up $3.7 billion of resources, that is, cut their spending by this amount, something more than $3.7 billion in tax would be required, for they would meet the tax in part by cutting savings. If they took one-third of the tax out of savings, $5.55 billion of tax would be needed. To avoid possible confusion it must be pointed out that this $5.55 billion of tax is not to be given a multiplier effect; the cut in taxpayer *A*'s income, which causes his spending to decrease, does not result in a net decline in the income of *B*, from whom *A* is accustomed to purchase; for *B*, released from *A*'s demands, is taken over by the government, which increases its dollar expenditure *pari passu* from the level reached by the $5.3 billion increase, to a still higher level, by adding another $3.7 billion of expenditures. *B* sells to the government, instead of to *A*. On p. 60, on the other hand, a multiplier effect had to be reckoned with because, at that stage, in those particular computations, the level of the government's dollar expenditures was already as it was postulated to be for June, 1942.

The third block of taxes is required to deal with the fact that consumers want to spend a larger proportion of their income in June, 1942, than in October, 1941. The first block of taxes has prevented them from getting any more disposable income out of the increase in output; the second block has cut their spending by the necessary amount below the spending level indicated by the October spending pattern; a third block is needed to counteract their increased desire to spend. The increased desire to spend was evaluated at $1.4 billion. Disposable income must be reduced enough further by taxes to reduce desired spending by this amount. If one-third of the tax comes out of saving, $2.1 billion is needed to accomplish this result.

The sum of the three tax blocks is $12.3 billion, the same answer that was reached under the other method of computation on p. 61.

TOTAL TAX REQUIREMENT, ASSUMPTIONS B, C, AND D

Returning to the method employed on pp. 53–63, the results obtained under Assumptions B, C, and D will be described; they are stated in Table XIII.

The added revenue from new measures happens to be $6.6 billion under Assumption B, virtually the same as under Assumption A. There is slightly less need, than under A, for new taxes merely to keep consumer disposable income unchanged; under B there is much greater diversion of resources to defense than under A, and the larger the diversion, the greater the tendency for consumers and civilian producers to save their money because the things they are accustomed to purchase are not available. Somewhat counterbalancing this factor is the assumption of a $10-billion increase in defense spending, in contrast to $9 billion under Assumption A.

There is slightly more need, than under A, for new taxes to reduce consumer spending after an unchanged disposable income has been guaranteed; the defense needs are greater and the postulated increase in total output is less than under A.

Under C the added revenue needed from new measures rises to $8.4 billion. This may at first appear odd, since the postulated increase in total output is greatest under C. The explanation lies in the large volume of taxation needed in the first stage of the analysis, that is, merely to keep consumer disposable income unchanged; $5.7 billion is required for this purpose ($4.3 billion under A). The added $1.4 billion is necessary largely because the government is spending $10.0 billion more instead of $9.0 billion more and the consumers are tending to spend somewhat more freely. The latter tendency results from the greater change in the distribution of the unchanged disposable income; a change that in turn is a product of the need to shift a larger amount around by taxation. In the second stage, reduction of spending, C requires only slightly more tax revenue than A; the less thrifty consumers of C, faced with a larger defense demand, have a somewhat larger increase in national output to help them out than their fellows under A.

The added revenue needed from new measures is lowest of all under

Table XIII

COMPUTATION OF ADDITIONAL TAX REVENUE, JUNE, 1942, OVER OCTOBER, 1941, REQUIRED TO MAINTAIN PRICE LEVEL UNCHANGED

Annual Rates, in Billions of Dollars

	ALTERNATIVE SETS OF ASSUMPTIONS CONCERNING INCREASE IN OUTPUT AND DEFENSE SPENDING, AND DIVERSION (SEE TABLE II)			
	A	*B*	*C*	*D*
2. Assumed increase in defense spending (Table II)	9.0	10.0	10.0	10.0
21. Net increase in civilian spending, if consumer disposable income is unchanged (Table XI)	1.4	–0.1	2.2	–2.0
26. Total increase in spending, hence, increase in drain on resources, under unchanged disposable income (item 2 plus item 21)	10.4	9.9	12.2	8.0
1. Assumed increase in total output (Table II)	5.3	4.4	6.7	3.0
27. Reduction in civilian spending required (item 26 minus item 1)	5.1	5.5	5.5	5.0
28. Assumed reduction in civilian spending caused by an additional billion dollars of income tax	2.0	2.0	2.0	2.0
29. Tax revenue needed from additional legislation, to bring civilian spending to required level, after enough taxation has been levied to maintain consumer disposable income unchanged	2.55	2.75	2.75	2.5
25. Tax revenue needed from additional legislation, to maintain consumer disposable income unchanged (Table XII)	4.3	3.9	5.7	2.1
24. Increase in tax payments or reserves under legislation in force October, 1941 (Table XII)	5.5	5.5	5.5	5.5

TABLE XIII (continued)

COMPUTATION OF ADDITIONAL TAX REVENUE, JUNE, 1942, OVER OCTOBER, 1941, REQUIRED TO MAINTAIN PRICE LEVEL UNCHANGED

Annual Rates, in Billions of Dollars

	ALTERNATIVE SETS OF ASSUMPTIONS CONCERNING INCREASE IN OUTPUT AND DEFENSE SPENDING, AND DIVERSION (SEE TABLE II)			
	A	*B*	*C*	*D*
30. Total additional tax revenue needed in June, 1942, over October, 1941, to avert inflationary price rise (excluding inflation induced by concerted action) (items 29, 25, and 24)	12.3	12.1	13.9	10.1
31. Total additional tax revenue needed from new legislation (item 29 plus item 25)	6.8	6.6	8.4	4.6

D—only $4.6 billion. This again looks odd, for it is under D that total output expands least. The answer again lies in the large amount of diversion that is forced by just this inability to expand output very much. The diversion is twice as great under D as under A. Consumers are deterred somewhat by this increase in diversion; but the important difference is in the field of civilian capital formation. It drops to a level $5.3 billion below that of October, 1941 (Assumption A shows a drop of only $2.3 billion). Consequently only $2.1 billion of new tax revenue is needed to maintain consumer disposable income unchanged. At the second stage—reducing consumer spending—the tax requirement is virtually the same as under A, just as it was under B and C.

Table XIV brings together the data for Assumptions A, B, C, and D in Tables II–IV, VI–XIII.

Table XIV

COMPUTATION OF AMOUNT OF ADDITIONAL TAX REVENUE NEEDED IN JUNE, 1942, COMPARED TO OCTOBER, 1941, TO AVERT INFLATION, UNDER THE ASSUMPTIONS GIVEN CONCERNING DIRECT CONTROLS

Annual Rates, in Billions of Dollars

	ALTERNATIVE SETS OF ASSUMPTIONS CONCERNING INCREASE IN OUTPUT AND DEFENSE SPENDING, AND DIVERSION			
	A	*B*	*C*	*D*
1. Assumed increase in total output	5.3	4.4	6.7	3.0
2. Assumed increase in defense spending	9.0	10.0	10.0	10.0
3. Assumed diversion to defense	4.0	7.0	4.0	8.0
a. Change in consumer spending	−2.5	−4.0	−2.5	−3.0
(i) Change in net spending of installment-credit money (i. e. change in rate of change of installment credit outstanding)	−1.2	−1.5	−1.2	−1.3
(ii) Change in spending of cash (i. e. the negative items represent gross blockage of cash spending resulting from diversion to defense through priorities, allocations, and other measures)	−1.3	−2.5	−1.3	−1.7
b. Change in net capital formation	−1.5	−3.0	−1.5	−5.0
4. Consumer spending (cash) on other goods, induced by gross blockage of cash spending on usual goods	1.1	1.9	1.1	1.5
5. Net change in consumer spending caused by diversion, through priorities, allocations, and other measures, of consumer goods (or the agents producing them) to defense (item 3a minus item 4)	−1.4	−2.1	−1.4	−1.5

TABLE XIV (continued)

	ALTERNATIVE SETS OF ASSUMPTIONS CONCERNING INCREASE IN OUTPUT AND DEFENSE SPENDING, AND DIVERSION			
	A	*B*	*C*	*D*
6. Change in anticipatory buying due to fear of further unavailability of goods	2.2	2.4	2.2	2.3
7. Elimination of lag in adjusting cash buying to recent upward change in disposable income	1.0	1.0	1.0	1.0
8. Change owing to savings-bond campaign and other patriotic appeals to reduce consumption	–0.1	–0.1	–0.1	–0.1
9. Change owing to altered distribution of disposable income	1.7	1.5	2.5	1.1
10. Change owing to increased turnover of employment	0.3	0.5	0.3	0.5
11. Total change in amount consumers would want to spend out of unchanged disposable income	3.7	3.2	4.5	3.3
Change in capital formation owing to:				
12. Altered rate of rise of consumption	–2.0	–2.3	–2.0	–2.3
13. Change in composition of consumption	0.5	0.8	0.5	0.5
14. Private financing of defense	1.4	1.4	1.4	1.4
15. Diversion to federally financed defense	–1.5	–3.0	–1.5	–5.0
16. Speculation	0.2	0.2	0.2	0.2
17. Change in location of population	1.0	0.7	1.0	0.5
18. Diversion to privately financed defense	–1.1	–0.9	–1.1	–0.5
19. Change in export balance	–0.8	–0.2	–0.8	–0.1
20. Total change in producer spending (change in capital formation)	–2.3	–3.3	–2.3	–5.3
21. Total net change in civilian spending (item 11 plus item 20)	1.4	–0.1	2.2	–2.0

TABLE XIV (continued)

COMPUTATION OF AMOUNT OF ADDITIONAL TAX REVENUE NEEDED IN JUNE, 1942, COMPARED TO OCTOBER, 1941, TO AVERT INFLATION, UNDER THE ASSUMPTIONS GIVEN CONCERNING DIRECT CONTROLS

Annual Rates, in Billions of Dollars

	ALTERNATIVE SETS OF ASSUMPTIONS CONCERNING INCREASE IN OUTPUT AND DEFENSE SPENDING, AND DIVERSION			
	A	*B*	*C*	*D*
22. Total initial increase in spending (hence, initial increase in disposable income) if not counterbalanced (item 2 plus item 21)	10.4	9.9	12.2	8.0
23. Increase in corporate retained income other than effective tax reserves	0.6	0.5	1.0	0.4
24. Increase in tax payments or reserves under legislation in force October, 1941				
(a) Corporate income and profits taxes	2.0	2.0	2.0	2.0
(b) Other	3.5	3.5	3.5	3.5
25. Tax revenue needed from additional legislation, to maintain consumer disposable income unchanged (item 22 minus items 23 and 24)	4.3	3.9	5.7	2.1
26. Total increase in spending, hence, increase in drain on resources, under unchanged disposable income (item 2 plus item 21)	10.4	9.9	12.2	8.0
27. Reduction in civilian spending required (item 26 minus item 1)	5.1	5.5	5.5	5.0
28. Assumed reduction in civilian spending caused by an additional billion dollars of income tax	2.0	2.0	2.0	2.0
29. Tax revenue needed from additional legislation, to bring civilian spending				

TABLE XIV (continued)

	ALTERNATIVE SETS OF ASSUMPTIONS CONCERNING INCREASE IN OUTPUT AND DEFENSE SPENDING, AND DIVERSION			
	A	*B*	*C*	*D*
to required level, after enough taxation has been levied to maintain consumer disposable income unchanged	2.5	2.7	2.7	2.5
30. Total additional tax revenue needed in June, 1942, over October, 1941, to avert inflationary price rise (excluding inflation induced by concerted action) (items 29, 25, and 24)	12.3	12.1	13.9	10.1
31. Total additional tax revenue needed from new legislation (item 29 plus item 25)	6.8	6.6	8.4	4.6

FORMULA STATEMENT

The method of computation explained on pages 53 to 63 can be expressed in a formula as follows:

G = change in government spending, at prices of the initial date
I = change in national income (output) at prices of the initial date
C = estimated change in rate at which consumers will want to spend if consumer disposable income remains unchanged, and prices are unchanged
F = estimated change in gross private capital formation if consumer spending changes by C, and prices are unchanged
R = estimated change in retained profits and reserves, other than effective tax reserves, of corporations
M = decrease in civilian spending to be obtained by imposing one dollar of new taxes, after enough taxes have been imposed to maintain consumer disposable income unchanged (includes multiplier effects)
T = increase in tax revenue needed to maintain price level unchanged, under the given assumptions concerning size of defense program, degree of allocation and rationing, and so on
t = increase in revenue to be expected from existing laws
T′ = T-t = increase in revenue from new tax measures, needed to maintain price level unchanged

Then, in view of the fact that G and C and F create income to consumers, except for the amount siphoned off as R,

$G + C + F - R$ = the increase in tax revenue needed to maintain consumer disposable income unchanged;

and, in view of (1) the failure of I to increase as much as G, and (2) the existence of C and F, viewed now as drains on the resources of the community (rather than as creators of additional money incomes to the recipients),

$[(G - I) + C + F]$ = necessary change (decrease) in civilian spending—the spending that would be occurring if disposable income were merely kept unchanged; and

$\frac{1}{M}[(G - I) + C + F]$ = dollars of tax necessary to decrease civilian spending by $(G - I) + C + F$.

Consequently,

$$T = G + C + F - R + \frac{1}{M}[(G - I) + C + F]$$

and $$T' = G + C + F - R + \frac{1}{M}[(G - I) + C + F] - t$$

SHORT-CUT METHODS OF COMPUTING TAX REQUIREMENTS

Short-cut computations of the tax requirements may be made by ascertaining only the increase in total output and the increase in defense spending (the first two items in Table II on p. 26) and foregoing the kind of estimating contained in pp. 21–51, where the chief forces influencing the volume of civilian spending were analyzed one by one.

If no more tax revenue at all is being collected in June, 1942, than in October, 1941, the situation viewed prospectively (ex ante) is as follows, using Assumption A, and all figures being in October, 1941, prices.

The national income will increase by \$5.3 billion. Consumers' incomes will increase by \$4.7 billion, since \$0.6 billion will be held up in corporations as retained profits. What must the consumers do with the \$4.7 billion? They must save it all, for none of the increased \$5.3 billion output is available for them. Defense needs absorb all of it. Not only that; defense requires another \$3.7 billion (\$9.0 billion minus \$5.3 billion). Hence, consumers and civilian producers together must somehow save another $3.7 billion. "Out of" their increase in income of $5.3 billion they must save $9.0 billion. Without strict rationing, they will not do so. The picture is an impossible one, internally inconsistent. The consumers and civilian producers will of course save something out of the added $5.3 billion. Suppose business saves $0.6 billion (as already noted) and consumers, $1.2 billion. This still leaves $7.2 billion to be cut from civilian spending ($9.0 billion minus $1.8 billion). By how much, then, must the disposable incomes of consumers be cut, to get a reduction of $7.2 billion in spending—that is, to make an increase of $5.3 billion in income compatible with a reduction of $3.7 billion in spending? On the average, the dollar taken in tax forces some cut by the taxpayer in his spending, but not a full dollar's worth. Suppose that the taxpayer meets each added dollar in tax by cutting his spending two-thirds of a dollar and his saving one-third of a dollar. Then the $7.2 billion decrease in spending can be achieved by $10.8 billion added tax, which results also in a decrease of $3.6 billion in saving. The picture has become possible, internally consistent, and is as follows:

Changes, June, 1942, Compared with October, 1941 (in billions of dollars):

Increase in national income	5.3
Increase in defense spending	9.0
Decrease in civilian spending	3.7
Net decrease in saving by consumers and business (3.6 – 1.8)	1.8
Amount by which disposable income is reduced from the level of June, 1942, by additional tax revenue	10.8

The simplicity of this approach masks its dangers. The crucial estimates are (1) what increase in consumers' savings would accompany an increase of $4.7 billion in income? (2) what change in capital formation would accompany the change in consumers' spending? and (3) how much taxation would be needed to cut civilian spending by $7.2 billion? The steps involved in the computation of items (1) and (2) are essentially the same as those on pp. 21–51, made somewhat more difficult, perhaps, by assuming that consumer disposable income is $4.7 billion higher in June than in the preceding October, instead of being unchanged. By omitting a detailed study of items (1) and (2), greater dependence is placed on some general multiplier or successive-effects assumption.[28]

Still another and simpler approach is to ask: Since civilian spending must decrease \$3.7 billion (Assumption A), what decline in savings will probably be associated with this decline in spending? The sum of these two is of course the shrinkage in the savings-plus-spending uses of the national income. The remaining use is for tax payments. Since the national income is to increase by \$5.3 billion, the tax-payment use of the income must rise by the arithmetic sum of all three items. A decline in spending is usually associated with a somewhat smaller decline in savings. Suppose therefore that savings decrease by \$3.0 billion. Then taxation must increase by (billions of dollars) $3.0 + 3.7 + 5.3 = 12.0$ The income has increased by \$5.3 billion while the spending-saving segment has shrunk by \$6.7 billion. The gap (this time a "tax gap") is therefore \$12.0 billion.

Obviously, all the problems that are encountered in the other simplified approach are found here, too.

In any case, a sense of perspective may be heightened by casting the quantities in terms of absolute totals at both initial and terminal dates instead of working merely with increases and decreases from unspecified levels of the initial date. And of course the levels must be in mind, if the increments and decrements are to be handled intelligently. But as a method of computation, the incremental technique has the advantage of compelling an unwavering attention to the margin; changes in rates of change, especially, are less apt to get neglected.

The chief purpose in publishing these computations, now that the estimates themselves are obsolete, is to invite improvements or entirely new approaches to the basic problem faced. The computations should also serve to emphasize the extent to which greatly needed data on consumer spendings, capital formation, and so on, are still unavailable.

In view of the paucity of data and the danger of ignoring important factors, were the estimates of total tax requirements in the last line of Table XIV suitable for transmission to policy-making officials? Some

[28] See page 60.

safeguard against relying too heavily on any one figure was supplied by pointing out the breadth of the range—from $4.6 billion to $8.4 billion—covered by the answers. Moreover, there was available at the time no other definite estimate of tax requirements to avert inflation with an accompanying detailed explanation of the reasoning by which it had been obtained. Two other estimates were at hand, but one employed numerous short-cuts and gave no detailed explanation of the procedure, while in the other the computations bore chiefly on the size of the inflationary gap without a definite statement of the amount of taxation needed to close it. Both in the Treasury and elsewhere the figure for tax requirements to avert inflation, so far as that aim was specified, was being reached by a process of individual intuition, strongly colored by guesses of what Congress or the public at large would be willing to accept. Crude as are the steps followed in the present study, they are presumably superior to the intuitive process. There is at least somewhat more chance to discover the mistakes.

Part II

TAXES AVAILABLE TO AVERT INFLATION

BY CARL SHOUP

BEFORE COMPUTING the amount of revenue needed to avert inflation, it is necessary to determine the kind of tax that is to be used. Taxes differ in the degree to which they compress consumer spending. Moreover, other considerations are important, including generally accepted standards of fairness, or at least absence of gross discrimination; administrative feasibility, including speed of application; preservation of incentive to work, especially overtime work in war industries.

Even the kind of tax revenue that comes entirely out of saving and hence does not check consumer spending at all is of some importance, since it lessens the size of the post-war debt. The present computations indicate that inflation can be averted with an amount of taxation that is by no means large enough to balance the annual budget. The public debt can grow, though inflation is held in check. After the war, taxes necessitated by the interest on this greatly increased debt might discourage private enterprise, chiefly because business is so largely a problem in risk-taking; taxation, especially taxation of income, shifts the odds against the risk-taker. Consequently, there is some reason for setting the total amount of tax revenue to be raised during the war at a level above that needed merely to avert inflation, this extra taxation being designed to come chiefly from funds otherwise idle. But this problem is deliberately excluded from the scope of the present work, aside from a brief reference to it in comparing the income tax with the sales tax; [1] and even there the comparison between the two taxes assumes tax rates with equal consumption-inhibiting, not revenue-raising, power. An adequate treatment of the total revenue problem would involve the possibility of creating deposit money without an interest charge, the prospects of a consumer-pur-

[1] See point 9 on p. 103.

chasing boom as soon as the war ends, and several other matters of similar importance and complexity.

POSSIBILITIES OTHER THAN THE INDIVIDUAL INCOME TAX AND SALES TAX

The choice among tax measures for purposes of the present study was narrowed to the sales tax and the individual income tax. Several possibilities were discarded either because their novelty required more research than the present project was equipped to undertake, as with the spendings tax, or because they appeared inadequate quantitatively, as with the tax on increases in personal incomes and the corporation income taxes.

Tax on increases in personal incomes.—It has been suggested that individuals should pay an "excess income" tax, measured by the increase in their personal incomes, presumably after deduction of the ordinary income tax. The individual's income for the taxable year after ordinary tax would be compared with his income after ordinary tax in a base period, for instance, the year 1939 or an average of several years, as 1937–39. The excess would be subject to a special tax. The suggestion rests largely on the view that those individuals who benefit financially from the war should defray more of the war's costs than they would under other taxes. The point is especially pertinent with respect to the profits of partnerships and sole proprietorships, since the present excess-profits tax applies only to corporate profits. The proposal also reflects a view that, regardless of the reason for the increase in income, an individual who has recently risen from a lower level can pay more tax with less sacrifice than his neighbor who has been on the higher level for a number of years and has adjusted his standard of living to it.[2] The first view is usually unopposed, at

[2] "The degree of acuteness of the sacrifice is largely determined by the extent to which the payment of the tax impinges upon the habitual commitment [of expenditure]. . . . If equality of sacrifice is to be achieved, the dynamic as well as the static condition of the income must be considered." R. W. Green, "An Excess Income Tax," *Economic Journal,* Dec., 1920, pp. 543–44. Green proposed a tax on the excess of an individual's total income (if above £2,000) over the average of his income for the three immediately preceding years; the exempt amount would therefore rise gradually as income rose. When the year's income fell below the standard, a tax refund would be granted at two-thirds the regular tax rate. *Ibid.,* pp. 545–49. See also J. H. Myers, "Excess Profits Tax on Individuals," *Taxes,* Dec., 1941.

least in general terms (but see the exceptions suggested below). The second view is by no means generally accepted. But even if it were, so many exceptions to the rule would be urged or admitted that the tax, as finally enacted, would be unlikely to check consumer spending substantially.

The exceptions concern chiefly those who were receiving no money income at all, or only relief or work-relief income, in 1939: young men and women recently out of schools and colleges, housewives, superannuated workers, and workers from the home-relief rolls or, more often, the work-relief rolls. It seems unlikely that the community would accept a special tax on these groups as a fair tax, especially at a rate of more than, say, 10 percent.

The wage-earning wife could complain of a double discrimination. The present income tax tends to deter her from seeking employment in defense industries, if she must hire someone to do part of the housework, for she is not allowed to deduct this expense in computing her net income. To tax her still more on the grounds that her money income is greater than it was in 1939 would indicate virtually no comprehension at all of the effort required by housework.

Another group of exceptions commonly urged covers those workers whose earnings are higher chiefly because of longer hours, or new jobs away from home, or in new homes (farm boys and girls moving to the city). Here, part of the increased earnings are needed to defray the increase in living expenses: greater calorie intake is required, working clothes wear out sooner, transportation and rental costs are higher. Furthermore, hours of overtime will not be forthcoming, in the present state of human nature, without at least some pay; more than that, the rate of pay per hour will commonly have to be higher than for the normal hours. Leisure is a commodity highly prized when it is scarce, especially because the need for it grows at the same time, from accumulation of fatigue. Whether the tax would give rise to effective demands for higher wage rates, as some observers fear, depends on methods and aims of wartime wage control, but the possibility is one to be considered.

For a third group, the increased earnings are in large part the reward for having undergone expenses of training, or at least for having passed up better-paying jobs for the time being in order to work at learners' wages. Skilled workers in industry, professional men and women, and many other cases come readily to mind.

A fourth exception, somewhat resembling the third, includes those whose increased incomes are due to promotions or to professional prominence (moving-picture stars, for instance) that would have occurred anyway, in the normal course of events; but the difficulty of identifying most of the members of this group would probably be insuperable.

A fifth exception that has been urged in some discussions embraces entire industries that were depressed before the war and in which wages were much lower than they would be over a longer period—coal mining in Great Britain, for instance.[3]

And a sixth exception might include those whose increase in income had been no more than enough to allow them to discharge added responsibilities of marriage or children; in computing the taxable change in income, it might be necessary to allow a credit for change in marital status and in number or average age of dependents.

If profits of unincorporated concerns were to be included in the tax, some special allowance might have to be made for selecting a base period long enough to reveal a fair average of pre-war income.

These exceptions do not destroy the case for a tax on certain kinds of increase in personal income, imposed on grounds of equity, and yielding a modest revenue; [4] but they do make it a weak instrument for checking inflation.

Even in its more modest role, the tax would pose some difficult problems. In many cases there would be no record of the individual's income in the pre-war period. Partners and proprietors of unincorporated concerns, being taxed on increase in profits, would be ready to raise all the numerous claims to special treatment, on the grounds of an "abnormal" profit experience in the pre-war period, that have made a legal maze out of the excess-profits tax.[5] Stockholders would

[3] "The Black Market," *Bulletin*, Institute of Statistics, Oxford, March 14, 1942, p. 100.

[4] Cf.: ". . . there is a good deal more to be said for a moderate excess profits tax (say 60 or 70 per cent) combined with a drastic excess income tax (rising to 100 per cent) than there is for a drastic excess profits tax (80–100 per cent) taken alone." J. R. Hicks, U. K. Hicks, and L. Rostas, *The Taxation of War Wealth*, Oxford, 1941, p. 69. The question arises whether the tax would be "drastic" in the size of its rate or in the width of its base.

[5] See Internal Revenue Code, §§ 711 (b) and 722.

escape the tax to the extent that earnings were retained and not paid out in dividends until after the war, when the tax had been repealed. Meanwhile, bondholders receiving back payments of interest on bonds that had gone into default during or before the pre-war period would claim relief; so would recipients of accumulated preferred dividends.

An increase in the price level would lessen the absolute significance of the increases in money incomes, though it would not lessen their significance relative to those incomes that had remained unchanged or that had decreased. In effect, the tax would reach those whose real incomes had not fallen by more than a certain proportion (the proportion in which the price level had risen).

Germany imposed a tax on increases in personal incomes, with numerous exemptions, in March, 1939, but reduced the rate from 30 percent to 15 percent in April, 1939, and repealed the tax in August, 1940. The tax was based on the increase in income of the taxable year over the income of the immediately preceding year, not over the income of some fixed pre-war period. Hence, only an ever-increasing income could be continually taxed.[6] In 1941, the Price Commissar issued a decree forcing the surrender of professional income in excess of that of the base period. Small professional incomes were exempted; so was income from extra work.[7] According to available information, the excess-income tax has not been introduced by any of the other major belligerents in the present war.

In 1915, Denmark, Sweden, and Norway, in the order given, imposed taxation on increases in income over the pre-war years,[8] including increases not only in profits, corporate and otherwise, but also in salary, wage, and investment income. However, the application of these taxes to individuals was considerably softened by exempting anyone whose net income for the taxable year was less than 8,000 kröner (Denmark) or less than 10,000 kröner (Sweden and Norway); in addition exemption was granted to a certain minimum amount of war income (that is, the excess of net income over the pre-

[6] The tax was also imposed on increases in profits. H. W. Singer, "The German War Economy in the Light of Economic Periodicals," *Economic Journal,* June–Sept., 1941, p. 214.

[7] H. W. Singer, "The German War Economy," *Economic Journal,* April, 1942, p. 29. Apparently the whole "skimming-off" technique has since been abandoned. Singer, *Economic Journal,* June–Sept., 1942, p. 202.

[8] The Danish base period included the tax year 1914–15.

war income, so far as it was attributable to the war). The Netherlands war-income tax of 1916 similarly applied to individuals, but with important exceptions: salaries and wages of public employees; salaries and wages that were not above going rates; and dividends.[9]

In 1916 and 1919 Germany imposed a tax on increment in wealth of individuals measured from the level of December 31, 1913, and in 1918 and 1919 a tax on the increase in personal incomes of those years over that of the last year of peace, except that only the excess over 10,000 marks was taxed, with a further deduction of 3,000 marks. The Austrian tax on increase of incomes, including individual incomes, did not apply to government salaries, and exempted a large block of increase in income of other employees (4,000 kronen in 1916, plus 3,000 kronen vanishing exemption; 20,000 kronen in 1918, plus 5,000 kronen vanishing exemption).[10]

Belgium, France, Great Britain, Italy, Russia, and the United States did not attempt to tax increases in wage and salary income.[11]

Taxes on corporate profits.—Several billions more of tax revenue have been obtained in the past few years by increasing the corporation income tax and introducing the corporation excess-profits tax. However, further increases in these taxes did not seem suitable methods for obtaining substantial increases in revenue with respect to the limited objectives of the present study.

A tax on corporate income runs a double danger of being paid out of savings rather than out of money that would otherwise have been spent; to this extent it fails to check inflation. First, the corporation may decide not to cut its dividends by the full amount of the tax increase. Second, most of the dividends paid to individuals go to those whose incomes are high enough to enable them to meet a substantial part of a cut in dividends by diminishing their current saving (or drawing on their accumulated capital) rather than by restricting their consumption.

An increase in corporation income or excess-profits taxes will pro-

[9] Karl Bräuer, "Die Besteuerung der Kriegsgewinne in den Europäischen Staaten," *Finanz und Volkswirtschaftliche Zeitfragen*, p. 45; Institut Solvay, "*L'Impôt sur les bénéfices de guerre*, pp. 115 ff.; M. J. Van der Flier, *War Finances in the Netherlands up to 1918*, pp. 79–93.

[10] Bräuer, *op. cit.*, pp. 14–16.

[11] The United States tax of 1917 to which J. R. Hicks and others refer (*op. cit.*, p. 65) was merely an 8 percent tax on current individual net income in excess of $6,000.

duce several indirect effects on inflation, many of them tending to increase it. A high tax rate reduces management's resistance to demands for wage increases, especially where resistance would invite labor trouble and absorb much time and effort. The high tax rate also reduces the reward for care in the purchase and use of materials and machinery. Moreover, if the high rate is thought to be temporary, there is a rational case for concentrating in the current year maintenance expenditures that would otherwise have been made some time later. A maintenance deduction means more tax saving in a year of high tax rates; the net cost of maintenance may therefore be lessened by moving the expenditure into the year of high taxation. Further, the high rates may increase the pressure on businessmen to crowd into the category of maintenance and replacement (from the category, expansion of the business) all that the Internal Revenue agents will stand for; and a high degree of success in this attempt might induce a larger total amount of capital expenditure, replacement plus expansion, than would occur under low tax rates. In the aggregate, these inflation-increasing characteristics of high rates on corporate income, or business income in general, may be important.

On the other hand, in so far as the tax prevents the appearance of large corporate profits, it removes an obvious stimulant to demands for higher wages.

More direct effects are possible. A heavy tax on corporate incomes might deter to some extent the purchase of capital equipment to expand the business, thus reducing civilian spending in the producers' goods sector. But the impossibility of predicting even roughly the amount by which a given rate would reduce such purchases would make the tax an undependable instrument of inflation control. Moreover, the amount of reduction in spending that might ensue would probably be small unless the tax promised to be in force for some years to come. Corporate spending on mere maintenance of already existing capital equipment is not directly checked by a tax on net income, since these maintenance expenditures are deducted in computing net income, and indeed, as indicated above, they may be encouraged by the high rate.

With respect to excess profits, a tax close to 100 percent on all increase in corporation profit would still allow inflation. Consumers spending a block of newly created money, or drawing on hoards, would push the price level up a notch. If the resulting increase in spending ended up as windfall profits of corporations, it would be largely absorbed in taxation. The second stage of inflation, a respending of the profits, would therefore be barred. In fact, however, some of the increase in spending would result not in windfall profits of corporations, but in higher wages, salaries, or rents, or higher profits of unincorporated enterprises, and would therefore escape the excess-profits tax. Moreover, consumers could appear again with another block of new money created for them by the government, and, if it were substantially larger than the first, it would probably push prices up another notch. The prospective size of the arms program guaranteed that ever-increasing blocks of new money would, in fact, be needed if additional tax revenue was to come from corporate taxes alone.

So long as the undistributed profits of a given year are not included in the stockholder's statement of taxable income for that year, there remains a case—not necessarily conclusive, of course—for corporate taxation of some sort by the Federal Government. And excess-profits taxation might be supported on the further grounds of absorbing some income that is a surplus in the sense that it is not a necessary reward to get things done, though the present excess-profits tax law almost surely goes much farther than this in many instances and falls short of it in others. The analysis above does not imply that these taxes should not be used. It merely explains why they were not selected for the restricted aim of the present study.

Spendings tax.—The individual income tax might be altered, with respect to further rate increases, by exempting all saving from the increase in rates, taxing only spendings. This spendings tax would exert a somewhat more powerful anti-inflationary effect for every 1 percent of tax rate than would the source-collected income tax to be described below; and, unlike the sales tax, it could have a progressive rate scale with personal exemption and credit for dependents that would allow for differences in economic status and also put a powerful check on marginal spending. The tax was not selected for purposes of the present study, however, chiefly for two reasons. First, to exert an immediate pressure against inflation it needs to be collected monthly or at least quarterly, which in turn implies either collection at the source or quarterly self-assessments on the current year's spendings. These considerations raise important problems of technique that could not be adequately studied in the present project. Second, more study was needed of the administrative problem of insuring a reasonable degree of accuracy in the taxpayer's statement of savings (or spendings), especially at low income levels. The most troublesome problem is expenditure on housing accommodation; to insure a reasonable degree of equity, either homeowners must be taxed on their imputed expenditure, or actual rental expenditure for dwellings must be exempt. The discrimination against renters that the existing income tax exercises is serious, but it would probably appear even more so under a spendings tax.[12]

Other possibilities.—A series of heavy excises—production taxes or sales taxes on selected consumer goods—could exert the necessary anti-inflationary pressure only if imposed on so broad a front as to become virtually a general sales tax with exemptions, a possibility discussed on pp. 98–99. The excises may be useful in a minor role: levied on articles made with labor, materials, and plant that are specially needed in the war effort, the taxes can drive civilians away, releasing the resources for government use without a bidding-up of price that would intensify inflation. In the United States, in the latter part of 1941, however, it was evident that direct controls would be used to clear the way for the government's demands.

Taxation of the purchase of capital goods by business firms might be useful in lessening civilian drain on scarce materials, labor, and plant that had slipped through the allocation or priorities net, but the quantitative aspects of this problem seemed unpredictable on the basis of readily available information, at least for the present study.

An increase in existing payroll taxes would reach only a part of those who are receiving salaries and wages. It would also leave investment income completely free of the added burden except in so far as the tax came out of profits. Moreover, the lack of any exemption

[12] In the comparison between a sales tax and an income tax, on pp. 91 ff., it will be seen that many of the points apply as well to a comparison of a spendings tax and an income tax, since a spendings tax is in essence a progressive retail sales tax collected from the buyer. But, as indicated in the text above, there are other important points applicable to a spendings tax but not to a sales tax.

for individuals with extremely low incomes, the failure to recognize differences in marital status and responsibility for dependents, and the refusal to allow any deductions for expenses incurred in earning the income would be further grounds for considering that a high-rate tax levied without promise of future benefits would be far too discriminatory. The imposition of a higher rate in connection with an extension or increase of benefit payments would of course exercise a significant check on inflation, at least for the time being, but the consideration of such a program involves forming a judgment on the desirability of further benefit payments, a matter outside the scope of the present study.

Direct property taxation is for all practical purposes forbidden the Federal Government under the constitutional clause that requires apportionment of such taxes among the states on the basis of population.

INDIVIDUAL INCOME TAX

Individual income taxation could not be reasonably effective in checking the threatened inflation if it took the form simply of an addition to the rates of the existing tax, which was being collected with a lag of about a year. Income received in January–December, 1942, would result in tax payments in March, June, September, and December, 1943. In the absence of a heavy tax on 1941 incomes additional to that already imposed by the Revenue Act of 1941, the flow of revenue that would be required in June, 1942, could not be obtained under traditional income-tax methods.

Two other possibilities remained: quarterly prepayment in 1942 on the estimated income of 1942; and collection at source during 1942 on 1942 income.

Collection at source would not be applicable to partnership and proprietorship income, including farm profits and income from professions, nor to the numerous small rents paid by individual tenants, nor to interest paid by individual debtors. These incomes might be reached by a prepayment system. The Treasury would send each of these taxpayers a bill based on one-quarter of his preceding year's reported net income, with an option to pay on his actual income for the quarter, and a requirement to pay on it if he had filed no return the preceding year. The regular annual return after the close of the year would allow adjustment for overpayments (refunds) or underpayments.

With respect to much the largest segment of the income stream—wages and salaries in general, dividends, and, in part, interest—three considerations tipped the balance in favor of collection at the source. It might be necessary to change the rate of the supplementary income tax at some time other than the quarterly dates; and, even if the changes could be restricted to those dates, there would be some confusion and errors in payment. Secondly, it would be difficult to induce millions of small taxpayers to file quarterly returns on estimated quarterly 1942 income. Finally, taxpayers would find it less embarrassing financially to pay smaller amounts weekly or monthly at the source than larger amounts quarterly, both because the amount of any one payment would be smaller, and because it is less painful to receive a smaller income than to give up a corresponding part of a larger one already pocketed.

The withholding tax and its quarterly prepayment complement would carry personal exemptions and a credit for dependents, and perhaps also a flat percentage of income as a preliminary estimate for deductions like interest, taxes, and so on, with a final reckoning made at the time of filing the annual return for the regular tax, in the succeeding March. Personal exemptions of $500 for a single person, $1,000 for a married taxpayer, and $300 for each dependent were assumed. The employee would file with his employer a certificate of family status, and the employer would deduct tax only on the excess of the pay check above the monthly, semimonthly, or weekly prorated part of the annual exemptions. Tax on dividends (and interest, if subject to the collection-at-source mechanism) would have to be withheld without accounting at the time for family status, since any given investor commonly receives such income from several sources, and might temporarily succeed in claiming several sets of exemption and credit. Exceptions could be made in special cases of potential hardship, however. In any case, the annual return in the subsequent year would contain the necessary adjustments.

A withholding tax without any personal exemption or credit for dependents whatever would be difficult to collect with a high percentage of completeness: witness the exclusion of domestic servants and farm workers from the social-security taxes. Most of them would not be taxable under a system with personal exemptions. Moreover, a tax without exemptions would cut into the subsistence of those with incomes so low that the decrease in consumption forced by the loss of a dollar in tax would probably cause a decrease of more than a dollar in working energy or efficiency; and the equity of imposing further taxes on the extremely low income groups is at least very doubtful. Finally, there would be serious discrimination between two taxpayers on the same level, if one were a single person without dependents and the other a married taxpayer with a number of dependents. Here, too, the issues of efficiency and equity both arise.

The government itself, for every dollar that it gained in tax from the very lowest income group, or from the very large family, would probably lose directly at least part of a dollar and perhaps more, either immediately or years later, through increased demands for cash relief, free food, free medical service, and so on, that would result from the decrease in the taxpayer's power to buy such things with his own money.

On the other hand, a given amount of revenue could be obtained at a lower rate than if exemptions and credits were granted, and a lower rate generally results in less evasion. There would also be a possible benefit to morale from the knowledge that the special tax effort was universal, unless exemption were retained for income from tax-exempt state and local bonds. But on balance, the case for granting exemptions and credits for family status seems much the stronger.

SALES TAX

While there is only one type of income tax that promises effective control of inflation, there are several types of sales tax available: a general sales tax, or turnover tax, on all transactions, as in Germany; a manufacturers' sales tax, as in Canada; a wholesale sales tax, as in Great Britain and Australia; or a retail sales tax, as in several states of the United States.

The only major advantage of the turnover tax is that for a given amount of revenue a smaller rate is needed, and consequently the inducement to evasion of the tax at any one point is somewhat smaller.

But there are many more taxpayers, hence many more points of potential evasion.

The turnover tax would greatly favor the vertically integrated concerns, where the product passes from raw to finished state with no sales, and hence no tax, en route. Taxation of intra-firm transfers has been tried in Europe, but the difficulties of this remedy are presumably severe. Unless farmers are effectively included, the turnover tax also favors the kind of finished product that, dollar for dollar of finished value, is produced with less than average processing and marketing costs (and with more than average farm cost). Chiefly for these reasons, the turnover tax was discarded in the present study.

The manufacturers' sales tax, applied only to the finished manufactured product as it leaves the hands of the last manufacturer, involves fewer taxpayers than the other forms of sales tax. But it requires the highest rate, to raise a given amount of revenue. And it necessitates an estimate of what a manufacturer's price would be at point of manufacture, for those transactions where he in fact sells direct to consumers, or to retailers, or at a price that covers transportation or other services. Otherwise, such sales will be taxed more heavily than sales made at the lower, factory price, without services. Similarly, there are difficulties in providing for the uniform inclusion or exclusion of the value of packages and containers, and selling and advertising expenses.

All purchasers who are likely to be working on raw materials or partly finished articles are licensed and allowed to purchase such goods free of tax by quoting their license number to the vendor. Some licensing difficulties may arise from complicated channels of flow of finished goods among manufacturers, wholesalers, and retailers.

The wholesale sales tax applies the technique of the manufacturers' tax, one stage further down. Sales by wholesalers to retailers or to consumers are taxed. The difficulty of getting a uniform price base for all sellers is perhaps somewhat less in the aggregate than under the manufacturers' tax and so, too, is the problem of granting exemption in all cases where the article is to be further processed. There would be more taxpayers, but a lower tax rate. In the absence of a more thorough examination, the manufacturers' tax and wholesale tax seem not to offer much choice.

Both taxes may result in some pyramiding; that is, the retailer and, under the manufacturers' tax, the wholesaler also, may apply their customary percentage mark-ups to a cost price that includes the sales tax, thus obtaining a profit on the tax. In some cases the "profit" on the tax will merely cover a necessary expense to the merchant, in so far as his expenses—commissions, wages, rent, interest, and personal property taxes—tend to rise and fall more or less automatically with the total cost of goods sold.

Conversely, there is somewhat more chance that market imperfections may cause at least a part of the tax to stay with the businessman and come out of his profits, when it has to be passed on two or three times before it reaches the consumer.

The repeal of a sales tax is likely to prove embarrassing to the business world when it has been levied at the manufacturing or wholesale stage. Upon repeal, the retailers' stocks of goods (and the wholesalers' too, under a manufacturers' tax) would be left with a "tax content" [13] that might prove difficult to work off in the face of newly produced tax-free goods.

The retail sales tax includes a much larger number of taxpayers than either of the other two, unless complete exemption is granted to those with a yearly turnover of less than about $50,000. But the tax rate, to produce a given amount of revenue, would need to be only about half or three-quarters that of a manufacturers' sales tax, with consequent lessening of inducement to evasion. The retail sales tax presents somewhat less difficulty, in the aggregate, with respect to putting all sales on a comparable base. Where credit, delivery, and other services are rendered, they will be taxed, but it may be argued that such services are properly taxable as part of the final product the consumer buys. The question is different under the wholesalers' or manufacturers' tax: there the problem arises from taxing such services in some cases, and exempting them in others, merely because the taxpayer-vendor is not always the businessman who performs them.

The proper treatment of trade-ins is another problem more or less peculiar to the retail sales tax.

The retail tax is better adapted than the others to a system of

[13] H. R. Ways and Means Committee, *Hearings, 1942 Revenue Revision*, p. 511; see also p. 1730.

blanket price control; the tax can be stated separately. When a tax must be carried down as a separate item from producer to wholesaler to retailer it is more difficult to isolate: and if it is isolated the consumer, by some simple arithmetic, can compute the margin the retailer is getting on each article.[14] Blanket price control was not in immediate prospect in the fall of 1941. But the point is useful anyway, for it shows that tax consciousness, through a separate stating of the tax, is more readily achieved under the retail sales tax.

Several states are using the retail tax. Politically, this fact makes a similar federal tax less available. Administratively, it has perhaps the reverse effect. Not only can the Federal Government draw on the experience of the states; some form of joint administration might be worked out.

Another possibility, a tax on value added, has not been utilized by any country, but has been discussed recently in Washington. The tax would be imposed on every business firm, including, in some versions, all wholesalers and retailers. The tax base would be, roughly, the gross income less cost of materials and fuel and power; it would therefore be the amount of value added by the concern's activities to the things it purchased. (Strictly, this approach would also call for the deduction of depreciation.) To raise a given volume of revenue, this tax could be imposed at a lower rate than any of the others, except a universal turnover tax. It would also make unnecessary the taxation of sales of machinery and fuel to business concerns. Although these sales are not to ultimate consumers, and hence should in principle be tax-free, there is some difficulty in distinguishing them from sales of the same articles to ultimate users like homeowners. It is the opinion of some students of sales taxation (in which, however, the present writer does not concur) that this difficulty is great enough to justify ignoring the status of the purchaser and taxing all such sales under an ordinary sales tax.[15]

The value-added tax has the disadvantage of making impracticable any very important degree of exemption of any class of goods—for

[14] If an article sells at retail for $1.00 and carries in addition a wholesalers' sales tax of 7 cents, and if the rate of that tax is known to be 10 percent, the price to the retailer, before tax, was obviously 70 cents, and his mark-up, therefore, about 43 percent. We are indebted to Dr. John F. Due for this point.

[15] See p. 103.

example, food. And in number of taxpayers it would present a larger problem than any of the other taxes.

In the light of all these considerations, a retail sales tax appeared to offer the best alternative to a withholding tax.

WITHHOLDING TAX WITH PERSONAL EXEMPTIONS VERSUS RETAIL SALES TAX

Making a choice between an income tax collected at the source and a retail sales tax is more of a technical venture than is commonly realized. In the first place, each tax can do a number of things that the other cannot. The list given below is designed to cover all the major points on which the two taxes differ.

In the second place, the respective rates at which the two taxes would be levied must be kept in mind. Roughly, it appears that a retail sales tax would have a tax base not far from $50 billion, and the withholding tax, under exemptions of $1,000, $500, and $300, a tax base of slightly over $30 billion (figures for calendar year 1942). To raise an equal amount of revenue, the rate of the income tax would have to be about two-thirds again as high as the retail sales tax rate. A comparison of a 10 percent retail sales tax, for example, with a 17 percent withholding tax (with the exemptions as given above) would be consistent from the point of view of revenue. But equality of revenue is not quite the proper test for purposes of this study; equality of consumption-inhibiting power is sought. A careful comparison on that basis would be a complex task. It is not needed at this point, where only an approximate equivalence of rates is required to help set the stage for a choice between the two taxes. Roughly, then, the withholding tax will be assumed to carry a rate double that of the alternative retail sales tax. If food is exempted under the retail sales tax, about one-third of the tax base is lost, and the respective rate proportions would be about 10 to 13 instead of 10 to 20.

In the third place, although either tax alone is capable of supplying all the revenue needed to avert inflation, it might be preferable to use both. A particular disadvantage of one tax or the other that would be unimportant so long as the tax rate were low might be intolerable under a high rate. The tendency to outright evasion is an illustration. Other disadvantages may not grow nearly so rapidly as the tax rate rises. This is a field to which little study or speculation has yet been devoted. Experience indicates, however, that any given tax, viewed as an alternative to some other tax, is subject to a tendency of decreasing relative advantage (relative, that is, to the advantage of using the alternative tax) as the tax rate rises. For instance, the most desirable combination of Tax A and Tax B, when X dollars is needed, may be Tax A at 10 percent and none of Tax B; but if 2X dollars is needed, a second 10 percent on Tax A may have more undesirable effects than a first 10 percent (or whatever the equivalent is) on Tax B. In other words, a diversified tax system may be needed, not merely because Tax B can do some things that Tax A cannot do at all, but also because the relative advantage of Tax A may weaken as its rate rises. Conceivably, too, this relative advantage may rise as the rate rises, as with a customs duty designed to promote some domestic industry, or with respect to some fixed overhead cost of administration. No attempt to gauge relative advantages at various rate levels will be made in this study. Largely for the sake of convenience, a definite choice between the two is made, instead of a mixture; but the possible superiority of a mixture, if rates have to go very high, must be kept in mind.

Advantages of a sales tax over an income tax.—A (10 percent) retail sales tax can, while a (20 percent) source-collected income tax cannot, accomplish the following aims:

1. Collect the tax in very small amounts, day by day, thus avoiding involuntary delinquency due to improvidence. The best that an income tax can do, in practice, is week-by-week, in correspondingly larger amounts; and for many taxpayers the interval must be longer. But the sales tax loses this advantage so far as the consumer buys on credit and pays his bills, and hence his sales tax, once a month.

2. Exercise a relatively small deterrent to work in war industries. Virtually no study of this crucial point has been made. Common sense, however, suggests that an income tax, cutting as it does so directly into the reward offered for additional work, is a greater deterrent to overtime work or to intense labor under piece rates, or to steady daily attendance on the job, than a sales tax, which cuts the reward indirectly. Moreover, the sales tax affects the reward only as it is spent on certain things, not saved or spent on tax-free items like rent. The

further fact that the rate of the income tax is substantially higher than that of the sales tax makes the presumed advantage of the sales tax on this point almost a certainty. The difference in rate of the two taxes arises of course from the fact that the income tax allows complete exemption for the reward of the first hours of work, through the personal exemption, and hence must strike the reward of the last hours of work much more severely than the sales tax, which takes a piece out of each hour's reward, even the first. The marginal impact of the income tax is therefore much greater. Perhaps certain technical changes that would reduce the marginal impact are practicable; the income-tax rate might be applied to the taxpayer's entire net income, once he became taxable at all by rising above the personal exemption level. This would allow a somewhat lower rate, though still not so low, probably, as the sales tax. The chief difficulty would be the abrupt jump from complete exemption to fairly severe taxation just by crossing the personal exemption line. Some sort of "notch" provision might be practicable to ease the transition, even in a source-collected tax, but the marginal effect on taxpayers in the notch might still be so severe and affect so many workers that it would counterbalance the advantage gained by the lowering of the marginal rate for all whose incomes extended beyond the notch.

The advantage of the sales tax may conceivably take the form of a larger incentive, rather than a smaller deterrent, to work. The absolute amount of either tax may press so hard on the standard of living that there develops a powerful inducement to work more and earn more, an inducement that overshadows the contrary tendency caused by the fact that as one's income increases, the dollars he must pay in tax increase, too. The relative advantage would still be with the sales tax.

That labor incentive is not purely a hypothetical problem is evidenced by the measures Germany is reported to have taken. Early in 1940 it was reported that exemption from the special 50 percent increase in the wage tax (not 50 percent of the wage, note) was granted to wages for overtime, Sunday, and night work.[16] Later in 1940 (September) this exemption was withdrawn, when full overtime rates,

[16] H. W. Singer, "The German War Economy in the Light of Economic Periodicals," *Economic Journal,* April, 1941, p. 25.

which had been somewhat restricted, were reintroduced.[17] But in November of the same year the exemption was restored, and extended to include the regular income tax.[18] About a year later, the "iron savings" program was introduced. Wage and salary earners are given the opportunity to save (a) either 12 marks or 24 marks a month, (b) plus all overtime bonuses up to 12 marks a month, (c) plus all Christmas bonuses, and so on, up to 480 marks—all by direct payroll deduction. The amounts so saved are exempted from the income tax, the wage tax, and the social-insurance contributions. They remain blocked for the duration of the war, and after the war a year's notice of withdrawal must be given. "This special treatment of overtime earnings is intended to increase the incentive for increased output." [19] In Great Britain, too, there is evidence that taxation—and also rationing—have caused some decrease in work.[20]

In many cases, but by no means all, the hours of work in a working day are fixed. But even then, a lack of incentive may show up in increased absenteeism. Piece-rate work is always sensitive to reward. Finally, even if hours are fixed, with no piece rates, and only a small amount of absenteeism exists, there remains the problem of inducing workers to leave nonessential civilian employment for war work and essential civilian work. This shift, involving as it does some added expense and inconvenience to the worker, may be retarded by a tax that directly lowers the nominally higher wages offered as an inducement to make the change.

A possible impairment in incentive of high-salaried executives and investors must also be considered. Incentive at high-salary levels is largely a matter of seeing a chance to rise higher, and the income-tax increase could be leveled off in the upper brackets to allow always

[17] Singer, *Economic Journal*, June–Sept., 1941, p. 200. A literal reading would indicate that the exemption had been from the entire wage tax, not merely the wartime increase. It is therefore not clear, at this writing, which is the case.

[18] *Ibid.*, pp. 200–201.

[19] Singer, *Economic Journal*, April, 1942, p. 34; Christmas bonuses not so saved now became subject to the wage tax. *Ibid.*, p. 25.

[20] W. J. Hughes, "An Alternative to the Last Two Budgets," *Economic Journal*, Dec., 1941, p. 506; *Economist*, Feb. 7, 1942, p. 176. On the other hand, a recent survey of the causes of absenteeism in the British cutlery trade does not give a prominent place to the income tax. F. A. Wells, "Voluntary Absenteeism in the Cutlery Trade," *Review of Economic Studies*, Summer, 1942, pp. 158–76.

some possibility of a net increase in salary, if this kind of incentive should prove necessary for wartime.

Wartime investment is so surrounded by direct controls, and the government is so prepared to spend whatever it needs to get whatever investment is necessary, that it seems doubtful whether the difference between the tax measures here under consideration would be significant on this point.

3. Minimize wasteful use of business resources. For the same reason that it is a smaller deterrent to extra work, the sales tax is not so likely to induce laxity in managing the affairs of an unincorporated business. When he knows that a substantial proportion of any saving will be taken away in tax, the independent proprietor or partner may slacken his efforts to get the best use out of his materials, plant, and labor supply. In the aggregate, this factor is less important than the effect on labor incentive. The volume of business that is carried on in unincorporated form, particularly of business that might impede the war effort by its wasteful use of men, plant, and materials, is relatively small. A similar conclusion applies in so far as the tax dampens a willingness to take business risks.

4. Avoid discrimination according to age. The amount a man spends throughout his life fluctuates somewhat less than the amount he receives as income. A high income-tax rate, levied for only a few years, discriminates among different age groups somewhat more capriciously than a sales tax does. The extraordinary, temporary income-tax rates become a special tax on those who happen at that particular time to be at the peak of their earning power but also at the peak of their saving. Correspondingly, elderly individuals who are living partly on their capital (as on annuities, for instance) are spared. Possibly this is just the pattern the legislator desires, but it is not commonly and explicitly advocated.

5. Avoid decreasing one of the rewards offered for postponing consumption, that is, interest (or a part of profit). The income tax is imposed on income whether it is saved or spent. If the income is saved and invested, the resulting interest or profit is taxed. Consequently the net return for waiting (and for risk-taking, too) is decreased. The sales tax does not have this effect. On the advisability of main-

taining the reward for postponing consumption, opinions differ in peacetime; in wartime, this aim probably has general acceptance. The point involved is the one that has been discussed by Irving Fisher under the label "double taxation."

6. Avoid awkward situations arising from contracts to repay debts. Some individuals committed themselves to ambitious saving programs through repayment of debts, before they had reason to foresee the high tax rates of the war period. In some of these cases release from the commitment—for instance, amortization payments on a home—is necessary if the income tax is to be paid without a considerable postponement of repayment or without a sudden and severe lowering of the standard of consumption. Release from the commitment is sometimes possible only through a sacrifice that is wasteful and, compared to the sacrifices that other taxpayers must make, unduly severe; giving up the home, for example. The sales tax, which automatically exempts income devoted to savings, has much less tendency to create such a problem.

7. Give the taxpayer some option to escape part of the tax by restricting his consumption of taxed goods below the level it would reach under an income tax. The offering of such an option may be desirable because of the numerous, largely unforeseeable, situations where the individual can meet the last few dollars of his tax obligation only by making a sacrifice that (in comparison with virtually all other taxpayers) is out of all proportion to the number of tax dollars involved. This argument is capable of only a narrow application. In practice, the taxpayer's demands for goods and services are too insistent to leave him with much option, under a general retail sales tax.

8. Reach every family and single individual. On the advisability of this aim, opinions differ; but to those who think it important that everyone contribute something toward the increase in tax revenues (in this case, increase over the revenues of the 1941 Revenue Act), the sales tax is the better tax with respect to this point. The source-collected income tax could in principle be imposed with no personal exemption at all. In practice, however, as suggested above, there would be enormous if not prohibitive administrative difficulty in reaching every small employer, including farmers and householders

employing domestic servants, and, on March 15 of the following year, every small income recipient.

9. Avoid undue exemption of farmers. A common charge against the income tax is its failure to tax the farmer; and the sales tax is presumed to do a somewhat better job. But the issues, and the facts, too, are not very clear. Part of the failure of the income tax to reach the farmer results from the farmer's failure to attain an income level comparable to that at which urban workers are taxed, even after all adjustments for comparing the two have been made. Part is traceable to the failure of the income tax to adjust to regional differences in cost of living, a point to be considered below. Part is due to the fact that a considerable proportion of food, fuel, and shelter consumed by the farmer is provided directly by his own farm and so is not required to be included in taxable gross income. That part of the farm expenses allocable to such items is not supposed to be deducted in computing net income, but it may be doubted that this provision is effective in practice. However, there is no prospect that the sales tax would reach these items either. Ignorance of tax responsibilities or even outright fraud may be important factors under the income tax; the retail sales tax avoids these issues with respect to the farmer, since he rarely engages in retail trade. Finally, the sales tax is likely to get at least something out of every farmer, owing to its failure to provide any personal exemption [21]—a characteristic that from a certain point of view is a disadvantage,[22] but that here has the virtue of canceling, to some extent, the failure to reach farm-produced income in kind. The income tax provides no such fortuitous canceling.

10. Allow, perhaps, for regional differences in cost of living. The chief factor in such differences is probably dwelling rental. The retail sales tax, as customarily conceived, exempts this kind of consumer outlay. Thus, undesignedly to be sure, the tax carries an exemption that varies directly with the regional cost of living. This advantage of the sales tax rests, however, upon a supposition rather than an ascertained fact: the supposition that the consumer's demand for housing accommodation is strong enough, in the high-cost regions, to result in his devoting a larger part of his total expenditure to housing

[21] But see pp. 98–99.
[22] See pp. 99–100.

than he would in the low-cost areas. It is possible that the high cost of housing drives him to purchase other things and to restrict his use of housing so greatly that he devotes a smaller part of his expenditures to housing than he would in a low-cost area. To the extent that this occurs, the exemption of housing under the retail sales tax puts a heavier burden on the family living in a high-cost area than on a family with the same real income (but lower dollar income) in a low-cost area. The data available are not adequate to demonstrate what the typical situation is. Common observation suggests that the family in the high-cost area does devote a larger part of the total expenditures to dwelling than a similar family with the same real income in a low-cost area, but the question must still be regarded as unsettled.

There may be a constitutional bar to varying the personal exemption of the income tax from region to region in the United States; moreover, the political repercussions would almost surely make such a plan unacceptable.

11. Tax individuals who receive all or most of their income in the form of interest on state and local bonds. Such interest is completely exempt from the federal income tax. Congress shows no disposition to tax either the interest or future issues or outstanding issues, and even if it did, there is at least some question whether a constitutional amendment would not be necessary. A sales tax, even at 10 percent, would be a small burden on wealthy holders of tax-exempt bonds, but for some of them it would be heavier than a 20 percent additional income tax.

Advantages of an Income Tax over a Sales Tax.—On the other hand, a source-collected income tax can, and a retail sales tax cannot, accomplish the following aims:

1. Allow complete exemption, from the increase in taxation, to individuals with very low incomes. This is accomplished through the use of a personal exemption.

Perhaps such an exemption could be made a part of the retail sales tax, by giving each consumer a book of coupons with an aggregate face value equal to the exemption. The retailers would present the coupons to the government in payment of the tax. This device has apparently never been utilized, and would therefore incur some risk in facing unknown difficulties, besides the customary problems that accompany all coupon plans—chiefly loss of coupons, by consumer or by retailer, and counterfeiting. The task of registering every consumer, or every household, and printing and distributing the coupon books would be larger than is generally realized. Transferability of the coupons would probably have to be allowed, in view of the difficulty in enforcing nontransferability. The coupon suggestion has promise, but, until it has been studied thoroughly, the income tax must be considered superior to the sales tax in so far as one of the aims is to exempt completely from the increase in taxation all those below a certain income level.

The test for lowness of income is commonly on a per capita basis, or something approaching it. For instance, a family with an income of $1,900 with three children may be regarded as no better off than a family at the $1,000 level but with no dependents, or a single person with $500. All three cases could be exempted completely from the increase in taxation, under the low-income test, by using the customary personal exemptions and credit for dependents (here assumed at $300). The sales tax, unless the coupon plan would work, would not only grant no relief on account of the dependents, but would tax the family more just on that account; a family with dependents finds it correspondingly harder to save, and saving is one of the ways to escape a sales tax.

The aim of exempting very low per capita incomes from further increases in taxation is important partly because, in the opinion of many, it would not be fair to ask them for a further sacrifice in addition to the direct and indirect taxes they are already paying. A second point involves a factual question rather than differences of opinion: further taxation of persons with very low per capita incomes will almost surely in some cases cause them so to reduce their consumption of food, clothing, and medical service as to impair their working efficiency, and consequently impair the war effort. The worker who is temporarily unemployed as his industry converts to war production, but who will be expected to build tanks a few months later, is granted a respite from further taxation during this period if an income tax is utilized. A sales tax might force a restriction in his consumption that would show up later in a smaller output per hour in the tank arsenal.[23]

[23] See also p. 87.

2. Allow progression of the tax rate as incomes rise. The income tax can accomplish this in two ways.

First, it can, as it customarily does, allow the personal exemption to be deducted from income even after the income has risen above the exemption. For example, let the personal exemption be $500 for a single person and $1,000 for a married couple; if the net income in question is $2,000, the single person is taxed on $1,500, and the married couple only on $1,000. Even if the tax rate is proportional, the result is a progressive tax on the entire net income. If the tax rate is 10 percent, the single person's tax is 7½ percent of his net money income, while the average per capita tax of the married couple is only 5 percent of their average per capita net money income. The rate differential will be even greater in terms of real income, if the family receives, as it normally does, some imputed income from the work of the housewife, since the results of this work increase the household's real income but not its taxable income. On this point, however, the retail sales tax can claim as much, since it, too, does not reach imputed income.[24]

Second, graduation can be accomplished directly, by varying the tax rate as net income after personal exemptions and credit for dependents varies. Under a monthly source-collected tax, however, rate graduation either must be confined to two or three broad brackets, to avoid undue difficulty for the employer in computing the amount to be withheld from each taxpayer, or must be effected by inserting in the law a lengthy tax table that shows the dollars in tax due on an income falling within a specified narrow range.[25] For instance, the table might show that for a single person with no dependents the tax due

[24] For example: If a married couple were receiving $2,000 in money income, and a single person the same; and if the married couple also received $500 in imputed income from the housewife's services; and if the money incomes were all spent on things subject to a 10 percent sales tax; then the tax, as a percent of per capita real income, would be 8 percent for the married persons, whose per capita real income is $1,250, and 10 percent for the single individual, whose per capita real income is larger ($2,000). The comparison is complicated by the exemption of rent and savings.

[25] For a tax table that takes account not only of marital status, dependents, and a graduated rate, but also a post-war refund and a credit for tax already collected, see "Table of Tax Deductions" in the *Canada Gazette*, Vol. LXXVI, No. 89, Aug. 26, 1942. The part of the table that specifies monthly deductions gives withholding requirements for each of 164 income ranges and each of 14 marital and dependent status possibilities.

would be $210 if his net income before deduction of personal exemption was between $2,000 and $2,099 inclusive, and $231 if his income was between $2,100 and $2,199. Using the mid-points for purposes of illustration, the tax would, in the first case, amount to 20 percent of the net income after a personal exemption of $1,000, and 20.1 percent in the second case. One difficulty is that the rate is regressive throughout any given range; another is that the marginal rate rises to over 100 percent in the first few dollars of each range (a taxpayer with $2,099 income would be better off than a taxpayer with $2,119 income).

The retail sales tax can be graduated in the sense of higher rates for luxury articles commonly bought only by those of large incomes. But the result is bound to be somewhat erratic, especially since the well-to-do use their purchasing power to buy not only different things but better qualities of the same things, and differences in quality are in practice difficult to isolate for taxation at special rates. The sales tax will be progressive up to perhaps $1,000 or $2,000 of income if food is exempt, since the proportion of income spent for food is much greater in the low-income groups. But above those levels the tax will become regressive, owing to the fact that the larger the income the smaller, ordinarily, is the proportion that is spent at all, so that a flat-rate sales tax becomes a smaller and smaller percent of income, as income grows.

Even if the addition to the income-tax structure becomes regressive at some point, as it becomes crowded in between the ceiling of a 100 percent total rate and the floor of an already high rate under the existing income tax, the comparison with the sales tax holds good; indeed, it is enough, on this score, to show that the addition to the income tax is not so regressive as the sales tax.

3. Allow for dependents, at the same income level. Of two families with the same income, one may have a number of children, the other no dependents of any kind. The income tax can make allowance for this difference by granting a credit for the dependents. The sales tax will tend to tax the family with dependents more heavily than the other family, since the former is under greater need to spend a large proportion of its income.

This distinction was introduced above in discussing the level at which complete exemption from the tax is granted. The point to be emphasized here is that the difference between the two taxes persists even above the level of complete exemption.

4. Avoid creating a demand for inflationary wage increases. A uniform urge toward an increase in wages would be avoided by an income tax providing personal exemptions and credits for dependents. In any one shop, for instance, some of the employees would be affected not at all or very little by the new tax, owing to their marital status or to dependents. They would presumably not feel under the same pressure as their unmarried fellow employees to demand a wage increase. A retail sales tax would, in appearance at least, raise prices for all alike.[26] Even a coupon system of exemptions might not do much to break up the feeling of a community of interest. These remarks are not inconsistent with the conclusion reached above that the income tax would probably be a stronger deterrent to overtime work. That is a matter of the individual's reaction as one person; the wage question involves group action.

However, it must be agreed that on this question of which tax would be the more likely to give rise to widespread demands for inflationary wage increases there must remain much uncertainty. The income tax would have at least some tendency in that direction.[27]

The granting of substantially higher money wages throughout industry is assumed here to be undesirable because of the resultant tendency to raise prices and stimulate an inflationary spiral under present conditions. The tendency exerted by the tax diminishes in practical importance as direct wage control becomes effective.

5. Avoid creating a demand for inflationary "parity-price" increases in farm products. The price level of farm products will be permitted to rise if there is a rise in the cost of things that farmers buy. This cost would be higher under a retail sales tax than under an income tax. Again, the practical importance of the point decreases as price ceilings become more rigid.

6. Minimize administrative expense. Adequate administration of

[26] The qualification, "in appearance," covers the possibility that in fact some part of the sales tax might come out of profits, wages, etc.

[27] Representatives of the retail trade have expressed the opinion that the income tax would be the more likely to provoke demands for wage increases. H. R. Ways and Means Committee, *Hearings, 1942 Revenue Revision*, pp. 1731, 1750.

the source-collected income tax would require a substantial addition to the existing staff of the Bureau of Internal Revenue, and the somewhat higher rate needed under the income tax would create more pressure for evasion at any one point, but, in view of the large number of taxpayers under the retail sales tax and the novelty of the tax, the administrative difficulty would probably be greater than under the income tax.

7. Create intelligent tax consciousness. Even with collection at source, the income recipient would have to make out and file a return once a year. This act probably does more to create a realization of the meaning of government and its financial needs than the repeated payment of a retail sales tax. The contrast becomes complete if the sales tax is hidden in the price instead of being stated separately; but it is here assumed that the existence of blanket price control would make necessary the stating of the tax separate from the price, all prices being quoted ex-tax.

8. Avoid unplanned changes in methods of production. The retail sales tax, as commonly imposed in the states of the United States, applies not only to consumer goods, but also to durable producer goods like machinery and office furniture and to supplies like fuel. This extension of scope is a concession to administrative convenience or necessity; it is argued that sellers of fuel, or hand tools, for instance, cannot be required to distinguish between consumer-purchasers and producer-purchasers.[28] The result, under a substantial tax rate, would almost surely be some reshuffling of the proportions in which various means of production were employed—conceivably beneficial, but probably not. In any case, the result would not be one expressly desired by the legislator. The income tax is free from this particular defect.

9. Provide more revenue to lessen the growth in the public debt. So long as the public debt carries an interest charge, post-war budgets may fail to provide for a substantial amount of public services that would otherwise have been undertaken with the marginal dollars of public expenditure, as viewed by the legislator, that are absorbed in debt service. Or, alternatively, rates of taxation may be somewhat higher in post-war budgets, with some consequent deterrent to risk-

[28] See p. 90.

taking by private enterprise. The income tax, for a given degree of inflation checking, would provide somewhat more revenue than the sales tax, since it would be paid to a greater extent from savings. The difference in revenue yield would become marked when widespread and intense scarcity of consumer goods developed. Money incomes before tax would continue large, and the income-tax revenue would thrive accordingly, while the yield of the retail sales tax would decline, especially if the tax were really effective in checking consumer purchases. In this latter aspect the retail sales tax would resemble a protective tariff, which does its best when it yields little or no revenue.

10. Avoid forcing an arbitrary change in the pattern of consumer spending. The income tax removes some of the consumer's income and leaves him free to spend the rest as he chooses. The retail sales tax leaves his income as before, but partially blocks some of his spending channels while leaving others freely navigable. The road to consumption of food and clothing, for example, is made more difficult, while a free way is left open to expenditures on dwelling rental and medical services (assuming these would not come within the scope of the tax). There is nothing gained thereby, and very likely something lost, with respect to the consumer's getting the greatest possible satisfaction out of his total spendings. He did not want to spend more on rent and less on food; he is now induced to do so merely to escape a newly arisen evil, the tax. If the war effort demands a greater restriction of food than of dwelling use, compared to what those uses would be under an income tax, then this aspect of the sales tax becomes an aim to be achieved; but this happy coincidence cannot be counted on. A retail sales tax patterned on this aim would turn into a series of special excises.

11. Lessen uncertainty about the distribution of the tax burden. The burden of the income tax is probably more apt to rest in fact where the legislator wants it to. This is so, not only because of the considerations discussed in points 4 and 5 above (increases in wages and farm prices to offset tax increases) but also because the retail sales tax, to do its job properly, must be shifted at least one stage (retailer to consumer), and shifting is apt to be impeded somewhat

by friction. The difference between the two taxes in this respect is probably not great, however.

12. Avoid diminishing the price differential against black markets. If black markets arise, they will of course be high-price markets. Dealers in the black markets would, almost by definition, evade payment of a sales tax. The introduction of a sales tax would therefore reduce the price differential between the two markets, compared to what it would be if the revenue were obtained by an increase in the income tax. The income tax, even when evaded by the black-market dealers, absorbs from all other income recipients, with impartiality, dollars of income that would have been spent on black markets and on legal markets.

Relative importance of the several advantages.—The fact that about the same number of accomplishments are listed above for both the retail sales tax and the source-collected income tax is a coincidence with no particular significance. One or two advantages may outweigh all the rest. The present writers' choice of the income tax, for purposes of this study, rests largely on the importance they attach to the complete exemption, from further tax increases, of families and individuals with very low incomes (point 1, p. 98) and to a smaller increase in tax for those who have dependents than for those, on the same income level, with fewer or no dependents (point 3, p. 101). The element of graduation alone, or regressivity (point 2, p. 100), is not so important; whatever undesirability the sales tax introduces in this respect can be largely counteracted by a change in the rates of the regular income tax. In so far as the source-collected tax would in fact cause less demand than the sales tax for inflationary wage increases and increases in farm prices, considerable importance must be attached to these points. And over the longer term, tax consciousness (point 7) and a slowing down in growth of the interest-bearing public debt (point 9) are important also.

On the other hand, the sales tax is especially attractive in that its deterrent effect on war work is probably smaller (point 2, p. 92). This is so important that it would be unsafe to depend on a source-collected income tax alone to check inflation beyond a point where the lowest rate of that tax had to be, say, 40 percent or more (this level is selected more or less at random, for illustration). Beyond that uncertain point, a further advance in the rate of the source-collected tax would need to be mitigated, if not forestalled altogether, by recourse to the sales tax.

If the demand for housing is inelastic enough so that among families with identical real incomes those living in high-cost areas do pay a greater proportion of their income in rent, the sales tax partly avoids a serious defect of the income tax at low-income levels.

The kind of sales tax analyzed in the comparison on pp. 91–105 carries no personal exemption or allowance for dependents. If these features could be added by use of the coupon method mentioned on pp. 98–99, the list of aims that can be accomplished by an income tax but not by a sales tax would have to be shortened by omitting item 1 (complete exemption, from the increase in taxation, to individuals with very low incomes), part of item 2 (graduation of the tax rate, indirectly, through personal exemptions), item 3 (allowance for dependents), and possibly item 4 (avoidance of a demand for inflationary wage increases). In view of the importance attached to these items (see p. 105 above), a successful coupon scheme might be enough to make the sales tax the favorite, or at least enough to justify introducing it sometime before income-tax rates reached the very high levels otherwise indicated. This statement implies no preference for the sales tax as a normal part of a peace-time revenue system.[29]

COMPULSORY LENDING

Another possibility is compulsory lending: the obligatory purchase of government securities not redeemable until after the war. The amount of bonds that any one person would be required to purchase would doubtless be expressed as a percentage of his income or his expenditures. If the income method were employed, the results of

[29] A point that is unimportant quantitatively for the economy as a whole, but that might be important for certain taxpayers in some states, results from the provision usually found in state income-tax laws that in computing net income the individual may deduct the taxes that he has personally been liable for and has paid, with certain exceptions. A federal retail sales tax would be an excise tax on the dealer, not legally imposed on the consumer, who would therefore be unable to count it as a deduction in computing his income subject to state income tax, while in twenty-three states unlimited deduction is allowed for federal income tax paid. (Roy G. Blakey and Violet Johnson, *State Income Taxes*, p. 28a.)

the present study with respect to the number of billions of dollars required to avert inflation would be applicable to compulsory lending also. One modification would be necessary: a dollar taken in compulsory lending probably inhibits consumer spending somewhat less than a dollar taken in tax. Under the lending program the consumer considers himself less impoverished for the long run. The money is coming back to him eventually, and he forgets about the possible corollary of higher taxes to redeem, or pay the interest on, the bond he has bought; or, if he does think of it, he may believe that the post-war tax burden will be borne chiefly by someone else.

The present study did not pursue the computations in these terms, for in the writers' opinion the time had not come for compulsory lending in place of added taxation. Compulsory lending does indeed offer some marked advantages over a tax levied on the same basis. It has a less harmful effect on the incentive to overtime work, regular attendance, and intense piece-rate work. It makes possible the granting of special exemptions on account of savings commitments under home-amortization contracts and similar agreements on debt repayment. Such exemptions would surely be considered undue favoritism if granted in computing income subject to tax; yet some sort of relief may be necessary in these cases if a large amount of meaningless sacrifice is to be avoided, as giving up a home that does not even indirectly help house defense workers. Another advantage commonly urged for a forced-lending plan is that it allows the release of purchasing power to consumers (through redemption of the bonds) after the war, when a depression might develop. Actually, however, this is scarcely an advantage compared with an equivalent tax; the use of a tax now does not preclude the creation and distribution of purchasing power later. Perhaps the particular pattern of post-war spending that would follow redemption of the forced-loan bonds could not be achieved in any other way, but that pattern is itself to a large extent unpredictable. The compulsory-lending plan does of course assure now, in the political sense of assurance, that the money will be passed out; it also commits the government, now, to a particular way of passing it out, and gives everyone advance knowledge of how much he is to get. But just because it does tie the government's hands in this way with respect to the post-war monetary situation, and also because a substantial dose of compulsory lending would probably make it politically impossible to resort to increased taxation at all after that time, the present study was devoted to computing the effects of added taxation instead.

RATES NEEDED FOR THE SUPPLEMENTARY INCOME TAX

In order to convert the estimates of the amount of income tax needed into a tax proposal with specified rates and exemptions, it was necessary to have estimates of the tax base for selected exemption levels.[30] Estimates were prepared for three levels of exemptions: (1) $2,000 for a married couple, $800 for a single individual, and $400 for each dependent—the exemptions of the 1940 Revenue Act; (2) $1,500, $750, and $400—the exemptions of the then pending Revenue Act of 1941; and (3) $1,000, $500, and $300. It was clear from these estimates that the exemptions would have to be lower than those of either the 1940 Revenue Act or the 1941 Revenue Act, if the necessary amount of revenue was to be raised with tax rates that were not inordinately high. The third set of exemptions—$1,000, $500, and $300—gave a sufficiently large tax base.

Estimating the tax base for exemptions lower than those for which data from *Statistics of Income* are available necessarily involves bold extrapolation and the piecing together of fragmentary data. Most of the scanty data for lower income levels are of little use for estimating an income-tax base. Like the data underlying the income distribution prepared by the National Resources Committee,[31] they are ordinarily in terms of "families" or "consumer units" and total income or consumer income. For tax purposes, data are needed in terms of "tax units" and net taxable income. A single "consumer unit"—say a family of four—may include four "tax units," since the husband, wife, and two children may each have a separate income. Similarly, total income may include items not includable in taxable income—imputed income from owned home, value of home produced food, tax-exempt interest, and so on—and it makes no allowance for deductions permitted in computing net taxable income—interest paid, contributions,

[30] These estimates were prepared primarily by George E. Lent, under the general direction of Milton Friedman.

[31] *Consumer Incomes in the United States*, Washington, D.C., Aug., 1938.

taxes paid, and the like. These discrepancies in concept are sufficiently serious to make the derivation of a distribution of net taxable income from a distribution of consumer income a hazardous undertaking.

Faced with this problem in their work in the Twentieth Century Fund's *Studies in Current Tax Problems,* Susan S. Burr and William Vickrey derived a distribution for the year 1933 by ingeniously piecing together income tax data [32] of Delaware, Kansas, and the Federal Government. This distribution for 1933 was taken as the basis of the present estimates for the lower part of the income distribution. For 1933 incomes above $5,000, *Statistics of Income* data were used.

The general principle followed in extrapolating the distribution to 1941 was to keep the proportionate distribution of income (the "Lorenz curve") the same. Scattered studies of changes in income distribution over time suggest that whatever changes may occur in the Lorenz curve are exceedingly small in magnitude. Indeed it is not firmly established whether change in the distribution occurs in the direction of greater equality or inequality as national income rises, though there is a growing weight of evidence that the two ends of the distribution change in opposite directions.

The number of tax units shown by the 1933 distribution was adjusted for the estimated increase in the number of income recipients and for the extension of the coverage of the income tax to state and local government employees, and the income classes were shifted to allow for the estimated increase in income per income recipient. The extrapolation was done in such a way as to yield separate distributions for single individuals with no dependents, with one, and with two dependents, and for married couples or heads of families with no, one, two, three, and four dependents. This procedure avoids the errors involved in using the average number of dependents for each income class and facilitates the estimation of the tax base.

The number of taxpayers and the tax base under each set of exemptions were derived from these distributions by interpolation within the income class containing the income level exempt from tax.

The final results were, of course, far removed from the basic 1933 distributions on which they rested. In order to test their validity, the

[32] "Estimating Income and Estate Tax Yields," *Studies in Current Tax Problems,* New York, 1937.

same procedure was used to derive estimates for prior years that could be compared with actual data for those years. These comparisons showed a comforting measure of agreement, the discrepancy being uniformly less than 10 percent. However, this test is necessarily restricted to the upper end of the income distribution and hence offers only indirect evidence on the validity of the lower end of the distributions used in the present study.

The final estimates of the tax base for an assumed level of income payments in 1941 of $85 billion were as follows:

EXEMPTIONS			
Married	*Single*	*Dependent*	*Tax Base (in billions)*
$2,000	$800	$400	$14.7
1,500	750	400	18.5
1,000	500	300	26.4

The actual level of income payments for 1941 turned out to be $92 billion, so that the above estimates are decidedly too low for 1941. For 1942, the estimates were raised to allow for an increase in income. The adjustment was entirely inadequate in light of the very large actual increase in income payments (from $92 billion to an estimated $114 billion or $115 billion). However, a large part of this increase reflects the substantial price rise that the recommended taxes were designed to avert.

Part III

METHODS OF PREDICTING THE ONSET OF "INFLATION"

BY MILTON FRIEDMAN

"INFLATION" has its genesis in an increased volume of spending by consumers, business, and government. This increase in spending can ordinarily be matched only in part by an expansion in the volume of commodities and services offered for sale; the rest is absorbed by a rise in the prices at which these goods sell. During the early stage of an upswing, the large volume of unutilized resources available enables the bulk of the increase in spending to be absorbed by an increased output of goods. This is essentially what happened during the expansion from 1933 to 1937 and again from 1938 to 1940. As expansion proceeds and the volume of unutilized resources decreases, a larger and larger part of the increase in spending is absorbed by rising prices.

Table XV shows that this is what has been happening in recent months. From the second to the third quarter and again from the third to the fourth quarter of 1940, none of the increase in national income was absorbed by rising prices; indeed, prices fell slightly during this period so that the increase in real output was larger than the increase in money income. From the fourth quarter of 1940 to the first quarter of 1941, 10 percent of the increase in national income was absorbed by rising prices; and successively larger percentages from then on, so that by 1942, more than two-thirds of the increase in national income between the first and second quarters was absorbed by rising prices. The steady rise in the percentage of the increase in national income absorbed by price rises is interrupted only once, by a minor decline from the last quarter of 1940 to the first quarter of 1941.[1]

This process of price rise may not be entirely attributable to "inflation" as that term is used in this study.[2] To determine the precise point at which "inflation," in the technical sense, began, would require the price rises to be traced to their causes. We shall not attempt to define the point of inflation so precisely, or to distinguish among different types of price rises. Instead, we shall regard the procedures to be outlined below as procedures for determining not the precise date at which inflation, in any exact sense, begins, but the part of expansions in purchasing power that will be absorbed by price increases in one or more stated periods.

As this discussion indicates, there are two major parts to the forecasting problem: on the one hand, the amount by which spending will increase over any period of time; on the other, the amount by which output will increase. Both parts of the problem can be further subdivided. On the spending side, we can ask how much of the additional spending will be done by consumers and how much by enterprises (public and private). On the output side, we can try to determine, first, the amount by which output could conceivably increase if all available resources were to be employed and, second, the part of this potential increase that is likely to be realized. Of course, a more detailed breakdown of both the increased spending and the increased output by types of commodities and services is possible, and, in any thorough-going analysis, highly desirable.

Under present conditions, the dominant impulse toward increased spending is the armament program; all the procedures that we shall outline in this essay take government spending as the major independ-

[1] The table presents only rough estimates of the way increases in income have been divided between increases in output and increases in prices. Deflation by the cost-of-living index number is unsatisfactory, first, because it is appropriate only to part, and to a declining part, of the national income, second, because during a period of rapidly rising prices the cost-of-living index number inevitably understates to an increasing degree the actual rise in prices. This understatement is inevitable because the index cannot take full account of such factors as transactions at prices other than legal maximum prices, and changes in quality and in services rendered along with the sale of commodities.

[2] See pp. 5–6.

TABLE XV

DIVISION OF CHANGES IN NATIONAL INCOME BETWEEN CHANGES IN REAL OUTPUT AND CHANGES IN PRICES

YEAR AND QUARTER	NATIONAL INCOME, CURRENT PRICES, (seasonally adjusted annual rate in billions of dollars)[a]	B.L.S. COST OF LIVING INDEX NUMBER (1935–39 = 100)	CHANGE IN NATIONAL INCOME (Annual rates in billions of dollars)		PERCENTAGE OF CHANGE IN NATIONAL INCOME ACCOUNTED FOR BY	
			Current prices	*Prices of preceding quarter*[b]	*Change in output*[c]	*Change in prices*[d]
(1)	(2)	(3)	(4)	(5)	(6)	(7)
1940						
April–June	75.6	100.5				
July–Sept.	77.2	100.4	1.6	1.7	106	–6
Oct.–Dec.	81.2	100.3	4.0	4.1	102	–2
1941						
Jan.–March	86.0	100.9	4.8	4.3	90	10
April–June	92.4	103.2	6.4	4.3	67	33
July–Sept.	97.6	106.5	5.2	2.2	42	58
Oct.–Dec.	103.0	110.0	5.4	2.1	39	61
1942						
Jan.–March	108.4	113.1	5.4	2.4	44	56
April–June	112.2	115.8	3.8	1.2	32	68

[a] Milton Gilbert and Robert Bangs, "National Income and the War Effort—First Half of 1942," *Survey of Current Business*, Aug., 1942, p. 14.

[b] Derived by deflating national income in current prices given in column (2), by ratio between B.L.S. cost of living index numbers given in column (3) for current and preceding quarter.

[c] Column (5) as a percentage of column (4).

[d] 100 minus column (6).

ent impulse and try to estimate the total increase in spending over a given period to which the government spending will lead. Similarly, the output side is greatly complicated by the specialized form of the expansion. The needs for armaments must take precedence, making it inevitable that any expansion in other types of output will differ widely from the expansion that takes place during an ordinary upswing in business conditions. The consequent distortion in the composition of total output makes the estimate of potential expansion of output in "over all" terms particularly hazardous; yet practically all the workers in this field have made their estimates in such terms.

The increase in income that will accompany expanded outlays on armaments depends on a complex of interrelated factors, many of which cannot be observed before the event: who receives the increased outlays, how much of it they decide to save, what kinds of goods they try to purchase with the part they plan to spend, the reactions of consumers to price changes, the anticipations of consumers about future price movements and availability of supplies, the extent to which enterprises try to expand their capital equipment, the costs that enterprises must incur to expand output, their anticipations about future price movements and hence their inventory policy, the flexibility of wage rates and prices of other factors of production, the demand for credit, the policies adopted by the banking community about loans and reserves, and so on. Many of these factors clearly affect also the expansion in output that will accompany the increase in income. In addition, the expansion in output depends on the quantity and kind of unutilized resources, the mobility and transferability of these resources, the rapidity with which output can be increased, the degree of competition in different sectors of the economy, the kind and amount of controls imposed by the Federal Government, and so on.

Despairing of their ability to reach quantitative answers by a direct analysis of these complex interrelationships, most investigators have sought refuge in empiricism and have based their estimates on historical relationships that have appeared fairly stable.

Two general methods have been used to estimate the expansion in spending that is likely to result from the armament program. One is based on the historical relation between changes in the stock of money and changes in income; a second, on the historical relation between investment and national income or gross national product.

The estimates of possible increases in output are made either by estimating the volume of unemployed resources, or by estimating the amount of employment that corresponds to any given national income (or gross national product) on the basis of historical relations and comparing the resulting estimate with the amount of labor available.

Comparison of the estimated increases in spending with the estimated increase in output reveals the probable degree of price change.

The four sections that follow discuss in more detail various approaches that have been followed in the past few years. The first is devoted to the work of James W. Angell, who bases his estimate of the expansion in spending on the relation between changes in the stock of money and changes in income, and his estimate of the expansion in output on the aggregate volume of unemployed resources. The second section discusses the work of the Iowa group, which was concerned primarily with estimating the increase in output both for the economy as a whole and for various categories of consumer goods. The third section is concerned less with actual forecasts than with a recently developed method of analysis, centering on the concept of the "inflationary gap." The fourth section is devoted to methods using the relationship between investment and income—methods that have been widely used by government agencies. One example of this class of methods, that used by Richard V. Gilbert and Victor Perlo of the Office of Price Administration, is discussed in detail.

None of the theoretical structures that implicitly or explicitly underlie these alternative approaches is entirely satisfactory or generally accepted. In consequence, the confidence to be placed in the results of the different methods must turn very largely on the empirical stability of the historical relations used.

The writers whose work is discussed in this essay were pioneering in largely unexplored territory. True, there had been extensive work on the behavior of economic activities in the business cycle, and on the development of formulas for forecasting business activity. But the former was largely descriptive, and the latter was primarily the work of business and financial writers and had little scientific basis. Conscious of their limited knowledge on a quantitative level of economic processes, the professional and academic economists had largely shied off from forecasting.

The pressing nature of the immediate problem made some attempt at quantitative forecasts imperative. As we shall see, the first attempts by the bolder investigators were none too successful. Anything else was not to be expected. Final mastery of the problem will be achieved only through repeated unsuccessful experiments. The mistakes of initiators are necessarily the basis for further developments. This essay is an attempt to evaluate these early experiments in terms of both their internal logic and the agreement of the results with experience. This task of criticism is much easier, albeit less pleasant, than that of exploration. The writers who were bold enough to predict the future deliberately exposed themselves to the test of experience. The critic, with the aid of hindsight, can easily point to mistakes. But these mistakes are evidence of the courage of the writers, rather than of the quality of their work.

JAMES W. ANGELL

Angell has published two almost identical sets of estimates: one in his book *Investment and Business Cycles* (1941), the other in an article in the May, 1941, *Review of Economic Statistics*. These estimates differ in unimportant details; the basic method is the same. In both, Angell considers his estimates "optimistic"; that is, he tries to determine how long inflation can be postponed, given conditions as favorable as is possible.

Angell defines inflation in the short period in terms of spending on consumer goods. Consequently he centers attention on the consumer goods industry. His general method is to estimate for a given future period, (1) the increase in money outlays on consumer goods that will result from government deficit financing; (2) the possible expansion in the output of consumer goods. If (1) is greater than (2) price rises are in prospect.

INCREASE IN OUTLAYS ON CONSUMER GOODS

The estimate of the increase in outlays on consumer goods that will result from government deficit spending is based on three items:

(a) The government deficit. This is taken as equivalent to an increase in the stock of money.

(b) The marginal circular velocity of money. This is the ratio between a change in national income from one year to the next and the associated change in the stock of money.

(c) The percentage of an increase in income that is spent on consumer goods.

The product of (a) and (b) is the estimated increase in income. The product of (c) and the estimated increase in income is the estimated increase in outlays on consumer goods. Item (b) is estimated as probably 1.75 but possibly as low as 1.65. This estimate was derived from the slope of the linear regression between national income and the stock of money computed from data for 1933–39. Item (c) is estimated as 88.2 from Kuznets' national income data for 1923–28.[3] To allow for a lag between an increase in the stock of money and the resulting increase in income, the estimates are assumed to apply to calendar years, though the deficits are for fiscal years.

Using Hansen's estimates of the deficit as $6.2 billion in fiscal 1941 and $9.2 billion in fiscal 1942,[4] Angell estimates the increase in outlays on consumer goods, in billions of dollars, as

Calendar 1941	9.0 – 9.6
1942	13.4 – 14.2
1941 and 1942	22.4 – 23.8

Certain general difficulties with Angell's method are clear. It makes no explicit allowance for the nature of the government expenditures and revenue structure. A change in the deficit as a result of taxes levied solely on high incomes might have a very different effect from an equal change in the deficit as a result of taxes levied on very low

[3] These and all later figures are taken from Angell's *Review of Economic Statistics* article rather than from his book. As noted above, the differences between the two are relatively minor.

[4] See A. H. Hansen, *Fiscal Policy and Business Cycles*, New York, 1941, p. 429.

incomes. Angell's method would, however, evaluate both as having the same effect. This difficulty is not serious for Angell's own estimates, since the historical data he uses presumably reflect a tax system much like the present one, but it does mean that his method would be of limited usefulness for estimating the influence of changes in the tax system. To take such changes into account it would be necessary to modify items (b) and (c).

More specifically, the validity of Angell's estimates depends on the accuracy of his estimates of the three basic items, (a), (b), and (c).

Item (a). By identifying the change in the deficit with the change in the volume of circulating money, Angell implicitly assumes that there is no private hoarding or dishoarding, and that the stock of money does not change for any other reason. He recognizes that the government deficit need not be financed entirely by the issuing of new money, but he argues that putting into active circulation money formerly held as idle money would have the same effect as the creation of new money. This may well be so. At the same time, it should be noted that Angell's estimate of item (b) is based on historical data showing the actual changes in the stock of money, and makes no explicit allowance for such reactivation of formerly idle money as might have taken place during the period to which his data relate. This procedure therefore implicitly assumes a constant relation between the changes in the total stock of money and the amount of reactivation of formerly idle money.

Data are now available to permit a test of Angell's assumption for the two years for which he made forecasts. As the accompanying table shows, Angell's assumption is not supported by the data. For 1941

FISCAL YEAR	NET BUDGET DEFICIT [a]	INCREASE IN CIRCULATING MONEY [b]
	(in billions of dollars)	
1941	5.1	6.9
1942	19.6	8.0

[a] *Bulletin of the Treasury Department.*

[b] *Federal Reserve Bulletin,* defined as adjusted demand deposits plus currency outside the banks. This differs from the definition used by Angell only by excluding U.S. Government deposits.

the deficit was considerably smaller than the increase in circulating money; and for 1942, more than twice as large.

Item (b). Basic to Angell's analysis is the assumption that the marginal circular velocity of money may be considered as fairly stable. This assumption is based on an analysis of the past relation between national income and the stock of money, from which Angell concludes that:

> The data for the first period, 1899–1929, reveal an extraordinarily stable relation between changes in income and changes in money stock during this period. It may be doubted if any other important and directly measurable economic magnitude, except the average circular velocity of money itself, has shown equal stability over as long a period as 30 years, at least in modern times.[5]

However, this conclusion is not supported by the data on which it is based; and these data do not justify the use made of item (b) in the present connection. Angell bases his conclusion primarily on a chart on which national income is plotted against the stock of money. This chart may be adequate for studying the average circular velocity of money; or for studying the relation between long-period changes in national income and the stock of money; but it seriously misrepresents the relationship between year-to-year changes in the two variables, as Angell himself recognizes at other points. The long-time upward trend of both national income and the stock of money is bound to give a close correlation between the two totals, no matter how loose the relation between year-to-year changes in them.

A more appropriate basis for judging the relation between year-to-year changes is given by Chart 1, based on the data used by Angell, which plots the *change* in the national income from one year to the next against the associated change in the volume of circulating money. As this chart shows, the relation between the year-to-year changes is extremely unstable.

In the five years from 1934 to 1939 in which both national income and the stock of money increased, the ratio between changes in the two varied from 1.08 to 6.05, the intermediate figures being 1.45, 2.14, and 2.37. Even if we disregard the extreme ratio of 6.05, which was for the confused year 1937, and use as a possible range 1.08 to 2.37,

[5] *Investment and Business Cycles*, pp. 148–53.

we get a much wider difference between a minimum and maximum estimate of the expansion in spending—using Angell's values for (a) and (c)—than Angell does, namely,

Calendar 1941	5.9 – 13.0
1942	8.8 – 19.2
1941 and 1942	14.7 – 32.2

Item (c). Angell estimated the percentage of an increase in income that would be spent on consumer goods by expressing the average volume of consumer outlay during 1923–28 as a percentage of the average national income. This is clearly erroneous. The logic of his method requires the comparison of the *increase* in consumer outlay with the *increase* in income; that is, the computation of the marginal rather than average propensity to consume. For 1923–28, used by Angell because it was "another period of expansion," the relation between year-to-year changes in consumer outlay and national income is very irregular. The change in consumer outlay ranges from 15 percent of the change in national income to 534 percent, the intermediate figures being 57, 61, 120, and 123. On the average, 84 percent of the change in income rather than 88 percent—the figure used by Angell—was absorbed by a change in consumer outlay.[6]

The relation between year-to-year changes in consumer outlay and national income is considerably more regular, though very different, for a more recent period of expansion, 1935–40. During these years, the change in consumer outlay ranges from 41 to 63 percent of the change in national income, the intermediate figures being 43, 53, 57, and 60. On the average, 54 percent of the change in national income was absorbed by the change in consumption. Total consumer outlay averaged 91 percent of total national income. If we use 43 to 63 as the possible range, the minimum and maximum estimates of the expansion in consumer spending just cited are illustrated in the following tabular arrangement (money figures in billions of dollars):

[6] Following Angell, these figures are based on Simon Kuznets' estimate. However, we have used annual data, whereas Angell used 3-year moving averages.

CHART 1

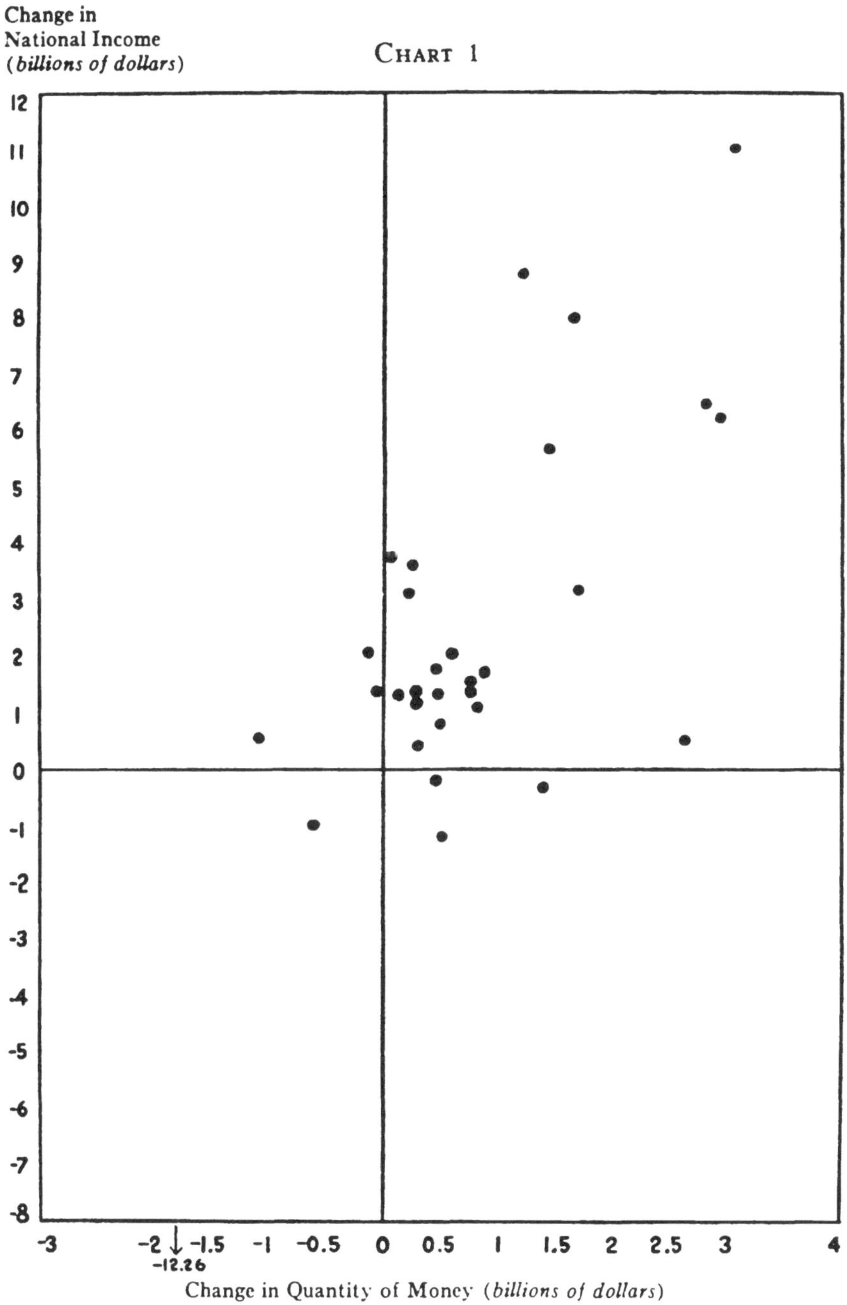

RELATION BETWEEN CHANGE IN NATIONAL INCOME AND CHANGE IN THE STOCK OF CIRCULATING MONEY, 1899–1929

Source: James W. Angell, *Investment and Business Cycles*, New York, 1941, pp. 337–8

	Minimum (b) = 1.08 (c) = .43	*Maximum* (b) = 2.37 (c) = .63
Calender 1941: (a) = $6.2	$2.9	$ 9.3
Calendar 1942: (a) = $9.2	4.3	13.7
1941 and 1942	$7.2	$23.0

THE POSSIBLE INCREASE IN OUTPUT OF CONSUMER GOODS

Angell's estimate of the possible increase in the output of consumer goods is based primarily on two items:

(a) possible increase in the labor force of the consumer goods industries and the industries that supply them;

(b) the addition (at constant prices) to the value of annual output of consumer goods per additional worker employed.

The product of (a) and (b) is the estimated increase in the dollar value of output at unchanged prices. Item (a) is estimated from available data on the labor force, unemployment, etc. The figures Angell cites in the *Review of Economic Statistics* justify a range of four to seven million additional laborers in 1941 and 1942; he selects the figure of "not over five million." (The figures in the book justify a range of 4.5 million to 6.0 million by 1941, 5 million to 6.5 million by 1942.) Item (b) is estimated as $2,000. This is a rough estimate obtained as follows:

In 1940, for the country as a whole, the average money income per person employed was roughly $1,500 a year. This means that the *average* value of the output of finished consumers' goods and services sold and of net additional investment goods sold was substantially $1,500 per person. . . . The *marginal* value, however—the increase in physical output and hence in sales proceeds, when employment is increased—is probably substantially higher in most cases where output was previously well below capacity, because of the spreading of overhead costs over a larger output. Suppose the marginal value is not $1,500 but $2,000 a year.[7]

Combining the estimates of (a) and (b), Angell estimates the possible increase in the output of consumer goods at not over $10 billion for the two years 1941 and 1942. By alternative combinations of the underlying data, it is possible to derive a range of $8 billion to $14 billion.

[7] *Investment and Business Cycles*, pp. 311-12.

In his estimate of the possible increase in the labor force engaged in the production of consumer goods, Angell (1) neglects possible additions to the labor force from present nonworkers, (2) makes no allowance for increased hours and (3) implicitly assumes no increase in the number of workers employed in producing new private investment goods. His allowance for (4) frictional unemployment and (5) unemployables is higher than that made by most other estimators. On the other hand, like other estimators, he (6) allows for 2 to 3 million workers now engaged in agriculture and in other occupations who could be spared without a decrease in output. It is hard to believe that this figure is not much too high. Further, Angell (7) assumes only a half a million to a million workers absorbed in the defense industries during 1941 and 1942. Items (1), (2), (4), and (5) make for an underestimate of the possible expansion in consumer goods output; items (3), (6), and (7), for an overestimate.

COMPARISON OF INCREASED OUTLAYS WITH INCREASED OUTPUT

Comparison of Angell's estimate of the increase in outlays on consumer goods with his estimate of the increase in the output of consumer goods should reveal whether inflation seems imminent for the period covered by the estimates. If the estimates were made for sufficiently detailed time periods, this comparison would also reveal the point at which "inflation" would begin.

Angell has made separate estimates of the increase in consumer outlays for calendar 1941 and 1942; but for output, he presents an estimate only for the two years together. For this two-year period, the estimates are summarized in the table on p. 124.

The optimistic combination—in the sense of the least inflationary pressure—is obtained by pairing the minimum estimate of the increase in consumer outlays with the maximum estimate of the increase in output; the reverse pairing yields the pessimistic combination.

If we compare Angell's estimates, there is a clear indication of strong inflationary pressure, since both the optimistic and pessimistic combinations reveal larger increases in consumer outlays than in the supply of consumer goods. However, the modified estimates, which

	ANGELL'S ORIGINAL ESTIMATES		MODIFIED OUTLAY ESTIMATES [a]	
	Optimistic combination	*Pessimistic combination*	*Optimistic combination*	*Pessimistic combination*
	(In billions of dollars)			
Increase in				
Consumer outlays	22.4 [b]	23.8 [b]	7.2	23.0
Output of consumer goods	14.0	8.0	14.0	8.0
	(Percent)			
Indicated price rise [c]	10	21	None	20

[a] Using range of 1.08 to 2.37 for marginal circular velocity of money, and range of .43 to .63 for proportion of increased income devoted to consumption.

[b] These are the only figures in this table that are explicitly set forth by Angell; the others are derived by the present writer as indicated in the text and in table notes a and c.

[c] Estimated by adding estimated increases in consumer outlays and output of consumer goods to consumer expenditures in 1940 and dividing total outlays obtained in this way by total output. Consumer expenditures in 1940 were taken as $66.2 billion, from Gilbert and Bangs, "National Income and the War Effort," *Survey of Current Business,* Aug., 1942, p. 15.

we have derived by using for the critical items a range based on experience during a five-year period, are not so consistent. The optimistic combination shows a possible increase in output almost twice as large as the increase in outlays; the pessimistic combination, a possible increase in output only slightly more than one-third as large as the increase in outlays.

In terms of indicated price increases, Angell's estimates yield a range of 10 to 20 percent; the modified estimates, a range of zero to 20 percent. The indicated timing of the onset of inflation is more significant from our point of view. According to Angell's estimates, increases in consumer outlays would begin to outrun increases in output either before the end of 1941 (pessimistic combination) or not until the middle of 1942 (optimistic combination). According to the modified estimates, the corresponding dates range from the latter part of 1941 to well after the end of 1942. Even Angell's estimates, therefore, give a range of about nine months in the estimated timing of inflation; and the modified estimates a range of more than fifteen months.

These wide ranges in the estimates of price increase and timing reveal the instability of the basic figures on which Angell's procedures are based—or alternatively, the sensitivity of the inflationary process that he is attempting to forecast. The existence of such wide ranges indicates that this method could not be expected to give a very precise estimate even if the logic of the method were accepted as correct and the estimated federal deficit as accurate.

COMPARISON OF FORECASTS WITH EXPERIENCE

The acid test of any method of forecasting is, of course, whether it works. This test of experience can be applied on two different levels. Most methods of forecasting proceed by estimating certain "initial" or "strategic" variables—in Angell's method of estimating the increase in consumer outlays, the federal deficit is the "strategic" variable—and then deriving from these variables the desired forecast by a specified procedure—in Angell's method, by multiplying the deficit by the marginal circular velocity of money and the percentage of an increase in income absorbed by consumer expenditures. A test of the *forecast* can be made by comparing it with experience; a test of the *procedure* by substituting the actual values of the strategic variables for the estimated values in deriving the desired forecast and then comparing this revised forecast with experience.

At the present stage of our knowledge, and for the period under discussion, the test of the procedure seems much more relevant than the test of the forecast. Methods are at the moment of more interest than results; and the fact that estimates of the strategic variables made in late 1940 or early 1941 did not envision December 7 is certainly no evidence against the method.

The necessary data for testing Angell's procedure of forecasting the increase in outlays on consumer goods are given in Table XVI.

In deriving his estimates Angell used $6.2 billion and $9.2 billion as the budget deficits for fiscal 1941 and 1942 respectively, whereas the actual budget deficits were $5.1 billion and $19.6 billion. As it happens, the errors in the assumed budget deficits, though in opposite directions, serve to improve the estimates in both years. In 1941 consumer expenditures increased more in response to the budget deficit than would be expected from Angell's procedure or the modification of it employed here; in consequence, the estimates in 1 and 2, based on too *large* a deficit, are closer to the actual figure than are

TABLE XVI

FORECASTS OF ESTIMATED MAXIMUM AND MINIMUM CHANGE IN CONSUMER OUTLAYS

	CALENDAR 1941		CALENDAR 1942		CALENDAR 1941 AND 1942	
	Minimum	*Maximum*	*Minimum*	*Maximum*	*Minimum*	*Maximum*
Budget deficits assumed by Angell [a]						
1. Angell's procedure	9.0	9.6	13.4	14.2	22.4	23.8
2. Modified procedure [b]	2.9	9.3	4.3	13.7	7.2	23.0
Actual budget deficits [c]						
3. Angell's procedure	7.4	7.9	28.5	30.3	35.9	38.2
4. Modified procedure [b]	2.4	7.6	9.1	29.3	11.5	36.9
Actual change in consumer outlays at current prices [d]	9.6		4.2		13.8	

[a] Taken from Hansen. $6.2 billion in fiscal 1941 and $9.2 in fiscal 1942.

[b] Using a range of 1.08 to 2.37 for marginal circular velocity of money; and of .43 to .63 for proportion of an increase in income absorbed by consumer spending.

[c] $5.1 billion in fiscal 1941, and $19.6 billion in fiscal 1942.

[d] Gilbert and Bangs, *op. cit.* For 1942, consumer expenditures are taken as $80 billion. This is a rough estimate based on estimates for first six months by Gilbert and Bangs, and on the apparent change since then.

the estimates in 3 and 4 based on the actual deficit. In 1942, on the other hand, consumer expenditures increased less in response to the budget deficit than would be expected from the procedures used, and hence, the estimates in 1 and 2, based on too *small* a deficit, are closer to the actual figures than are the estimates in 3 and 4 based on the actual deficit.

The forecasts based on the actual deficits—the figures relevant to a test of the *procedure*—do not agree well with experience. For 1941, they are in general too low, even the highest being almost $2 billion below the actual increase in consumer outlays. For 1942, on the other hand, they are uniformly too high, even the lowest being more than twice the actual increase in consumer outlays. The errors are in opposite directions in the two years, and hence are offset in the forecasts for the two years combined. The actual change falls within the range given by the modified procedure, using the actual budget deficit, but considerably outside the range given by Angell's procedure.

The general conclusion that emerges is that neither Angell's procedure nor the modified procedure provides an accurate method of forecasting increases in consumer outlay.

Angell's method of forecasting the increase in the output of consumer goods cannot be compared with experience in as great detail as his method of forecasting the increase in consumer outlays. Angell estimated the possible increase at not over $10 billion, at early 1941 prices, for the calendar years 1941 and 1942, and alternative combinations of his underlying data yield a range of $8 billion to $14 billion. The actual increase in output of consumer goods, at 1940 prices, between calendar 1940 and calendar 1941 was less than $5½ billion, and the output of consumer goods has been falling considerably since then.[8]

This discrepancy between the forecast and experience may reflect an error in Angell's estimate of increased employment in consumer goods industries rather than in his estimate of the additional value of output from each additional worker. However, the available data do not permit a test of the source of the error.

THE IOWA GROUP

The Iowa group [9] have not outlined any specific procedure for determining either the expansion in spending that will be associated with government expenditures on armaments or the expansion in output that can be attained. They have instead presented a series of *ad hoc* estimates that represent largely personal judgments based on rough general data. Unlike most of the other writers, however, they deal not only with output as a whole, or such broad subdivisions as consumer outlay and capital formation, but also with more detailed categories—food, clothing, and the like.

[8] Gilbert and Bangs, *op. cit.*

[9] A. G. Hart, E. D. Allen, and associates of the Economics staff of Iowa State College, *Paying for Defense*, Philadelphia, 1941, especially Chapter IV, pp. 36–48. The original draft underlying Chapter IV was prepared by Gale Johnson.

POSSIBLE EXPANSION IN NATIONAL MONEY INCOME

The only statement made by the Iowa group about the increase in national money income that is likely to result from government spending is

> The $80 billion level of [national income] . . . is a close approximation to the national income of the United States in the winter months of 1941. The $90 billion level is one which we are likely to reach, if the present pace of expansion continues, sometime late in 1941 or early in 1942. (Page 38.)

Using the National Resources Committee estimate of consumer expenditures at various levels of income, the Iowa group estimates that the 12½ percent rise in national income from $80 to $90 billion would be associated with a $6 billion or 10 percent rise in total consumption.

> "Food and tobacco" would expand by only 6.5 per cent, "automobile and operation" by 13.9 per cent. In general, the goods which people will buy in much greater quantity if their incomes rise are "durable goods," like automobiles and pianos; while their purchases of food and other "nondurables" expand in a smaller proportion. (Page 40.)

POSSIBLE EXPANSION IN OUTPUT

Starting with the general premise that output will be limited by labor, plant, or materials, whichever is scarcest, the Iowa group first estimates the expansion in total output that would be possible if labor were the only limiting factor, and modifies this estimate to take account of other limitations by sketching the possibilities of expanding the output of specific types of goods.

Total nonagricultural employment in early 1941 was estimated at 38 million persons working on the average 40 hours a week; possible additions to nonagricultural employment, at between 5 and 10 million persons; and possible increases in hours per week, at between 5 and 10. Adding 5 million men and raising average hours per week from 40 to 45 would increase the total number of man-hours by about 25 percent; adding 10 million men and raising average hours per week from 40 to 50, by about 60 percent. These estimates of the labor reserve were scaled down to allow for (a) the lower skill of persons in the labor reserve than of persons at work; (b) the fact that many skilled workers were already working overtime and hence the longer hours would affect mainly unskilled workers; (c) the lower productivity of additional hours worked, because of fatigue and the like; (d) the drain of men by the army and navy. (Pages 37 and 38.) In addition to these points listed by the Iowa group two others should be added: (e) the average work week of 40 hours on which the estimates are based is for manufacturing only and the work week is now probably more than 40 hours in other industries; (f) the length of the work week is a fairly arbitrary concept in many types of activities—for example, professional service, retail trade—and is not likely to be increased in a formal sense even though the quantity of work performed is increased; hence the length of the work week for other types of activities would have to be increased by much more than 25 percent to increase the average hours of all nonagricultural employees by 25 percent. "Making a crude allowance for the factors just listed," say the Iowa group, "we may place the actual labor reserve at between 10 and 40 percent of the labor now employed outside agriculture, allowing both for additional workers and longer hours." (Page 38.) A part of this labor reserve will of course be absorbed by defense production. Consequently, they conclude, "it is not unlikely that labor can be found for a ten or for a twenty per cent expansion of industrial production for civilian purposes within the next year or two." (Page 38.)

"Labor is not the only limitation upon production. When output must be raised it is roughly correct to say that it is limited by the available amount of unskilled or semi-skilled labor, key skilled workers, plant or key materials whichever is lowest." (Page 37.) Account is taken of these other limitations by analyzing each segment of consumer outlay separately. The findings are summarized as follows:

> The American economic system can probably provide at about present prices most of the food called for by a rise of national income to a $90 billion level or even higher, if no British demands for such goods come onto our markets. But if the British turn to us for food the amount available for domestic consumption may well fall considerably below present levels.
>
> As to other non-durable consumers' goods, clothing can expand sufficiently if materials are available, and the service trades and public utilities if the public will accept reductions in quality. Motor and household fuels

can be expanded at the source, but are likely to be pinched by transportation difficulties arising from transfer of tankers to the British.

Durable consumers' goods compete directly with defense. In consequence their production will doubtless have to be cut below present levels. On similar grounds, the supply of producers' durable goods for civilian uses will have to be cut and this will increase the difficulty of preventing shortages of consumers' goods.

The upshot is that the apparent promise of our large labor reserve cannot be quickly fulfilled. We shall have to work through a series of equipment and material shortages and train a good deal of fresh labor before we are able to expand output much, except for food. (Page 48.)

The Iowa group gives no indication how much of the 10 to 20 percent potential addition to the output of civilian goods that the labor reserve alone would permit can actually be realized. A rough estimate can, however, be derived by combining their qualitative conclusions with their estimates of the increase in consumer expenditures that would accompany the increase in national income from $80 billion to $90 billion. If, for each category of consumption for which the Iowa group says expansion is possible, we assume that the entire estimated increase in expenditures is matched by an increase in output with no increase in prices, we get a total increase in the output of consumer goods of about $5 billion, or about 8 percent. This estimate takes account solely of increases and makes no allowance for decreases; hence, it might best be considered an estimate of the possible increase in the supply of nondurable commodities and services, since the Iowa group concludes that the decrease in output will be concentrated in durable goods.

Even for nondurable goods and services, however, this estimated increase proved to be somewhat too large. From the first quarter of 1941 to the first quarter of 1942, the real output of consumer nondurable goods and services rose by about $3½ billion; and since then seems to have fallen slightly. War expenditures rose far more rapidly than was allowed for by the Iowa group (they were writing well before Pearl Harbor), and the output of consumer goods accordingly rose less.

In addition to the estimates summarized above, the Iowa group presented estimates of the amount of taxes needed to prevent inflation. These estimated tax needs were not, however, based primarily on the above estimates, but were largely derived independently from figures on government spending, and on possible nonexpansionary borrowing.[10]

THE "INFLATIONARY GAP"

Much recent English discussion of fiscal policy has centered on the so-called "inflationary gap" which achieved prominence when it was discussed at some length by the Chancellor in his budget speech in the spring of 1941.[11]

At a time of relatively full employment, if the government uses additional resources someone else must use less. This transfer of resources will be accomplished without a price rise if the increase in the government's demand for the additional resources is matched by a decrease in nongovernmental demand. Consequently, the "inflationary gap" is the "amount of the government's expenditure against which there is no corresponding release of real resources of manpower or materials by some other member of the community." (*Economist, loc. cit.*) If there is such a "gap," the government can get the real resources, but only by bidding up prices and thereby "forcing" others to release the resources.

Lady Macbeth's words, "I have thee not, yet I see thee still" describe the "inflationary gap" aptly. In retrospect, there can be no gap. The total value of resources used is equal to the value of the resources used by the government plus the value of the resources used by others; the former is also the government's expenditure on resources. Hence the government's expenditure is always equal to the value of the resources "released," that is, not used by others. In prospect, however, there may well be a "gap." At current prices, the total value of all resources available for use next year—roughly, next year's income at this year's prices—is some definite amount. The recipients of this

[10] *Ibid.*, p. 145.

[11] See *An Analysis of the Sources of War Finance and an Estimate of the National Income and Expenditure in 1938 and 1940,* Cmd. 6261; "The First War Budget," *Economist,* April 12, 1941; F. W. Paish, "The Budget and the White Paper," *London and Cambridge Economic Service's Report on Current Economic Conditions,* May, 1941, pp. 10–13. A second White Paper was presented with the budget statement of April, 1942, entitled *An Analysis of the Sources of War Finance and an Estimate of the National Income and Expenditure in 1938, 1940 and 1941,* Cmd. 6347. This second White Paper not only gives estimates for 1941 but also revisions of the earlier estimates for 1938 and 1940.

Table XVII

SOURCE OF BRITISH GOVERNMENT EXPENDITURES REQUIRING DOMESTIC FINANCE, CALENDAR 1940

(All figures in millions of pounds)

INCOME RECEIPTS *A*			DISPOSAL BY INCOME RECIPIENTS *B*		DISPOSAL BY BUSINESS *C*			INCOME PAYMENTS *D*		
1. Personal income received from			1. Expenditures on business goods	4,424	1. Income payments to			1. Paid by business to		
a. Government	2,545		2. Direct taxes	617	a. Persons	3,051		a. Persons	3,051	
b. Business	3,051		3. Accrued for tax liabilities	82	b. Others	211		b. Others	211	
c. Total		5,596	4. Other savings		c. Total		3,262	c. Total		3,262
2. Impersonal income[a] (after direct taxes) received from			a. Personal	473	2. Taxes			2. Paid by Government to		
a. Government	133		b. Impersonal (A-2-c)	344	a. Indirect taxes less subsidies	660		a. Persons	2,545	
b. Business	211		5. Total national income	5,940	b. Direct	92		b. Others	133	
c. Total		344			c. Total		752	c. Total[b]		2,678
3. Total national income		5,940			3. War risk insurance premiums		124	3. Total national income		5,940
					4. Depreciation allowances accumulated but not spent		286			
					5. Total receipts from sale of business goods (B-1)		4,424			

[a] Undistributed profits less business losses, plus miscellaneous government income plus investment income of charities, etc.

[b] In addition, government spent 759 abroad, covered by foreign disinvestment.

Source of data: see bottom of page 133.

amount will try to spend a fairly determinate part of it—how large a part depending of course on their saving and spending habits, the taxes they must pay, prices, and the like. In addition, government plans to spend a certain amount. The sum of what the government plans to spend plus what consumers will try to spend may exceed the total value at current prices of all resources available for use next year. The difference is the "inflationary gap." If there is such a "gap," one or more of these items must change: prices may rise and hence total income in money terms may increase; consumers may be rationed more severely and hence they may spend less than anticipated; and so on. In any event, at the end of the next year, the double entry books will necessarily balance; the "inflationary gap" will have done its work and exist no longer.

Notes for Table XVII

All estimates are based on figures given in the second White Paper, Cmd. 6347, and all references below are to Table and item numbers in that White Paper.

A-1-a and A-1-b. Obtained by subtracting A-2-a and A-2-b from D-1-c and D-2-c, respectively.

A-1-c. Item 8, Table II.

A-2-a and A-2-b. Obtained by apportioning A-2-c in the ratio of total government domestic expenditures to total private domestic expenditures. Total government domestic expenditures taken as item 7, Table I, plus items 4, 5, 6, Table II, plus figure in footnote of Table II, minus item 9, Table I. Total domestic private expenditures taken as item 6, Table I.

A-2-c. Items 1 plus 2, Table I, plus figure in footnote of Table II, minus item 1, Table II, minus item 4, Table IV, plus items 11 and 12, Table II.

B-1. Item 6, Table I.

B-2. Item 11 plus item 12, Table II.

B-3. Item 13, Table II.

B-4-a. Item 14, Table II.

C-1-a. Same as A-1-b.

C-1-b. Same as A-2-b.

C-2-a. Item 11, Table I, minus item 10, Table I, plus part of item 12, Table I, indirect taxes not directly on consumption. Part taken determined by using ratio indicated under A-2-a and A-2-b.

C-2-b. Part of difference between item 4, Table IV, and items 11 plus 12, Table II. This difference is total direct taxes paid by other than persons. Part taken determined by using ratio indicated under A-2-a and A-2-b.

C-3. Item 13, Table I.

C-4. Item 8, Table I.

D-1-a. Obtained by subtracting D-1-b from D-1-c.

D-1-b. Same as A-2-b.

D-1-c. Obtained by subtracting D-2-c from D-3.

D-2-a. Obtained by subtracting D-2-b from D-2-c.

D-2-b. Same as A-2-a.

D-2-c. Item 7, Table I plus items 4, 5, 6, and figure in footnote, Table II, minus part of item 12, Table I, not included in C-2-a, minus part of direct taxes paid by other than persons not included in C-2-b, minus item 9, Table I.

Using the figures given in the second British White Paper (Cmd. 6347), we can summarize the books for Great Britain for 1940. In the schematic summary on page 132 (Table XVII), we treat government as if it were an integrated enterprise that purchases all resources directly from individuals and makes payments to nonindividuals only in the form of interest, and the like. "Business" is occupied solely with selling goods and services not used by government. Unreal though it is, this treatment emphasizes the distinction that is most important for the present problem—namely, between (a) resources used directly or indirectly for government account, and hence engaged in producing goods not available for sale in the market, and (b) resources used directly or indirectly in producing goods available for sale. The summary is restricted to government expenditures requiring domestic finance, and neglects some £759 million financed from overseas sources (sale of investments, gold and silver, and so on).

The first column reveals the source of income receipts. Individuals received a total of £5,596 million, £2,545 million from government, £3,051 million from business. Impersonal income—undistributed profits less business losses of enterprises, investment income of charities, miscellaneous income of government—totaled £344 million, £211 million from business, £133 million from government. Total income was £5,940 million. The major part of this total, £5,585 million, represents payments for the use of resources; the rest, £355 million, essentially transfer payments—national debt interest, old-age pensions, social-insurance benefits. (The White Paper designates the first component, "net national income.")

Individuals spent £4,424 million on "business goods," paid £617 million in direct taxes, accumulated £82 million as a reserve against tax liabilities and saved £473 million in the form of cash, bank deposits, insurance reserves, and government bonds. The £344 million impersonal income is all treated as saved. All of these items other than the amount spent on business goods reflect the "release" of resources: received in the main as payment for the use of resources, they were available for the purchase of goods and services but were not so used.

Not all of the £4,424 million spent on "business goods" went to pay for the use of real resources. Only £3,051 million was paid to individuals for the use of resources as wages, salaries, rents, dividends; an additional £211 million was paid to others, that is, represented impersonal income. In addition to these sums paid for the use of resources, £660 million was paid as the excess of indirect taxes over subsidies, £92 million as direct business taxes, and £124 million as war risk insurance premiums, and £286 million was accumulated as depreciation reserves, etc., but not spent. This item of £286 million is not equal to the total allowance for depreciation, etc.; some part of the resources purchased with item C-1, the £3,262 million paid to individuals and others, may have been used to replace or maintain capital equipment. The £286 million represents essentially the depreciation not made good—i. e., domestic disinvestment. Items C-2 (taxes), C-3 (war risk insurance premiums), and C-4 (depreciation reserves), are further offsets to government expenditure. They represent sums received for the use of resources whose spending did not involve a corresponding drain on resources.

The final column is essentially a restatement of the first column. It summarizes the payments by business and government. Each item that enters into the total of this column also enters into the total of the first column, since what is paid by one party is necessarily received by another. Moreover, the total of this column must equal the total of the disposal column, since income received must end up somewhere—either as money spent, paid in taxes, or saved. The equality of the first and last column emphasizes the impossibility of a "gap" after the event.

The tabulation on page 136 summarizes the sources from which funds were available for government purposes.

The several items listed in this summary were not necessarily made directly available to the government. For example, personal savings were obviously not all invested in government securities. The relationship is, if anything, the other way. Government expenditure, possibly financed in the first instance by the creation of money, found its way into personal savings; that is, individuals were willing to hold these noninterest bearing securities. In effect the government received the use of part of individuals' incomes, though the individuals themselves may not have had the faintest notion that this was the case.

What now of the future? On the basis of a summary such as this,

Item	*Source*	*Revenue in £ million*
B-2	Taxes, direct personal	617
C-2-b	Taxes, direct impersonal	92
C-2-a	Taxes, indirect less subsidies	660
C-3	War risk insurance premiums	124
B-3	Tax accruals	82
B-4-a	Savings, personal	473
B-4-b	Savings, impersonal	344
C-4	Domestic disinvestment	286
	Total domestic expenditures	2,678
	Financed by overseas sources	759
	Total	3,437[a]

[a] Total government expenditure on goods and services is given in item 7, Table I of the second White Paper as £3,333 million. The difference between this figure and the figure of £3,437 million that we use is explained by our inclusion of transfer items and our exclusion of business taxes attributable to government purchases—these taxes are in essence paid by government to itself, as we have treated government.

how do we decide whether an "inflationary gap" is in prospect? The first step is to decide whether any of the items in the summary are misleading. For example, item B-4-a (personal savings), is estimated as £473 million in 1940. Does this correspond to the amount that people really want to save out of a total personal income of £5,596 million? Or does it represent funds in transit, the piling up of cash balances by individuals who had unexpected rises in income that they want to spend but have not yet had an opportunity to spend? As Mr. Paish puts it,

> the question of exactly what constitutes an inflationary gap is extremely difficult to answer. Broadly speaking, it involves finding the answers to at least four subsidiary questions:—(1) Has the financing of the budget deficit been accompanied by an increase in the quantity of money or bank deposits? (2) Do the people who own these increased balances wish to save as much, or are they intending to spend them on consumption goods at the first opportunity? (3) If they do wish to save as much, do they wish to continue to hold their savings in this form? (4) If they do spend them, are there sufficient resources available to enable the increased demand to

be met without a serious rise in prices? In the present case the answers to the first and last questions are clear. There *has* been a very marked increase in the volume of bank deposits, and there are *not* the resources available to enable these increased deposits to be spent without a serious rise in prices.[12]

Mr. Paish, through an ingenious analysis, gives a reasonably satisfactory answer to his second and third questions. Putting together the information in the White Paper and banking statistics, he comes to the conclusion that the bulk of personal savings went into savings-bank deposits, small investors' securities and other long-dated securities, and relatively little into what we should call demand deposits or short-term investments; that is, personal savings are primarily in forms that suggest they are "real" savings and not funds in transit.

A corresponding analysis must be made of other items in the summary to see how they could be expected to change in the coming period. For example, the £286 million in item C-4 may be less than could be secured in this way; some of the physical maintenance and replacement paid for out of the £3,262 million disbursed by business for the use of resources can perhaps be dispensed with next year, and so on. If every item in the summary is analyzed in this way, an estimate can be secured of the positive or negative "inflationary gap" that would accompany the *same* amount of government expenditure. Suppose, for example, that all items remain the same except that item C-1 (business disbursements for resources) can be expected to decline by £100 million and C-4 (unspent depreciation allowances), can be expected to increase by the same amount. Then there is a negative inflationary gap of £100 million; in other words, government expenditures can increase by £100 million without any inflationary tendencies, since business is releasing resources sufficient to match the increase in government expenditures.

To get the total "inflationary gap" for next year, the expected increase in government expenditures must be added to the estimate of the "inflationary gap" with the *same* amount of government expenditure. Suppose the latter is zero, so that, with the *same* government expenditure in 1941, all the figures in the summary would be the same

[12] "The Budget and the White Paper," p. 12.

as in 1940. Suppose, further, that government plans to spend an additional £1,000 million, so that this is next year's "inflationary gap," and that no explicit action is taken to close the gap. How will the "inflationary gap" be closed in the next year, as it clearly must since the books will necessarily balance at the end of next year? At one extreme, the government may simply order the transfer to government use of resources now used by "business" and fix the prices to be paid for resources. In this case, item D-1 will decline by £1,000 million, and item D-2 will rise by £1,000 million. Total income will still be £5,940 million, and hence consumers will still try to spend £4,424 million. Presumably, however, the transfer of resources will decrease the volume of goods available for purchase (this will not happen only if all of the decline in business expenditures can come out of replacement and maintenance, in which case the only effect would be a counterbalancing rise of £1,000 million in item C-4). If prices of business goods are not controlled, they will rise, and in addition, inventories may decline. To the extent that inventories decline, item C-4 will absorb some part of the £1,000 million. The rest will go into profits, here included in item C-1; item D-1 will not decline by the full £1,000 million and total income will not remain £5,940 million. In effect, the government will not have been successful in fixing the prices paid for resources, since the price paid to entrepreneurial resources will rise. In consequence of the rise in total income, the items in column B will change. The recipients of profits will try to spend some part on business goods and will save some part. Under the assumed conditions, this will lead to a still further rise in prices and profits. It is not possible, without further knowledge, to say what the books will look like at the end of the year, except that we know that the total of items B-2, B-3, B-4, C-2, C-3, and C-4 must rise by exactly £1,000 million.

If, in addition to fixing the prices of resources other than entrepreneurship, the government also fixes the prices of all business goods and rations the available supply, then, except for that part of the £1,000 million decline in C-1 absorbed by C-4, the net effect will be a decline in item B-1 and a counterbalancing rise in item B-4, savings. This is perhaps the most likely eventuality in England. As Mr. Paish says, in existing conditions, the emergence of an implicitly inflationary situation will probably be seen, not in an obvious rise in prices, but in an increasingly wide extension of the system of rationing and other limitations on the use of money. It is just as possible to raise forced loans from the public by giving them money they cannot spend as by taking from them part of the money they would otherwise have received. Whether the offer of money which can be spent, if at all, only after the war, would continue to provide an adequate economic incentive for increased exertions, and whether it would have to be supplemented by more direct incentives, beneficial or penal, are questions which cannot be answered in advance. It is clear, however, that great limitations on the use of money may in some cases give rise to almost as great a redistribution of wealth (for instance, between debtor and creditor) as inflation itself, while at the same time not providing that additional incentive to personal exertion which rising prices often provides.

If the prices of neither resources nor business goods are fixed, the result will be much the same as when only the prices of resources other than entrepreneurship are fixed, except that government expenditures may have to rise by more than £1,000 million if the same amount of resources are to be diverted. Government can get extra resources only by bidding them away from business, which will lead to a rise in the prices of resources. Hence item D-1 will decline by less than £1,000 million and may indeed rise. Again, the change in total income will cause modifications in columns B and C, prices of "business" goods will rise, and so on. About all one can say without more information and a more detailed analysis is that the total of items B-2, B-3, B-4, C-2, C-3, and C-4 must rise by whatever amount government expenditures rise.

Explicit action to close the "inflationary gap" would involve explicit increases in the items whose sum must equal government expenditures. Items B-2, B-3, and C-2, the tax items, can be changed most directly. In estimating the effect of changes in taxes, however, account must be taken of indirect repercussions. For example, if an increase in B-2, direct taxes, merely resulted in a corresponding decline in B-4, savings, the increased taxes would make no contribution toward closing the "gap." Item B-4 can be affected by a savings campaign, or by a forced saving plan; and so on.

In his budget for 1941–42, the Chancellor . . . placed the "inflationary" gap at about £500 Mn. This gap he proposes to fill, to the extent of £125 Mn. in a full year and £96 Mn. in the present year, by raising the standard rate of Income Tax . . . ; and to the extent of a further £125 Mn. in a full year and £54 Mn. in the present year by reducing the Personal and Earned Income Allowances. . . . For the closing of the rest of the "gap" the Chancellor relies on a still further increase in voluntary saving. (Paish, *op. cit.*, p. 13.)

The preceding analysis has assumed that no unutilized resources were available, a close approximation to the real situation in Great Britain. If unutilized resources are available, the government can use more resources without others' using less. Suppose that there had been £1,000 million's worth of unutilized resources in Great Britain at the end of 1940. It does not follow that government could have increased its expenditures by £1,000 million without a prospective "inflationary gap." For, if the government had done so, total income would have changed, and the items in column B would have changed also. The recipients of the £1,000 million would have presumably tried to spend some part of it, and this would have led to the kinds of results already described. Government expenditures can rise without creating an "inflationary gap" solely by an amount that will lead to a rise of £1,000 million in the sum of items D-1 and D-2.

This "inflationary gap" analysis does not give any specific technique for determining the rise in income or in prices that will be associated with a given increase in government expenditures. At the same time, it seems exceedingly valuable. It furnishes a significant framework for interpreting government policy, and reveals the basic factors on which its effects depend. It combines the monetary and "real" aspects of the problem in a way that gives each its proper place. It is the kind of analysis that underlies the specific and detailed techniques that we discuss in the other sections of this essay.

METHODS USING THE RELATION BETWEEN INVESTMENT AND INCOME

During recent years, methods of forecasting resting on the relation between investment and income have been widely used, particularly by government agencies. The Bureau of the Budget, the National Resources Planning Board, the Office of Price Administration, the Department of Commerce, and the Department of Labor have used methods that, while differing from one another, all take investment or "offsets to savings" as the strategic variable. Investment or "offsets to savings" is ordinarily broadly defined as the sum of private capital formation, including the net change in inventories and the net foreign balance, the net government contribution (roughly, government expenditures on goods and services less government receipts from income), and the net change in consumer credit outstanding.

In broad outline, the procedure typically consists in making independent estimates of changes in some future period in investment as a whole or in selected categories of investment. The change in investment is then translated into a change in income by use of historical relationships. The first approximation obtained in this way is examined for internal consistency to see whether, for example, the assumed changes in various investment items are consistent with the derived changes in income and consumer outlay. The process may then be repeated with investment items adjusted and further approximations derived.

This procedure gives an estimate of national money income (or gross national product). In order to determine what, if any, general price movements are implied by the estimate, it is necessary to have an estimate of the expansion in physical output that is feasible. This estimate is sometimes made independently, sometimes as part of the process of deriving estimates of national money income. The ratio of the national money income to the national real income gives the price rise to be anticipated; and the difference between the two gives the amount of income that the government must prevent from coming into existence if prices are not to rise.

The users of this method are wont to emphasize that its value is greatest when the supply of resources is relatively most elastic, and its value least, when relatively full employment has been reached and direct governmental control has superseded the control of the market in important segments of the economy.

The logical foundation of this procedure is often claimed to be the Keynesian analysis. According to this analysis, changes in income are brought about by discrepancies between ex ante saving, the amount that individuals and business enterprises want to save out of any given income, and ex ante investment, the amount that they want to invest—"planned" investment as it were. Changes in income continue until ex ante saving and investment are equal, provided of course the economic system is subject to no additional "shocks" in the interim. At equilibrium, when ex ante saving and investment are equal, there is a fixed relation between them, on the one hand, and the national income, on the other, a relation determined by the saving and spending habits of income recipients. Ex ante saving and investment cannot of course be measured. We can only measure actual (or ex post) saving and investment which as ordinarily defined are necessarily equal in any time unit. Actual saving will differ from ex ante saving because of unplanned saving or dissaving. For example, a business enterprise may find the price of its products higher than anticipated and in consequence a surplus may accumulate, or an individual may get an unexpected increase in income, much of which he may save until he readjusts his consumption pattern to his new income level. Similarly, actual investment may differ from ex ante investment. In the face of an unexpectedly large demand, a business concern may draw down inventories below the desired level, that is, it may disinvest.

Unable to measure ex ante saving directly, the users of the investment method implicitly derive their first approximation by adopting the hypothesis that ex ante saving next year is equal to ex post saving this year, that is, to investment this year. There is, of course, little basis in either theory or fact for this hypothesis in a changing world. They then estimate investment next year, and take the difference between this estimate and actual investment this year as equivalent to the difference between ex ante investment and ex ante saving.

This theoretical structure can more properly be considered a rationalization of the investment procedure than a justification. The links between the statistical estimates and the ex ante concepts are extremely loose; even more important, the relation between income and ex ante investment can be considered stable only under equilibrium conditions. The Keynesian analysis gives no reason to suppose that it will be stable when the system is not in equilibrium.

The validity of the procedure should therefore be judged on a largely statistical level. It depends on (1) the accuracy of the estimated change in investment and (2) the stability of the relation between changes in investment and changes in income.

1. In "normal" times it is exceedingly doubtful that much confidence could be attached to the estimated change in investment. This may not be so, however, at present when the government contribution plays so large a role. The most questionable item is probably the estimated change in inventory. However, if the forecasts are looked on not as predictions but as a step in deciding on proper economic policy, even this difficulty is not serious. For, if economic policy succeeds in preventing a rise in prices, as well as expectations of future price rises, there will be no reason to expect a speculative rise in inventories. Consequently, the estimate of the change in inventories could include only the change needed to conduct the changed volume of business and make no allowance for possible speculative changes. In terms of the theoretical structure, an additional justification for excluding speculative inventory change is that they can be assumed more like ex post than like ex ante investment. If this treatment of inventories is adopted, the estimated change in income must be interpreted as the change that would occur if there were no speculative change in inventories.

2. The proper relation between changes in income and changes in investment clearly depends on the treatment of inventories. If the estimated change in inventories is supposed to include all inventory changes, the relation called for is different than if it is supposed to exclude speculative changes. Data to judge the stability of the relation when all inventory changes are included are presented in the accompanying charts and table. As Chart 2 shows, while there is a decided positive relation between the change in capital formation and the change in national income, there is considerable scatter. The rank difference correlation between the two variables is .79. The ratio between the change in national income and the change in net capital formation (see column 7 of Table XVIII) varies from –56 to 9.1, a very wide range. However, the extreme negative item arises because net capital formation is almost zero. If we exclude this item the range is –2.0 to 9.1, still a broad range. During the period since 1935, the ratio varied from 1.4 to 7.6.

CHART 2

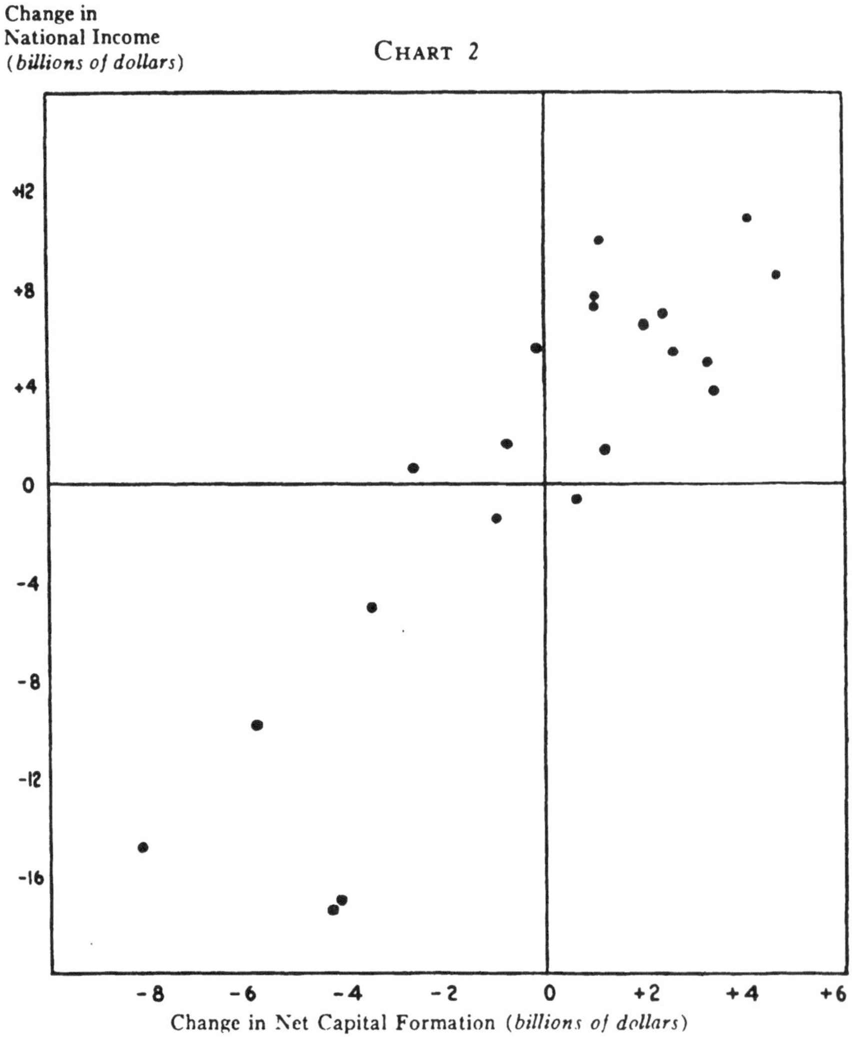

RELATION BETWEEN CHANGE IN CAPITAL FORMATION AND CHANGE IN NATIONAL INCOME, 1919–40

Source: Table XVIII, p. 145

Table XVIII

RELATION AMONG CHANGES IN CAPITAL FORMATION, NATIONAL INCOME, AND CONSUMER OUTLAY [a]

YEAR	NATIONAL INCOME	NET CAPITAL FORMATION	CONSUMER OUTLAY	CHANGE IN NATIONAL INCOME	CHANGE IN NET CAPITAL FORMATION	CHANGE IN CONSUMER OUTLAY	RATIO OF CHANGE IN NATIONAL INCOME TO CHANGE IN NET CAPITAL FORMATION
	(1)	(2)	(3)	(4)	(5)	(6)	(7)
1919	64.2	10.3	53.9				
1920	74.2	11.4	62.8	10.0	1.1	8.9	9.1
1921	59.4	3.3	56.1	-14.8	-8.1	-6.7	1.8
1922	60.7	4.5	56.2	1.3	1.2	0.1	1.1
1923	71.6	8.6	63.0	10.9	4.1	6.8	2.7
1924	72.1	5.9	66.2	0.5	-2.7	3.2	-0.2
1925	76.0	9.3	66.7	3.9	3.4	0.5	1.1
1926	81.6	9.2	72.4	5.6	-0.1	5.7	-56.0
1927	80.1	8.2	71.9	-1.5	-1.0	-0.5	1.5
1928	81.7	7.4	74.3	1.6	-0.8	2.4	-2.0
1929	87.2	10.0	77.2	5.5	2.6	2.9	2.1
1930	77.3	4.2	73.1	-9.9	-5.8	-4.1	1.7
1931	60.3	0.1	60.2	-17.0	-4.1	-12.9	4.1
1932	42.9	-4.2	47.1	-17.4	-4.3	-13.1	4.0
1933	42.2	-3.6	45.8	-0.7	0.6	-1.3	-1.2
1934	49.5	-2.6	52.1	7.3	1.0	6.3	7.3
1935	54.4	0.7	53.7	4.9	3.3	1.6	1.5
1936	62.9	5.4	57.5	8.5	4.7	3.8	1.8
1937	70.5	6.4	64.1	7.6	1.0	6.6	7.6
1938	65.5	2.9	62.6	-5.0	-3.5	-1.5	1.4
1939	72.4	5.3	67.1	6.9	2.4	4.5	2.9
1940	78.9	7.3	71.6	6.5	2.0	4.5	3.2

[a] For 1919 to 1938, data on national income, net capital formation, and consumer outlay from Simon Kuznets, *National Income and Its Composition, 1919–1938*, vol. I, 137, 269. For 1939 to 1940, estimates were derived by extrapolating earlier figures on the basis of Department of Commerce estimates.

Comparing the change in national income with the change in investment is somewhat misleading, since the change in national income equals the change in investment plus the change in consumer outlay. Consequently, there is necessarily a tendency toward a fairly strong positive correlation, since the change in national income is correlated with part of itself. It is more illuminating to compare the two parts of the change in national income, as is done in Chart 3. The relation between the change in capital formation and the change in consumer outlay is somewhat less close than between the former and the change in national income, the rank difference correlation being only .62.

THE GILBERT-PERLO METHOD

Of the several variants of the investment method that have been used, a detailed description has been published of only one—that used by Richard V. Gilbert and Victor Perlo, of the Office of Price Administration, and designated by them the "investment-factor" method. The other methods are described in confidential government memoranda. The description of the Gilbert-Perlo method appears in the July–October, 1942, issue of *Econometrica;* [13] a more general statement and some of the predictions based on the method appear in the December, 1940, *Savings Bank Journal.*

The Gilbert-Perlo method is based on the relation between offsets to savings and gross national product. It takes federal expenditures, the export balance, and, at times, net change in inventories, as the factors initiating expansion. The items and relations used are:

(1) federal expenditures
(2) export balance
(3) historical relations between:
  (a) offsets to savings and gross national product
  (b) gross national product and components of offsets to savings other than the net government contribution and the net foreign balance (plant and equipment expenditures, residential housing expenditures, net change in inventories, net contribution of state and local governments, net change in consumer credit)
  (c) gross national product and imports
  (d) gross national product and tax revenues, adjusted for changes in Revenue Act

[13] "The Investment-Factor Method of Forecasting Business Activity," pp. 311–16

CHART 3

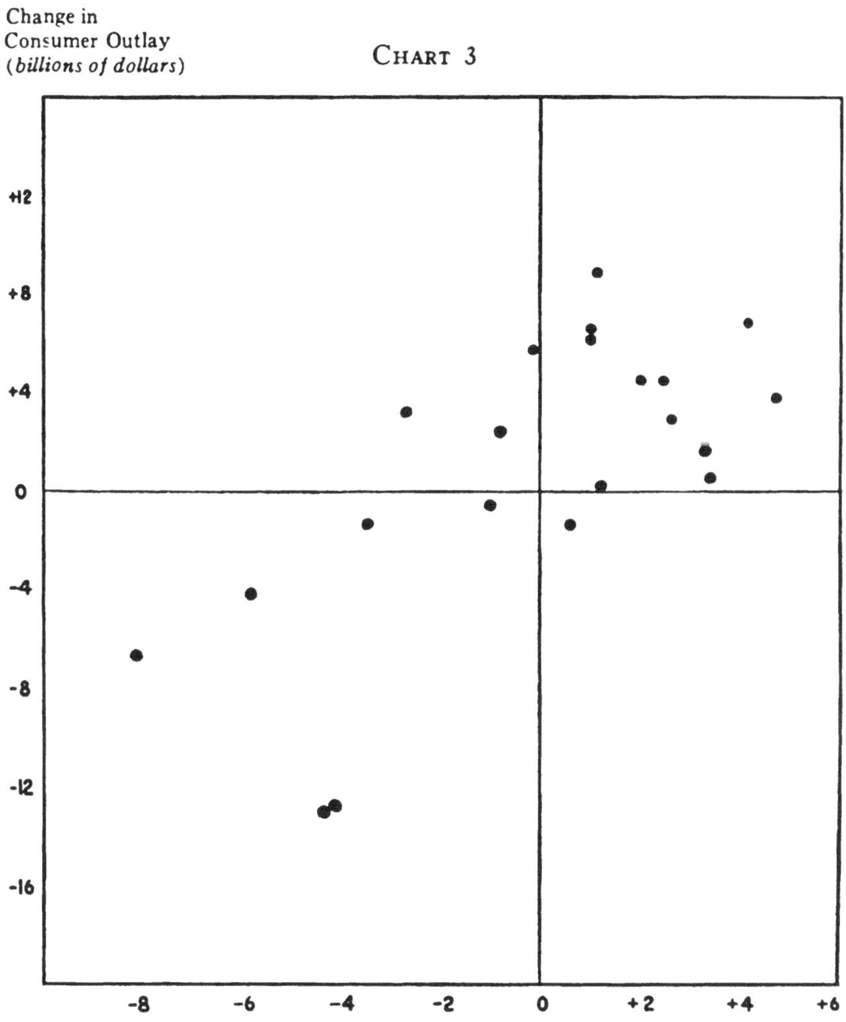

RELATION BETWEEN CHANGE IN CONSUMER OUTLAY AND CHANGE IN CAPITAL FORMATION, 1919–40

Source: Table XVIII, p. 145

(e) gross national product and index of industrial production
(f) gross national product and employment
(g) gross national product and national income

The procedure is to add estimated changes in (1) and (2) to the base year's offsets to savings. This gives a preliminary estimate of offsets to savings in the year for which the estimate is to be made. This total, combined with (3)(a), yields a preliminary estimate of gross national product. This preliminary estimate of gross national product, combined with (3)(b), yields an estimate of other offsets to savings; combined with (3)(c), an estimate of the change in imports that can be used to convert (2) into an estimate of the net foreign balance; and, combined with (3)(d), an estimate of tax revenue that can be used to convert (1) into an estimate of the net government contribution. Totaling these estimates gives a corrected estimate of offsets to savings. This process is repeated until successive estimates are identical.

The estimate of gross national product obtained by this process of successive approximations is then combined with (3)(e) and (3)(f) to estimate output and employment. In making these estimates, it is implicitly assumed that prices remain unchanged, or more exactly, that they change as they did during the period for which the historical relations were computed. Comparison of the employment estimate with the estimate of available labor force indicates whether the price assumption is tenable. If it is not, the gross national product at unchanged prices that corresponds to attainable full employment is estimated, apparently by using relation (3)(f) in reverse, and from this, using (3)(g), the corresponding national income at unchanged prices. The expected price change is then computed by dividing the national money income that corresponds to the initial estimate of gross national product by the national income at unchanged prices that corresponds to attainable full employment.

Account is taken of tax policy in two ways. First, in computing the net government contribution, tax revenues (actual receipts for personal taxes, accruals for corporate taxes) are deducted from government expenditures. However, this makes no allowance for changes in the structure of the tax system. Such changes are presumably taken into account by altering (3) (a). It is not entirely clear just how this is done. Apparently, the reduction in savings as a result of additional taxes is estimated, and *added* to the estimated offsets to savings; since the greater the amount that comes out of savings, the larger will tend to be the gross national product corresponding to offsets to savings computed without this correction. The amount of taxes that must be levied to prevent inflation can be computed by determining the net government contribution that would correspond to the national income at attainable full employment, and subtracting this from the net government contribution without additional tax changes.

Forecasts of national income made by the Gilbert-Perlo method late in 1940 for hypothetical fiscal years 1940–1944 are given in Table XIX. With the assumed defense expenditures, the estimates indicate that there would be no serious inflation problem (no price rise from approximately 1939 levels) until fiscal 1944, when defense expenditures were taken as $40 billion. At that time, about $15 billion of additional taxes would be needed to stem price rises, and real national income at 1939 prices would reach $129 billion. Price rises might apparently be expected to begin when defense expenditures were somewhere between $20 billion and $40 billion.

Defense expenditures actually reached a rate of $20 billion about October or November, 1941, and a rate of $40 billion about April, 1942. Prices, as measured by the sluggish Bureau of Labor Statistics cost-of-living index number, were well above the 1939 level by March, 1941, when defense expenditures were at an annual rate of less than $10 billion. Between March, 1941, and November, 1941, the cost-of-living index rose 9 percentage points and between November, 1941, and April, 1942, another 5 percentage points, or a total rise from March, 1941, to April, 1942, of 14 percent over the March, 1941, level of 101.2.

The national income in 1939 prices in the quarter in which defense expenditures reached an annual rate of $10 billion (second quarter, 1941) was approximately $88 billion; in the quarter in which defense expenditures reached an annual rate of $20 billion (fourth quarter, 1941), approximately $93 billion; and in the quarter in which defense expenditures reached an annual rate of $40 billion (second quarter, 1942), approximately $96 billion.[14] These are all substantially, and increasingly, lower than the national income (at 1939 prices) associated by Gilbert and Perlo with the corresponding levels of defense expenditures.[15]

These comparisons are not, however, an entirely fair test of the Gilbert-Perlo method. In the first place, the comparisons take defense expenditures as the single "initial" or "strategic" variable, whereas the Gilbert-Perlo method takes account of other strategic variables as well. More important, the actual expansion of defense expenditures to a $40 billion level took place in a much shorter space of time than was assumed—more than a year and a half less. Had Gilbert and Perlo been assuming an equally large expansion in war expenditure in so much shorter a time, they undoubtedly would have forecast a much smaller expansion in real output.

A test biased in the opposite direction is to compare the forecast levels of national income with the actual national income in the specified years, rather than with the national incomes associated with the specified levels of defense spending. As Table XIX shows, this comparison is much more favorable. For the years for which comparison is possible, the Gilbert-Perlo estimates are very close to the actual national income. Presumably this is the basis for their statement that "during the past two years the investment-factor method has given much better results than forecasts built up from individual industry forecasts." [16]

[14] Computed by deflating national income figures given by Milton Gilbert and Robert Bangs, *op. cit.*, p. 14, by Bureau of Labor Statistics cost-of-living index number.

[15] Some comments on a draft of this section transmitted to the author by Gilbert and Perlo state, with respect to this paragraph, "There was a technical reason for this. The method is set up to give gross national product estimates. To convert the gross national product into national income a simple formula . . . was used. This formula, having been based on past relationships, was valid as long as there were no substantial changes in the tax law because the gross national product is measured before taxes, while the national income is measured after [business] taxes. The forecast levels of national income therefore measured the national income after the old taxes but before the new. When adjustment is made for this factor, the difference is substantially reduced." While the factor mentioned may explain some of the discrepancy, the implicit assumption in this statement that increased business taxes do not affect gross national product but only reduce national income cannot be accepted.

[16] *Econometrica*, July–Oct., 1942, p. 315. The comments referred to in the preceding footnote say, with respect to this paragraph, "The following test was made: the final values of the investment factors and revenues were taken from the Department of

However, it already seems clear that the forecasts for fiscal 1943 and fiscal 1944 will not fare so well, since national income at 1939 prices is unlikely to exceed $105 billion in fiscal 1943. The Gilbert-Perlo estimates show a steadily accelerating rate of rise between 1940 and 1943, whereas actual figures already show a declining rate of growth.

The forecasts just discussed are apparently based in part on the estimates given in Table XX of national income at 1939 prices at attainable full employment for 40-, 43-, and 48-hour work weeks. Each length of work week was associated with a different number of men withdrawn from the labor force by the army and navy.

TABLE XIX

GILBERT–PERLO ESTIMATES FOR HYPOTHETICAL FISCAL YEARS 1940–1944; AND ACTUAL DEFENSE EXPENDITURES AND NATIONAL INCOME

FISCAL YEAR	ASSUMED DEFENSE EXPENDITURES	ACTUAL DEFENSE EXPENDITURES [a]	NATIONAL INCOME UNDER		ACTUAL NATIONAL INCOME	
			1939 and 1940 Revenue Acts	Additional taxes in 1944 [b]	Current prices [c]	1939 prices [d]
			(billions of dollars)			
1940	1.6	1.7	71.7		74.0	73.5
1941	5.0	6.3	80.8		84.2	82.7
1942	10.0	26.0	91.4		104.3	93.0
1943	20.0		118.4			
1944	40.0		176.6	129.4		

[a] Budget expenditures only.
[b] Special taxes yielding $14.8 billion, required to prevent inflation.
[c] Milton Gilbert and Robert Bangs, *op. cit.*, p. 15.
[d] Deflated by Bureau of Labor Statistics cost-of-living index number.

The estimates of the increased output attainable through lengthening the work week seem clearly too high. An increase in average hours from 40 to 43, associated with the withdrawal of over half a million

Commerce article in the May, 1942, *Survey of Current Business* and inserted into the relationships for 1940 and 1941. In each of these two cases the forecast underestimated the actual level of gross national product. For calendar 1940 the actual level was $97.1 billion, while the forecast gave $95.3 billion, while in 1941 the actual level was $119.5 billion, while the forecast was $113.3 billion." It is not clear whether this additional test took account of the point mentioned in the preceding footnote.

TABLE XX

GILBERT–PERLO ESTIMATES OF REAL NATIONAL INCOME UNDER ALTERNATIVE LABOR ASSUMPTIONS

LENGTH OF WORK WEEK IN HOURS	NUMBER OF MEN WITHDRAWN FOR MILITARY FORCES (*millions*)	NATIONAL INCOME (*billions*)	PERCENT INCREASE IN TOTAL MAN-HOURS	PERCENT INCREASE IN NATIONAL INCOME
40	2.6	$107.7		
43	3.2	118.4	6.3	10
48	6.4	129.4	6.3	9.3

men from the labor force, would increase total man-hours by about 6 percent; and an increase in hours from 43 to 48, associated with the withdrawal of about 3 million men, would increase total man-hours by about the same percentage. The first 6 percent increase, coming when there is already full employment, is supposed to increase total output by 10 percent; and the second 6 percent increase in man-hours is supposed to increase output by over 9 percent.

If these results are correct, then much of what we think we know must be discarded as fallacious. Extra hours bring extra strain and fatigue and can hardly be expected to be as productive as the initial 40 hours. True, in the early stages of recovery from a deep depression, these may be counteracted by better organization of work, by more intensive utilization of machinery, by concealed unemployment of individuals who could render more service in the same time with no extra cost (as, for instance retail dealers and operators of movie houses). But these counterbalancing forces must be almost completely absent when the expansion in hours takes place at a time of full employment.

There is the further question whether the assumed increases in average work week can be achieved. As noted in the comments on the work of the Iowa group, the average work week of 40 hours is probably valid for manufacturing alone. Hours may well be longer in other industries. Increases in hours have no meaning in many segments of the economy. What does an increase in hours from 40 to 43 or 48 mean for farmers, independent businessmen, independent professional men, bank clerks and other workers whose work week coincides with the period during which the service in question is being rendered? Manufacturing and mining are probably the two major industries in which lengthening of the work week would affect man-hours proportionately; man-hours would also be affected, though to a lesser extent, in transportation and trade. In plants now working continuously, an increase in hours per week could not increase output, but it would release labor for use elsewhere. The Gilbert-Perlo estimates are for total output. Consequently, the percentage increases in man-hours shown in the above table imply that the average work week for *all gainfully occupied* persons is increased by 7½ and 11½ percent respectively (40 to 43 and 43 to 48). To attain such increases would imply very much larger increases in those segments where hours per week can be increased. For example, an average work week of 48 hours for all gainfully occupied might well mean an average work week of 56 hours or more in manufacturing and mining.

Part IV

A TECHNIQUE FOR ANALYZING AND ANTICIPATING CHANGE IN NATIONAL INCOME

By Ruth P. Mack

THE WISH to prevent inflation has caused a praiseworthy gap-consciousness among men burdened with responsibility for the public interest. Various definitions and methods of measuring the gap have been devised. This essay may be regarded as another sheaf in the large harvest.

The major components of national income are highly sensitive aggregates, all of which are dependent as well as independent variables. The direction and extent of their change, moreover, rests on the manner in which many decisions by many individuals are made. Consequently, the relation between certain of these components—a "gap" between consumer income and goods available for consumer purchase, or between any other appropriate set of magnitudes, whether positive (an inflationary gap) or negative (a purchasing-power gap)—has boundary markers which float with only tenuous anchorage on a sea of individual decisions and capricious circumstance. The forecaster must learn the weight of the mooring and the length of the mooring chain and must attempt to predict the movement of the wind and current in order that he may surmise how the floated markers will shift.

To do this he must make, and this is the point to be emphasized, a great many assumptions about the way in which events take place and decisions are made. Yet even when the forces at work in an economy are as strong as they are today, the task is a perilous one. For though war expenditures mount towards the hundred billion mark and stipulated procedures reach into new areas, there are still an indefinite number of ways in which the decisions of individuals will affect the magnitude and proportions of national income, changing thereby the size of an inflationary gap and the way in which it is closed.

If, then, we face squarely the true nature of the problem of estimating national income, the inflationary gap, or taxes necessary to prevent inflation, we must trace the process of change in many if not all of its intricacies. Only in this way will the assumptions and judgments underlying the answers become explicit and therefore subject to correction.

We may, for example, start with the current situation and, following through the dynamics of the process with great care, estimate how national real income and its components, as well as prices of various classes of goods, will change. Then, if a price rise is indicated, we may make some further assumptions about change in taxation or the introduction of price control measures. This set of assumptions needs, in turn, to be incorporated in another detailed analysis of process, since many of the basic judgments used in the first set of forecasts will change as a result of the new measures and consequently the gap will no longer be the same. Thus the selection of remedial policy involves a series of approximations each step of which is sandwiched between a re-thinking of the process of change.

In the approach utilized in Part I, the problem of estimation is simplified in two main ways: 1. The effective limit to the output of goods and services is assumed to be not consumer demand but the availability of physical resources such as labor, materials and plants; this assumption eliminates the need to trace the spiral of changed income—demand—production—income. 2. The price level is assumed to remain constant during the interval for which estimates are made, thereby avoiding the necessity of evaluating the effect of changing prices on production and spending and income.

In this essay the second of these assumptions is removed. In order to know whether remedial measures should be taken and what they ought to be, it is helpful to know what the disease would lead to in the absence of medicine. Such knowledge may help not only in suggesting the appropriate prescription but also in getting it accepted by the patient. It is therefore useful to estimate changes in the total and components of national income which would occur were price change not estopped.[1] The analysis, although not the statistical computations, also deals with the problem of estimating national income when the other assumption—that output is limited by available physical resources and therefore insensitive to changing demand—is likewise removed.[2]

NOTES ON THE THEORETICAL FRAMEWORK

In order to trace the intricate process of change in national income, it is necessary to make many assumptions about how transitions from one level to the next occur. It is necessary, in other words, to understand the dynamics of change of national income. Knowledge in this field is more of an art than a science. It involves evaluations that are of necessity based on insufficient evidence and untested theory. Nevertheless, any estimate of the magnitude of income flows rests on such judgments. They should be explicit.

The analysis of process which underlies the estimating procedure herewith described is based on a number of major evaluations or judgments. A brief enumeration of them will provide a scaffolding sufficient to support the skilled climber likely to venture into the rarefied atmosphere of these pages:

1. Investment is not an independent variable to which a multiplier may be applied in order to estimate change in total national income. The magnitude of investment is, in significant part, a function of the size of national income and the direction and extent of its change. Similarly unrealistic is the use of a constant consumption function in deriving the appropriate multiplier figure.

2. There is a close correlation between consumer disposable income and spending when changes in a few important variables are allowed for. A similarly satisfactory correlation does not exist at other levels such as between gross income of producers and their purchases of materials to be processed, or between net income of producers and their purchases of capital goods. This relationship between consumer income (minus taxes) and spending provides a level at which the otherwise complete circularity of process can be ana-

[1] The reader will observe that this essay is presented approximately as it was completed in the fall of 1941 and does not attempt to take account of events that have occurred since then.

[2] See pp. 194 ff.

lyzed, providing it is possible to discern the sequence of action and reaction in the income—consumption—production—income circle. Accordingly we focus the analysis on the estimation of consumer income and spending.

3. In order to develop a pattern of action and reaction it is necessary to look not on the completed act alone, but on how it came to be made. Accordingly ex ante rather than ex post measurement is crucial in the analysis or forecast of change. The distinction must be clearly envisioned and stubbornly maintained. When this is done, it becomes apparent that not only is there an important difference on a statistical and analytic level between plans and actuality, but that the relationship between them at any given time is one of the more important factors bearing on new plans and consequently on future actuality.

The sequence of action and reaction, which is in reality continuous, must, for the sort of analysis here undertaken, be formalized into set periods: plans are made at a certain time for a certain period; a divergence from planned behavior may cause actual occurrences for the period to differ from plans. In order that an analysis of this sort be reasonably realistic, the time unit of analysis must be short. We have selected one month as a statistically convenient interval.

4. Bringing points 2 and 3 together, the analysis is made to focus on estimating, first, consumer income and the proportions of that income which consumers would plan to spend on commodities and services of various sorts—consumer ready purchase money (hereafter referred to as rpm)—and, second, the aggregate dollar value of consumers' commodities and services offered for sale at the price at which they were intended to sell—goods ready for sale (hereafter referred to as grs). The changing relations between rpm and grs are thought to be indicative of the way in which future production plans will move.

These rpm and grs concepts involve several applications of the distinction between ex ante and ex post levels:

(a) Consumer ready purchase money is the sum which, during a given interval of time, consumers plan to spend. Included in consumer income is the increase in installment and open book credit outstanding. Since purchase on the installment plan or through charge accounts is an accepted method of financing purchasing, new borrowing minus repayments is thought of as ready purchase money. Income used for the payment of taxes is, in effect, preëmpted by the government and therefore is not part of the fund the disposal of which consumers may determine. Planned saving represents the difference between current income and the amount that it seems proper or necessary to plan to spend. Actual or ex post saving may be more or less than this planned or ex ante saving. Often the difference is small. But when prices are changing rapidly, or when goods grow scarce, the difference may be substantial. In any event it is improper to assume without further ado that, for any period of time, consumers actually do spend the amounts that they had intended to spend.

(b) Goods ready for sale is planned sales. It is, in other words, finished consumers' goods produced minus a planned increase (or plus a decrease) in inventories. Although inventories of finished goods are ordinarily designed as a cushion between production and sales, there are certain changes that are desired or usual and others which are undesired. We need to distinguish, for example, between an increase in inventories necessary to support higher sales volume and the piling up of inventory when sales fall off unexpectedly. Goods ready for sale excludes the former and includes the latter.

(c) The price at which goods were intended to sell is the price which producers expected to get at the time when they determined their production schedules. In embodying this concept in estimates, it is necessary to make some sort of simplifying assumption concerning the relation of this price to current prices. We have assumed that producers planned this month's production last month and therefore at last month's prices. This particular formulation could be changed as circumstances suggested, although some sort of simplification is unavoidable.

The relation between consumer ready purchase money and finished goods ready for sale to consumers will affect retailers' plans and reorders. But these actions will in turn affect plans and reorders of wholesalers and this will influence expectations and actions of producers of the finished commodities and so on until the raw goods issue from the earth, air, or sea.

5. This process of demand transmission is in part the result of efforts to judge probable sales and related inventory change at each

level of the production and distribution of consumers' goods. It involves judgments made at each link in the chain from raw to finished goods. These judgments will be good and they will be bad. When they are bad, cumulative error will be transmitted backward and play its part in the decisions of others. We know bafflingly little about the nature of this entire process.

Dynamic factors, not essentially part of a circular flow analysis, also enter the picture—variations in harvests, speculative accumulation of stocks, shifts in foreign markets, technical innovation resulting in changed prices which alter the pattern of consumers' wants—this sort of influence must also be given due weight. It typically becomes more significant as the distance from the finished product widens.

Planned and unplanned inventory change is the net result of these myriad decisions. Total inventory change in the consumer-goods fields represents the difference between production and sales of all goods eventually intended to be embodied in finished consumers' goods.

When attention focuses on the process of decision-making, change in inventory attaches itself inseparably to the production-planning procedure. Total planned production in any enterprise consists of goods intended for sale plus goods intended to swell inventories (or minus the decrease in inventories that is desired). The boundary between the two is often very hazy and certainly needs to be considered in a time dimension, but to think of sales as commodity flow and of an increase in inventory as capital accumulation leads to serious difficulties.[3] Therefore, when interest focuses on dynamics of change, it is necessary to distinguish sharply between inventory change and other sorts of capital formation.

Another general point about the treatment of inventory is suggested: Net change, even in planned and unplanned inventory of any given category of goods, is only part of the story. Its meaning to fore-

[3] The difficulty of measuring inventories of undifferentiated goods destined for one use rather than another is reason enough for the statistical procedure which has typically been followed. But these practical difficulties need not obscure the fact that, on a conceptual level, the distinction is clear enough and that the process of determining production schedules is affected by and reflected in the relationship between changes in inventories and sales in identical establishments.

casters or analysts will differ depending upon whether a net change of, say, zero, is the result of no change throughout the group or of compensating changes of large or small magnitude in various sections of the total.

6. Investment, as well as production at the earlier stages of consumers' goods, is influenced by the rpm–grs relation. Machinery and buildings for both plant expansion and replacement tend to be installed when the business prospect is clearing. When, on the other hand, business is increasing more slowly or falling off, orders for new equipment, if not at first actual installations, tend to fall off sharply.

But here again, emphasis on the rpm–grs relation need not cause the analysis to be limited to the circular flow level. Independent dynamic factors enter strongly into the investment picture—more strongly, however, at some times and in some cases than others: Technological change and the driving spirit of competition cause the design and exploitation of new products and machines which, because they pay their way for the purchaser, literally create their own market. Housing seems to follow a course which is more nearly independent of the rate of operation of the economy than is true for plant and equipment.

Finally, government spending and its financing provide a group of independent elements in the panorama of change which today foreshorten the others. Under more usual conditions, one of the major purposes of analytic forecast of change in national income would be the thought that it should be of aid in the formulation of public policy, not only with respect to government expenditure and its financing but also with respect to the influence which ought to be exerted on investment, saving, inventory accumulation, and prices.

DESCRIPTION OF THE METHOD

The manner in which the theoretical considerations that have been enumerated are embodied in a technique of analysis and forecast of national income is described in the pages which follow. To illustrate the method, tables containing estimates have been prepared. These figures are the result of a mere toying with the statistical record, an adequate treatment of which would require the resources of a research institution and extended experiment and study. The tables should be regarded as illustrative of a method of arriving at forecasts rather than as the finished product of that method.[4]

Two sets of figures are required: (1) a set of monthly forecasts of change in national income and its components; (2) a set of current estimates of actual data which correspond to the quantities used in arriving at the forecasts and thus afford a basis for their constant revision. These current data must of course also provide the bridgehead to which the forecasted span attaches. June, 1941, was, when the figures were first prepared, the last month for which current data could be obtained. Accordingly, the forecasts start with July and are based on estimates of actual figures for June obtained by using a wide variety of statistical series.

Were this system of forecast put to use, the June base figures would presumably be extended as current data became available. Although the lapse of time since the assembly of the figures would have made an extension of this sort possible, it has not been attempted. As has been said before, the tables merely illustrate a method and the projections would add nothing to an understanding of the procedure. The description which follows, therefore, relates to the method of constructing the base figure for June, 1941, and the forecasts for July, 1941, through February, 1942. A detailed description of the base figures is given in Appendix A. The current estimates of actual data would be made by continuing the base-month calculations as the data became available. A description of the forecasts is given in Appendix B.

There are six major steps that must be taken to convert estimates of production, made under the assumption of a constant price level, to estimates of production and of income and its distribution when prices do change. (We assume that no new measures for controlling

[4] In rereading this manuscript before it goes to press, I find myself disagreeing with many of the detailed judgments embodied in the tables. Some, though not all, of these doubts are included in comments in the appendices. In this essay, as in so many research problems, it seems to be necessary to have completed the work in order to make adequately the judgments required at its beginning. No major revisions, however, have been made. The technique described is a highly flexible instrument, the application of which at any time or place would always involve a careful examination of the current scene guided by the analytic categories used in this analysis. Concerning the usefulness of these categories as well as the general nature of their subdivision, I have undergone no change of heart.

prices have been put into effect since the 1941 Revenue Act.) Moreover, the method of analytic forecast that has been developed is thought to have possibilities for forecasting changes in income and production when physical output is not primarily determined by limitations in available factors of production. This matter is discussed in the closing section.

STEP I

Step I estimates income currently produced and divides it between retained income of producers and income payments to individuals.

The current output of the economy is summarized under the following headings: durable producers' goods, nondurable and durable consumers' commodities, consumers' services, and government services represented by the sum of money disbursed directly by the government as salaries, wages, benefits, and interest. Government orders placed with private industries are included under the appropriate heading (ordnance is treated with durable producers' goods). The figures include production resulting in inventory increases as well as in sales of finished goods and services.

These aggregates combine to form a concept of gross product differing somewhat from that ordinarily used. Not only are all machines and plant buildings, whether constructed for replacement or expansion, for private industry or for governments, regarded as finished goods, but all government services and benefits are classed as services included in the gross national product. Although there is nothing in the method of analysis which demands this particular definition of gross national product, there are several reasons for using it.

The purposes to which an analysis of this sort is likely to be put require a measure of national income which is sensitive to short-term changes in the contribution of various sectors of the economy. The accuracy with which changes in net capital formation can be recorded depends on the accuracy with which changes in current depreciation accruals (actual and imputed) measure the using up of capital. There is every reason to believe that these measures are quite insensitive to short-term change, and it is not at all clear that they even record long-term change adequately.[5]

[5] See R. P. Mack, *Flow of Business Funds and Consumer Purchasing Power*, New York, 1940, Chapters II, VII, and VIII.

For analogous reasons, the measure of government contribution used by Kuznets seems inadequate for the purposes of this analysis.[6] It is highly questionable whether government services of certain sorts are susceptible of allocation to any branch of the economy. If the cost basis of evaluation is used and if government accounting permitted a rough allocation of cost, one is inclined to insist that the services of the army and navy, of the school system and post office simply cannot be cut into slices and assigned to this or that group or aspect of economic life. If the payment price basis is used, an additional problem enters. It is well known that there is no effort to collect taxes on the basis of services received. Entirely different concepts are used —ability to pay, political expediency, social justice. If the method of allocating government services to business and individuals bears little or no relation to either what the service is worth to the recipient or what it costs, then there is no reason to expect that changes in measures of allocation will reflect any real change in services received. If those measures are subject to drastic change, as they are, the difficulty is obvious.

In short, our interest in long and, especially, short run changes in output dictates erring on the side of including too much rather than too little. In so far as government and private accounting, as well as the nature of many government functions, makes it impossible to allocate benefits from various government functions to any one group in the economy, it is desirable to include all government expenditure in gross national income. Government services to business are therefore counted twice (just as plant replacement is counted twice in the usual concept of gross national income)—once as business taxes and once as a portion of income paid out by governments.[7]

[6] Kuznets divides government services, excluding capital formation, into two parts equal to the taxes paid by business and by private individuals. The former part is considered an intermediate product incorporated eventually in finished goods of various sorts; the latter is considered finished goods—consumer service. Government construction is included in capital formation. The procedure rests on the thought that taxes are a sort of "payment price" and represent a very rough evaluation of the value of services received. (See Simon Kuznets, *National Income and Its Composition, 1919–1938*, New York, 1941, pp. 32 ff.)

[7] There are other arguments favoring the use of gross concepts for the sort of purpose here envisioned but they are too problematical to discuss here. They have to do with changes in the prices of factors of production and the relative importance of various sorts of income payments which are likely to accompany a change in gross capital formation (accompanied by an equal change in depreciation) or a change in govern-

Table XXI

INCOME PRODUCED AND DISTRIBUTED, JUNE, 1941, TO
(IN MILLIONS

	June [a]	July	August
† 1. Income Produced (line 2 + 16)	10,160	10,270	10,409
2. Income produced by business enterprises (line 3 + 4)	8,976	9,084	9,221
* 3. Durable producers' goods	1,787	1,868	1,956
4. Consumers' goods (line 5 + 6 + 7)	7,189	7,216	7,265
* 5. Non-durable commodities	3,820	3,841	3,866
* 6. Durable commodities	1,036	1,021	1,022
* † 7. Services	2,333	2,354	2,377
* 8. Current retained income of business at prices of previous month (line 9 + 10 + 11 + 12)	2,839	2,844	2,871
† 9. Retained income of prev. m. at prices of prev. m.		2,839	2,881
† 10. Change from prev. m. related to change in total income (prices constant)		5 (lines 10–12)	−10 (lines 10–12)
† 11. Change from prev. m. related to change in prices			
† 12. Change from prev. m. related to change in taxes			
* † 13. Income distributed to individuals by business enterprises (line 14 + 15)	6,137	6,240	6,350
* † 14. Ownership income	1,964	1,947	1,981
* † 15. Labor income	4,173	4,293	4,369
16. Income distributed directly by government (line 17 + 20)	1,184	1,186	1,188
† 17. Ownership income (line 18 + 19)	148	148	148
* † 18. Federal Government	98	98	98
* † 19. State and local governments	50	50	50
† 20. Labor income and benefits (line 21 + 22)	1,036	1,038	1,040
* † 21. Federal Government	515	517	519
* † 22. State and local governments	521	521	521
* 23. Total income distributed to individuals (line 13 + 16)	7,321	7,426	7,538
24. Change from prev. m.	141	105	112
25. Ownership income (line 14 + 17)	2,112	2,095	2,129
26. Change from prev. m.	31	−17	34
27. Labor income (line 15 + 20)	5,209	5,331	5,409
28. Change from prev. m.	110	122	78

[a] June, 1941, figures are at current prices.
* Derivation of figures for base month, June, 1941, in Appendix A, pp. 207–13.

(STEP I)

JUNE, 1942, AT PRICES OF THE PREVIOUS MONTH [a]
OF DOLLARS)

SEPTEMBER	OCTOBER	NOVEMBER	DECEMBER	JANUARY	FEBRUARY
10,616	10,794	10.945	11,089	11,227	11,303
9,426	9,602	9,751	9,893	10,029	10,103
2,060	2,162	2,261	2,361	2,465	2,557
7,366	7,440	7,490	7,532	7,564	7,546
3,925	3,974	4,017	4,057	4,101	4,123
1,021	1,011	987	954	902	840
2,420	2,455	2,486	2,521	2,561	2,583
2,968	3,051	3,130	3,201	3,274	3,306
2,973	3,051	3,118	3,204	3,282	3,301
31	28	25	15	15	12
−36	} −28	} −13	−18	−23	−9
6,458	6,551	6,621	6,692	6,755	6,799
2,008	2,037	2,053	2,068	2,089	2,094
4,450	4,514	4,568	4,624	4,666	4,705
1,190	1,192	1,194	1,196	1,198	1,200
148	148	148	148	148	148
98	98	98	98	98	98
50	50	50	50	50	50
1,042	1,044	1,046	1,048	1,050	1,052
521	523	525	527	529	531
521	521	521	521	521	521
7,648	7,743	7,815	7,888	7,953	7,999
110	95	72	73	65	46
2,156	2,185	2,201	2,216	2,237	2,242
27	29	16	15	21	5
5,492	5,558	5,614	5,672	5.716	5,757
83	66	56	58	44	41

† Derivation of figures for July, 1941–February, 1942, in Appendix B. Lines 9 – 28, pp. 218–21; lines 1 – 7, p. 230.

The income resulting from this gross national product is divided between, on the one hand, income paid out to individuals in the form of wages, salaries, benefits, entrepreneurial withdrawals, dividends, interest, rents and royalties, and, on the other hand, income retained by business enterprises in the form of depreciation accruals, other increases in the accruals over the charges to reserve accounts, retained profits, and federal, state, and local taxes paid by business enterprises. The total income paid out is then divided between labor income and ownership income.

Table XXI presents, for Step I, the base figures for the month of June and the eight monthly projections. Except for June, production is recorded at the prices of the previous month. (See discussion under Step III). The methods used for arriving at the base figures for June, 1941, are described in Appendix A, pages 207 to 213. The figures for the other months, however, are the end product of the analysis and cannot therefore be adequately described at this point. Step VI and the related section in Appendix B explain their composition. It is well to bear in mind, however, that for the period under consideration, when physical capacity and availability of factors of production rather than demand provide the effective limits of output, the analysis here presented is primarily concerned with an estimate of change in prices, that is, with dollar volume rather than with physical volume of production, the latter having been estimated on the basis of criteria external to this study.

STEP II

The next step involves the estimation of the part of the current income (stated in prices of the previous month) computed in Step I that consumers will want to devote to the major types of expenditures —perishable and semidurable commodities, durable commodities, and services—and the part of current income that they will aim to save. We call the former aggregate "ready purchase money of consumers."

In order to estimate these quantities, we need first to corral the

ment services (accompanied by an equal change in business taxes). The problem exists on the level of money prices and also on the level of "real" prices.

factors which will influence the amount of current income that consumers will aim to spend.[8] The extent to which income has changed is, perhaps, the most obvious of these, and the new income minus marginal saving will enter the stream of ready purchase money. The proportion of marginal income saved may well differ with the location of the margin, the direction of its change and other contemporary circumstances. But it is quite as likely that forces will be at work on the total saving-income function. These factors—changes in taxes, in dishoarding of the last month's unintended saving, advance buying—need to be evaluated quite as carefully as changes in saving related to changing income. The particular list of factors which seem most important at any one time will change with changing conditions. Finally, changes in installment credit affect both the size of income,

[8] The application of the concept of ex ante consumer saving to monthly data raises an important question. Monthly expenditures vary widely for chance or seasonal reasons. Does this fact not destroy the causal stiffness that we attribute to saving and spending patterns? The distinction between ex ante and ex post saving would be meaningless if the irregularities of the time pattern of purchasing caused individuals to lose control over the relation of expenditure to income and of one class of expenditure to another. But as long as we hold to the central points—that individuals who save money have not satisfied all of their wants for commodities and services and that the saving patterns have stability—then it seems reasonable to attribute that stability to implemented intentions. If people are to enforce their intentions with respect to spending and saving, they must do so on a month-to-month and, in fact, day-to-day basis, otherwise their plans for the year would be mere dreams. There are many different schemes which are adopted—mother tries to put three dollars in the savings bank every week and when she knows that there will be school clothes to purchase in the fall she tries to save up enough cash over the summer to meet the September expenses; mother knows that expenses are heavier some months than others and that on the heavy months she can just about make the cash stretch and on the light months she can put something in the bank providing she buys only the familiar list of goods; the varieties are endless. They blur the edges of a concept such as ex ante saving but they do not seem to me to invalidate it. In fact, if it has no meaning in monthly terms, it has no meaning in annual terms.

The fuzzy nature of most plans about saving and spending mean that ex ante saving ought really be stated as a range rather than as a single figure. But *changes* in plans are more precise than their absolute levels, and since we are only interested in measuring change, the use of a figure rather than a range is not seriously unrealistic.

Since all the calculations are made with seasonally adjusted figures, it is necessary to face a technical problem of seasonal adjustment of ex ante saving and expenditure categories. Here, however, it is proper to lose the distinction between ex ante and ex post saving. We may assume that the seasonal pattern of an individual's actual purchases is the reflection of his judgment about the best time to purchase what he intends to buy. It therefore seems altogether proper to use the same seasonal adjustment for ex ante and ex post expenditure, and the adjustment for saving is adjusted income minus adjusted expenditure.

as we have defined it, and the saving-income function, since we have found it convenient to think of additions to installment credit outstanding as an increase in disposable consumer income at the same time that no part of the resultant income is saved.

After having determined the probable size of the aggregate funds entering the market, it is then necessary to estimate how they will be

TABLE XXII

CONSUMER READY PURCHASE MONEY, JUNE, 1941,

		JUNE	JULY	AUGUST
1.	Current consumer ready purchase money —rpm (line 2 + 3 + 9 + 19)	7,049	7,142	7,244
* 2.	Rpm of prev. m.	6,910	7,049	7,142
3.	Rpm increment over prev. m. related to change in income (line 4 – 5)	124	105	96
4.	Income increment (Table XXI, line 24)	141	105	112
* † 5.	Portion of income increment withheld by consumers (line 6 + 7)	17	0.1	15.8
* † 6.	35% of ownership income increment	11	–6.0	11.9
* † 7.	5% of labor income increment	6	6.1	3.9
* 8.	Rpm related to change from base month in the proportion of total income spent (line 10 + 12 + 14 + 16)		3	9
9.	Change from prev. m. (line 11 + 13 + 15 + 17)		3	16
† 10.	Related to change in taxes			
11.	Change from prev. m.			
† 12.	Related to advance buying		3	3
13.	Change from prev. m.		3	0
† 14.	Related to dishoarding of forced saving of prev. m.			16
15.	Change from prev. m.			16
† 16.	Related to other causes			
17.	Change from prev. m.			
*†18.	Rpm related to change in installment credit outstanding	100	85	75
* 19.	Change in the change	15	–15	–10
20.	Rpm applicable to the purchase of nondurable commodities (line 21 + 26)	3,606	3,660	3,717
* 21.	Rpm of prev. m.			
* 22.	Change related to change in income increment after taxes (52% of line 3 + 11)	3,540 64.5	3,606 54.5	3,660 50.0
23.	Change related to advance buying (50% of line 13)		1.5	
24.	Change related to dishoarding, etc. (50% of line 15 + 17)			8.0

divided between effective demand for consumers' durable and non-durable commodities and services. The relevant judgments cannot be made without regard for the source of the various additions or subtractions to the funds which consumers will plan to spend.

The following table and the relevant portions of Appendix A and Appendix B describe the procedure more fully.

(Step II)

TO FEBRUARY, 1942 (IN MILLIONS OF DOLLARS)

SEPTEMBER	OCTOBER	NOVEMBER	DECEMBER	JANUARY	FEBRUARY
7,335	7,409	7,473	7,532	7,482	7,440
7,244	7,335	7,409	7,473	7,532	7,482
96	82	64	65	55	42
110	95	72	73	65	46
13.6	13.4	8.4	8.2	9.6	3.8
9.4	10.1	5.6	5.3	7.4	1.8
4.2	3.3	2.8	2.9	2.2	2.0
24	26	36	35	−60	−139
5	2	10	−1	−95	−79
				−93	−163
				−93	−70
4	2	2	2	1	0
1	−2	0	0	−1	−1
20	24	34	30	32	24
4	4	10	−4	2	−8
			3	0	
			3	−3	
65	55	45	40	30	25
−10	−10	−10	−5	−10	−5
3,768	3,811	3,848	3,881	3,859	3,840
3,717	3,768	3,811	3,848	3,881	3,859
49.9	42.6	33.3	33.8	−19.8	−14.6
0.5	−1.0			−0.5	
2.0	2.0	5.0	−0.5	−0.5	−4.0

TABLE XXII—

CONSUMER READY PURCHASE MONEY, JUNE, 1941,

		JUNE	JULY	AUGUST
* 25.	Change related to change in installment credit outstanding (10% of line 19)	1.5	−1.5	−1.0
26.	Total change from prev. m. (line 22 to 25)	66.0	54.5	57.0
27.	Rpm applicable to purchase of durable commodities (line 28 + 33)	1,044	1,046	1,049
* 28.	Rpm of prev. m.	1,014	1,044	1,046
* 29.	Change related to change in income increment after taxes (13% of line 3 + 11)	16.1	13.6	12.5
30.	Change related to advance buying (50% of line 13)		1.5	
31.	Change related to dishoarding, etc. (zero)			
* 32.	Change related to change in installment credit outstanding (90% of line 19)	13.5	−13.5	−9.0
33.	Total change from prev. m. (lines 29 to 32)	29.6	1.6	3.5
34.	Rpm applicable to services (line 35 + 38)	2,399	2,436	2,478
* 35.	Rpm of prev. m.	2,356	2,399	2,436
* 36.	Change related to change in income increment after taxes (35% of line 3 + 11)	43.4	36.8	33.6
37.	Change related to dishoarding, etc. (50% of line 15 + 17)			8.0
38.	Total change from prev. m. (line 36 + 37)	43.4	36.8	41.6

* Derivation of figures for base month, June, 1941, in Appendix A, pp. 213–15.

STEP III

The estimation of the goods that are ready for sale to consumers at the price for which they were intended to sell is the next step.

The theoretical formulations of the introductory section suggest that goods ready for sale at the price for which they were intended to sell would be goods arriving in retail stores (or in other institutions selling directly to the public) during the given period, minus planned changes in retailers' stocks. When the period is short—say a day or a week—the amount of goods in retail stores during the period cannot be affected by a change in consumer demand and can therefore be taken as a more or less fixed quantity for the period. When, however,

(CONTINUED)

TO FEBRUARY, 1942 (IN MILLIONS OF DOLLARS)

SEPTEMBER	OCTOBER	NOVEMBER	DECEMBER	JANUARY	FEBRUARY
-1.0	-1.0	-1.0	-0.5	-1.0	-0.5
51.4	42.6	37.3	32.8	-21.8	-19.1
1,053	1,054	1,053	1,057	1,043	1,035
1,049	1,053	1,054	1,053	1,057	1,043
12.5	10.7	8.3	8.5	-4.9	-3.6
0.5	-1.0			-0.5	
-9.0	-9.0	-9.0	-4.5	-9.0	-4.5
4.0	0.7	-0.7	4.0	-14.4	-8.1
2,514	2,545	2,572	2,594	2,580	2,566
2,478	2,514	2,545	2,572	2,594	2,580
33.6	28.7	22.4	22.8	-13.3	-9.8
2.0	2.0	5.0	-0.5	-0.5	-4.0
35.6	30.7	27.4	22.3	-13.8	-13.8

† Derivation of figures for July, 1941, to February, 1942, in Appendix B, pp. 221–26.

we lengthen the period to a month, reorders or new orders, inspired by changed demand during the early part of the month, could affect the quantity of goods in stores at the middle or end of the month and thus influence the month's total of goods ready for sale. The provision of additional finished goods, however, would be contingent on the availability of stocks and/or additional production that could get under way in time to provide finished goods within the month. But the ability of the manufacturer of finished goods to increase his sales is, in turn, dependent on the labor and raw materials which he has on hand or can obtain; and this is also true of the manufacturers' suppliers and so on down the line.

Goods offered for sale by retailers during the month is, then, in part a function of current and earlier sales expectations of wholesalers and producers of consumers' goods and the preparations which have been made to fill forthcoming orders. If we assume that retailers must anticipate their sales by the two weeks which, let us pretend, are required for wholesalers to make deliveries, the goods ready for sale by retailers during the first two weeks of, say, June would depend on their forecast and resulting orders during the last two weeks of May, and their goods ready for sale during the last two weeks of June would depend on sales expectations and orders during the first two weeks of the month. Wholesalers who received these orders during the last two weeks of May and the first two weeks of June, would, in order to fill them, have had to anticipate changes in demand by an interval long enough to have the goods in stock, unless inventories carried the burden of change. If manufacturers also take two weeks to make deliveries, then an order which would eventually supply June consumer demand would have had to be placed with manufacturers by wholesalers in May. These manufacturers of finished consumers' goods would, in turn, have had to anticipate changes in demand by whatever interval was required to process the goods; whereas their orders, placed with their suppliers, must have anticipated their changed production schedules by the further interval required for delivery from these suppliers.

But a neat shingling of demand-transmission of this sort is doubtless highly unrealistic (and of course the regular two-week interval used in the example is in itself thoroughly atypical). In the first place, several intermediate stages of processing and distribution are eliminated in connection with some transactions: Many retailers buy most of their goods direct from manufacturers, and, for certain products, automobiles for example, there is a close tie between retail sales and manufacturers' production schedules. In the second place, inventory change does actually absorb much of the intermediate impact of change so that production is likely to lag behind anticipation, thus foreshortening the interval between changing consumer takings and changing preparations at earlier stages of production. Finally, in so far as current retail sales are used as an indication of probable future sales by producers or distributors all along the line, production and sales in the earlier stages of the process tend to relate more closely to current retail sales than they otherwise might.

It would seem, therefore, that goods ready for sale during the month would probably be influenced by changes in preparations made not only by retailers but also by wholesalers and many manufacturers of finished consumers' goods. For this group of enterprises, inventory change needs to be divided into planned change, which enters into production plans, and unplanned change, which results from the difference between plans and actuality and is reflected in the rpm–grs comparisons.

For the earlier stages in the process, the distinction between planned and unplanned sales or inventory change is of course equally important. However, it is necessary to make quantitative estimates on the basis of expectations which are shown to be true or false primarily by data only remotely related to the grs–rpm comparison. Future, rather than current, consumption and the way in which change in demand is passed back might be the crucial question here. In forecasting production, most careful consideration needs to be given to these matters. It might well be that information concerning the relation of actual to planned inventory change and sales at the earlier stages of production would be of great help in anticipating change in production all along the line. But these are considerations which would enter this analysis in Step VI. At this point, only total inventory change would need to be forecast or recorded for the earlier stages of production. And the distinction between planned and unplanned inventory change would relate to the later stages of production and distribution.

Goods ready for sale would thus be estimated by giving consideration to changes in the current output of retailers, wholesalers and finished goods manufacturers and to their planned inventory change.

In the case of the service industries, the goods ready for sale concept is not applicable. Preliminary estimates of current production, subject to correction at a later stage of the analysis, is all that is required.

A second problem in the estimation of the goods ready for sale to consumers at the price for which they were intended to sell involves adjustment for price change. Changes in production are recorded in

TABLE XXIII

CONSUMERS' GOODS READY FOR SALE TO DOMESTIC CONSUMERS,

	JUNE [a]	JULY	AUGUST
1. Nondurable commodities ready for sale to domestic consumers—grs (line 2 − (3 + 4 + 5))	3,674	3,736	3,761
2. Produced at prices of prev. m. (Table XXI, line 5)	3,820	3,841	3,866
* † 3. Planned inventory change	87	45	45
* † 4. Exports minus imports (including tourist expenditures)	−40	−40	−40
* † 5. Consumers' goods purchased by government	99	100	100
6. Durable goods ready for sale to domestic consumers—grs (line 7 − 8)	1.042	1,001	993
7. Produced at prices of prev. m. (Table XXI, line 6)	1,036	1,021	1,022
* † 8. Planned inventory change	−6	20	29
9. Services produced (first approximation) (Table XXI, line 7)	2,333	2,354	2,377

[a] June figures are given in June prices, and inventory change in line 3 and 8 relates to total, not planned inventory change during June.

physical terms. We need to translate them into dollars—the aggregate price at which goods were intended to sell. What sort of price index ought to be used in estimating base figures and as a guide to forecast? How can we distinguish between actual prices and those for which goods were intended to sell? The second question must be answered by a semi-arbitrary simplification. We shall assume that businessmen plan production one month ahead at current prices. This assumption would need to be changed were a serious price inflation under way, since then producers would probably plan a higher price next month than is quoted this month. The reverse would be true of deflation.

The first question—which price index is preferable—is difficult to answer. Theoretically, we ought to record changes in the price at which goods being currently produced, in whatever stage of production or distribution they are currently found, will be intended to sell when they reach the retail stage. We are forced to ignore the distinction between intention and actuality when dealing with price indexes. This leaves us a choice between using a price index which by proper

(STEP III)

JUNE, 1941, TO FEBRUARY, 1942 (IN MILLIONS OF DOLLARS)

SEPTEMBER	OCTOBER	NOVEMBER	DECEMBER	JANUARY	FEBRUARY
3,820	3,869	3,917	3,962	4,001	4,033
3,925	3,974	4,017	4,057	4,101	4,123
45	45	40	35	40	30
–40	–40	–40	–40	–40	–40
100	100	100	100	100	100
1,001	991	969	939	884	825
1,021	1,011	987	954	902	840
20	20	18	15	18	15
2,420	2,455	2,486	2,521	2,561	2,583

* Derivation of figures for base month, June, 1941, in Appendix A, pp. 215–17.
† Derivations of figures for July, 1941, to February, 1942, in Appendix B, pp. 226–27.

weighting on the basis of value added expresses current prices at each stage of production and distribution (in manufacturers' or wholesalers' prices), or using a retail-price index.

We may compare the results that would be obtained by the first method with the objective which we seek—the price at which currently produced goods will sell when they reach the retail stage: The index would, when, for example, prices are rising, overstate the prices of finished or nearly finished goods (since component parts would be priced at current, and therefore higher, levels) and understate the price at which goods now in the earlier stages of production would sell when completed (since later stages of production would be recorded at current and therefore lower prices). But this understatement would be reduced and the overstatement emphasized by the fact that price change tends to lose amplitude as the finished stages are approached. The opposite of these statements would apply when prices are falling. On balance, therefore, indexes of these sorts, would, relative to our standard, probably overemphasize price fluctuation.

A retail-price index would, on the other hand, provide an unduly conservative picture of change. On balance, however, it seems preferable, and we therefore use a retail-price index to convert quantity to dollar figures, though we choose it more because it is the lesser of various evils than well suited to our purposes.[9]

After having arrived at an estimate of goods ready for sale at the prices at which they were intended to sell, we must subtract the value of consumption goods purchased by the government (such as food and clothing for the army) as well as consumers' goods exported (minus imports of such goods). The resulting estimate of goods ready for sale to domestic consumers is given in Table XXIII.

STEP IV

The thought underlying the calculation of ready purchase money of consumers and goods ready for sale to domestic consumers is that these two aggregates exert forces in the market. Consumers attempt to spend the ready purchase money applicable to commodities and services of various sorts on those goods, and they shift, reduce, or increase their expenditures only as the result of other pressures; also, the income ordinarily assigned to savings is not spent on commodities or services without obstructing frictions. Similarly, enterprisers do not willingly draw down inventories below the levels that seem desirable without planning compensating measures. Moreover, when such measures are out of the question, as when shortages in labor and materials make it impossible so to increase production as to make up for forced reductions in inventories during the previous month, enterprisers are averse to selling more real goods than they planned to sell, although this does not mean that the aversion cannot be overcome.

After the sales have been consummated, consumers' purchases

[9] The deficiencies of a retail price index for the purpose at hand cannot be properly evaluated without further study. They involve questions such as the stability of retail price lines and the extent to which quality changes, imperceptible to both the cost of living pricing machinery and the consumer, slip into the price index (in so far as they are caught by the price record but undetected by the consumer a different problem arises). Another set of questions focuses around the role of mark-downs in determining the prices actually paid by consumers. Then too, there is legitimate doubt as to the extent to which the price behavior of articles included in retail price indexes is characteristic of the less standardized type of merchandise which, though ill suited for price comparisons, is nevertheless important in the average budget.

must, of course, equal retailers' sales. The rpm and grs concepts endeavor to go behind the ex post equality to the process which brought it about.

If ready purchase money (rpm) exceeds the aggregate price for which consumers' goods were intended to sell (grs), then one or all of several things can occur to cause the two diverse magnitudes to come together in the completed sale. The reaction will start at the retail stage and be passed back to wholesalers, producers, and their suppliers. Starting with the retailer, sales may be turned down, or, by lengthening delivery dates, they may in effect be turned down for the current period, thus automatically increasing consumer saving; retailers may draw down inventories, planning to restore them to desirable levels later on; [10] retailers may raise prices, thus absorbing the additional buying power (this would constitute a divergence between the price at which the goods were intended to sell and were actually sold; it could take the form of increased mark-up on new goods delivered during the month, of less than usual mark-down, or, in stores where bargaining is customary, of a stiffer trade). Finally, consumers may revise the amount they are willing to spend, thus saving more than planned, if, for example, prices rise sharply. These statements can be readily rephrased to cover a purchasing-power deficiency. At other stages of production, retailers' and consumers' reactions are recorded after due filtering and after the influence of other relevant factors is taken into account; adjustments, analogous to those described for the retail stage, take place to reconcile planned and actual sales.

To arrive at forecasts, it is necessary to evaluate the part played by lengthening delivery periods, by government price fixing and other pressures on prices, the possibility of physical expansion of output,

[10] An interesting problem in shifts within the various inventory categories relates to the phenomenon of retail price lines. One way in which excess ready purchase money may be utilized by consumers is in the purchase of more higher and fewer lower priced articles than the business world expected to sell. In that case, inventories in the lower price lines for a given commodity might move more slowly and those in the higher price lines for the same commodity more rapidly than planned, although the net change in inventories might be negligible.

This case provides an example of the need, mentioned on page 159, to go behind net changes in inventories to gross changes of various sorts when dealing with the dynamics of change in national income.

Table XXIV

RECONCILIATION OF RPM AND GRS, JULY, 1941,

	JULY	AUGUST
Nondurable commodities		
1. Rpm (Table XXII, line 20)	3,660	3,717
2. Grs (Table XXIII, line 1)	3,736	3,761
3. Excess (+) or deficiency (−) of rpm over grs (line 1 − 2)	−76	−44
† 4. Shift of rpm to or from other classes of goods (line 4 + 13 + 22 = 0)	80	80
5. Net excess or deficiency (line 3 + 4)	4	36
† 6. Application (+) of excess or source (−) of additional rpm (line 7 + 8 + 9)	4	36
† 7. Unplanned change in inventories (decrease +)		
† 8. Unplanned consumer saving (increase +)		
† 9. Price change (increase +)	4	36
Durable commodities		
10. Rpm (Table XXII, line 27)	1,046	1,049
11. Grs (Table XXIII, line 6)	1,001	993
12. Excess (+) or deficiency (−) of rpm over grs (line 10 − 11)	45	56
† 13. Shift of rpm to or from other classes of goods (line 4 + 13 + 22 = 0)		
14. Net excess or deficiency (line 12 + 13)	45	56
† 15. Application (+) of excess or source (−) of additional rpm (line 16 + 17 + 18)	45	56
† 16. Unplanned change in inventories (decrease +)		8
† 17. Unplanned consumer saving (increase +)	21	25
† 18. Price change (increase +)	24	23
Services		
19. Rpm (Table XXII, line 34)	2,436	2,478
20. Services produced (Table XXIII, line 10)	2,354	2,377
21. Excess (+) or deficiency (−) of rpm over supply (line 19 − 20)	82	101
† 22. Shift of rpm to or from other classes of goods (line 4 + 13 + 22 = 0)	−80	−80
23. Net excess or deficiency (line 21 + 22)	2	21
† 24. Application (+) of excess or source (−) of additional rpm (line 25 + 26 + 27)	2	21
† 25. Changed production of services (decrease +)		
† 26. Unplanned saving (increase +)		
† 27. Price change (increase +)	2	21

† Derivation of figures for July, 1941, to February, 1942, in Appendix B, pp. 227–29.

(STEP IV)

TO FEBRUARY, 1942 (IN MILLIONS OF DOLLARS)

SEPTEMBER	OCTOBER	NOVEMBER	DECEMBER	JANUARY	FEBRUARY
3,768	3,811	3,848	3,881	3,859	3,840
3,820	3,869	3,917	3,962	4,001	4,033
–52	–58	–69	–81	–142	–193
80	80	91	106	109	136
28	22	22	25	–33	–57
28	22	22	25	–33	–57
		3	3	–13	–20
				–20	–27
28	22	19	22		–10
1,053	1,054	1,053	1,057	1,043	1,035
1,001	991	969	939	884	825
52	63	84	118	159	210
		–19	–51	–90	–136
52	63	65	67	69	74
52	63	65	67	69	74
		5	5		
30	43	37	40	49	63
22	20	23	22	20	11
2,514	2,545	2,572	2,594	2,580	2,566
2,420	2,455	2,486	2,521	2,561	2,583
94	90	86	73	19	–17
–80	–80	–72	–55	–19	0
14	10	14	18	0	–17
14	10	14	18	0	–17
					–7
14	10	14	18	0	–10

the desire to hoard stocks, and the rest. These judgments must, of course, be primarily based on whatever objective data form a basis for prognosis, but the analysis itself provides an internal check of sorts. An assumption concerning a change in price, for example, must be consistent with the assumptions made concerning the size of rpm and grs and the other ways which could be used to bring them together. A change in one assumption will require corresponding changes in one or more of the others and these changes must seem sensible.

As data become available the extension of the base figures should indicate how forecasts may have erred in the past, thus providing a basis for the improvement of future predictions. A comparison of yesterday's forecasts, as they move under the eye of the present, with current information on actual inventory change, price change and consumer saving might cause a correction of estimates as to how these various factors would, in the near future, combine to bring ready purchase money and goods ready for sale together through the market mechanism.

The forecasting procedure is illustrated in Table XXIV on pp. 178–79. Appendix B describes some of the considerations that lead to the distribution of the excess purchasing power each month between changes in price, inventory, and saving. Since, for June, 1941, as well as for the other months, these allocations are essentially a part of the forecasting technique rather than a base figure calculation, Appendix A does not apply. The June figures are in fact ignored since grs is, it will be recalled, stated in current prices for June and the grs–rpm comparisons have therefore little meaning.

STEP V

Sales at current prices may now be estimated by adjusting goods ready for sale at the previous month's prices for unplanned inventory change and adding the increase in price (or subtracting the decrease) indicated in the previous step. Finally, the estimate for finished output at the previous month's prices, given in Step I, can be revised for change in prices during the month.

Table XXV presents these figures and brief comments on some of them appear in Appendix B.

STEP VI

It is now necessary to link the beginning and end of the analysis by estimating production for July at June prices. Up to this point we have made estimates of the amount of income retained by business, planned consumer saving, and planned inventory change. We have also, with the aid of the grs-rpm comparisons, estimated the divergence between actual and planned inventory change in the later stages of production and distribution of consumers' goods, the divergence between actual and planned consumer saving and between actual prices and the prices for which consumers' goods were made to sell.

In so far as changes in the volume of production during the following month depend on changes in demand, the size of the grs–rpm gap and the methods whereby it was closed—the varying proportions of inventory change, unintended saving, and price change—would be highly relevant considerations in predicting the probable extent and direction of change in future output. But as long as the effective limits to physical production relate to the availability of factors of production rather than the strength of dollar demand, these quantities tell us little concerning the output of tomorrow.

The period under consideration is one in which the pressing demand for armament and other goods for belligerent nations causes a great many production schedules to be set as high as the supply of materials and labor and plant capacity permit. Primarily, therefore, the supply of the wherewithal to produce, rather than matters relating to demand, need to be evaluated in arriving at a forecast of change in output.

If we assume that physical output will not be greatly affected by change in price, it will be possible to estimate the changing dollar volume of production in two steps. The first would be concerned with evaluating the possible physical expansion; the second, with the price change that would accompany it.

Table XXVI relates to the first step and presents estimates of change in output at June, 1941, prices. These estimates conform to the assumptions made in the preliminary report.[11] Probable expansion

[11] See Foreword p. vii.

TABLE XXV

SALES AND PRODUCTION AT CURRENT PRICES, JULY,

	JULY	AUGUST
Nondurable commodities		
1. Sold to domestic consumers at prev. m. prices (Table XXIV, line 2 – 7)	3,736	3,761
2. Sold to domestic consumers at current prices (line 1 + Table XXIV, line 9)	3,740	3,797
3. Price change as % of sales at prev. m. prices	0.1	1.0
4. Total change in inventories (Table XXIII, line 3 + Table XXIV, line 7)	45	45
† 5. Production at current prices (line 2 + 4 + Table XXIII, line 4 + 5) or (Table XXI, line 5 + Table XXIV, line 9)	3,845	3,902
Durable commodities		
6. Sold to domestic consumers at prev. m. prices (Table XXIV, line 11 – 16)	1,001	985
7. Sold to domestic consumers at current prices (line 6 + Table XXIV, line 18)	1,025	1,008
8. Price change as % of sales at prev. m. prices	2.4	2.3
9. Total change in inventories (Table XXIII, line 8 + Table XXIV, line 16)	20	37
† 10. Production at current prices (Table XXI, line 6 + Table XXIV, line 18)	1,045	1,045
Services		
11. Produced and sold to domestic consumers at prev. m. prices (Table XXIV, line 20)	2,354	2,377
12. Produced and sold to domestic consumers at current prices (line 11 + Table XXIV, line 27)	2,356	2,398
13. Price change as % of line 11	0.1	0.9
Producers' goods		
14. Produced at prev. m. prices (Table XXI, line 3)	1,868	1,956
† 15. Percentage price change (estimated)	0.4	1.1
16. Dollar price change (line 14 × 15)	7	22
17. Production at current prices (line 14 + 16)	1,875	1,978
Totals		
18. Production at current prices (line 5 + 10 + 12 + 17)	9,121	9,323
19. Sales of consumers' goods at current prices (line 2 + 7 + 12)	7,121	7,203
20. Sales of consumers' goods at prev. m. prices (line 1 + 6 + 11)	7,091	7,023
21. Total price change (line 22 + 23)	37	102
22. Consumers' goods (Table XXIV, line 9 + 18 + 27)	30	80
23. Producers' goods (line 16)	7	22
24. Price change of consumers' goods as % of sales at prev. m. prices	0.5	1.4

† Derivation of the figures described in Appendix B, p. 229.

(Step V)

1941, to February, 1942 (in millions of dollars)

SEPTEMBER	OCTOBER	NOVEMBER	DECEMBER	JANUARY	FEBRUARY
3,820	3,869	3,914	3,959	4,014	4,053
3,848	3,891	3,933	3,981	4,014	4,043
0.7	0.6	0.5	0.6	0	–0.2
45	45	43	38	27	10
3,953	3,996	4,036	4,079	4,101	4,113
1,001	991	964	934	884	825
1,023	1,011	987	956	904	836
2.2	2.0	2.4	2.4	2.3	1.3
20	20	23	20	18	15
1,043	1,031	1,010	976	922	851
2,418	2,455	2,486	2,521	2,561	2,583
2,434	2,465	2,500	2,539	2,561	2,573
0.6	0.4	0.6	0.7	0.0	–0.4
2,060	2,162	2,261	2,361	2,465	2,557
0.9	0.7	0.8	0.8	0.3	1.0
19	15	18	19	7	26
2,079	2,177	2,277	2,380	2,472	2,583
9,509	9,669	9,823	9,974	10,056	10,120
7,305	7,367	7,420	7,476	7,479	7,452
7,241	7,315	7,364	7,414	7,459	7,461
83	67	74	81	27	15
64	52	56	62	20	–9
19	15	18	19	7	26
1.2	0.9	1.0	1.1	0.4	–0.0

in physical production between June, 1941, and June, 1942, was estimated on the basis of judgments concerning available labor, materials, plant, and probable diversion of factors from private to public areas of the economy. The month-to-month changes were interpolated on the basis of a straight line progression except in the case of durable consumers' goods. (See Appendix B.)

TABLE XXVI

PRODUCTION, JUNE, 1941, TO JUNE, 1942, AT JUNE,

	JUNE	JULY	AUGUST	SEPTEMBER	OCTOBER	NOVEMBER
1. Durable producers' goods and construction	1787	1868	1949	2030	2111	2192
2. Current month as % of previous month			104.336	104.156	103.990	103.837
3. Consumers' goods (line 4 + 6 + 8)	7189	7216	7236	7255	7267	7269
4. Nondurable commodities	3820	3841	3862	3883	3904	3925
5. Current month as % of previous month			100.547	100.584	100.541	100.538
6. Durable commodities	1036	1021	999	976	946	906
7. Current month as % of previous month			97.845	97.698	96.926	95.772
8. Services	2333	2354	2375	2396	2417	2438
9. Current month as % of previous month			100.892	100.884	100.876	100.869
10. Government direct expenditures (line 11 + 14)	1184	1186	1188	1190	1192	1194
11. Ownership income	148	148	148	148	148	148
12. Federal Government	98	98	98	98	98	98
13. State and local governments	50	50	50	50	50	50
14. Labor income	1036	1038	1040	1042	1044	1046
15. Federal Government	515	517	519	521	523	525
16. State and local governments	521	521	521	521	521	521

* Derivation of base figures for June, 1941, is the same as that described in connection with Table XXI in Appendix A, pp. 207–13.

† Derivation of the figures for July, 1941, to June, 1942, given in Appendix B, pp. 229–30.

The percentage change in output between June and July at June prices as given in Table XXVI was then applied to production for June at current prices. Similarly, the percentage change between July and August in June prices from Table XXVI was applied to production for July at July prices as yielded in Step V of our analysis. Thus, although for this exceptional period changes in physical production were determined largely independently of the analysis here presented, the changes in price, and therefore in dollar volume of production, involve all of the steps of the analysis.

(STEP VI)

1941, PRICES * † (IN MILLIONS OF DOLLARS)

DECEMBER	JANUARY	FEBRUARY	MARCH	APRIL	MAY	JUNE	ANNUAL RATE, JUNE, 1941	ANNUAL RATE, JUNE, 1942	CHANGE IN ANNUAL RATE, JUNE, 1941, TO JUNE, 1942
2273	2354	2435	2516	2597	2678	2759	21444	33108	11664
103.695	103.564	103.441	103.326	103.219	103.119	103.025			
7261	7238	7210	7197	7199	7211	7233	86268	86796	528
3946	3967	3988	4009	4030	4051	4072	45840	48864	3020
100.535	100.532	100.529	100.527	100.524	100.521	100.518			
856	791	721	666	626	596	576	12432	6912	-5520
94.481	92.406	91.150	92.372	93.994	95.208	96.644			
2459	2480	2501	2522	2543	2564	2585	27996	31020	3024
100.861	100.854	100.847	100.840	100.833	100.826	100.819			
1196	1198	1200	1202	1204	1206	1208	14208	14520	288
148	148	148	148	148	148	148			
98	98	98	98	98	98	98			
50	50	50	50	50	50	50			
1048	1050	1052	1054	1056	1058	1060			
527	529	531	533	535	537	539			
521	521	521	521	521	521	521			

Theoretically, the estimated change in physical production should have been corrected for the change in output associated with change along the supply curve as prices rise. We did not, however, correct the figures in this way. In the first place, the original estimates, which were based on the work of several government bureaus, seemed to presuppose some increase in price, although it was far from clear to what extent this was so. In the second place, even a rough estimate of the reaction of supply to changing prices would require a careful analysis of the actual situations in many of the major industries of the country. Accordingly, no attempt was made to correct the estimates for any further change in price than was already included in them.

It will be recalled that the estimate for change in consumers' services arrived at by these overall estimates of change in physical production is regarded as a first approximation only and is subject to subsequent correction on the basis of the rpm–grs comparisons.

Were forecasts of change in income made under more normal conditions, this sixth step of the analysis would not be accompanied by a table showing change in physical production. Instead, it would consist of an effort to bring to bear on the question of probable change in production during the following month all of the information developed during the earlier stages of the procedure as well as other relevant data. The way in which the analysis could be used for this purpose is briefly discussed on pages 194–205 below.

THE STORY TOLD BY THE FORECASTS

Before discussing what the figures show, it is well to recall what sad affairs they really are. It is not clear whether it would in any event be possible to provide a self-respecting set of base figures and forecasts; but certainly were one to make a serious attempt to do so, continuous practice, a trained staff, and access to confidential government information would be required. The figures presented in the foregoing tables have been assembled without even a thorough survey and utilization of such data as are available. The base figures for June, 1941, obtained by projecting statistical series, should be regarded merely as illustrative of the procedure rather than as estimates on which any confidence ought to be placed; the forecasts for the following eight months should not be regarded as actual predictions but rather as the projection of certain stated assumptions in an effort to indicate what other facts need to be considered and what conclusions follow. The projections, made in the early fall of 1941, have not been revised in the light of subsequent events.

These figures are variations on a single theme: Consumer ready purchase money outrunning the value, at preëxisting prices, of consumers' commodities and services produced, with consequent upward pressure on prices. This is the motif of a boom period. And certainly armament expenditures increasing by $14 billion in the course of a year plus private capital formation of no puny proportions are reason enough for the redundancy of consumer purchasing power. In simplest terms, this means that individuals are receiving income from their contributions to the production of a vast quantity of goods which they cannot buy. Even after they have put aside a considerable portion of current income for a rainy day, and after the government has appropriated some of it through taxation, they still jingle in their pockets coin which exceeds, in the aggregate, the aggregate sales tags on the goods currently displayed in retail shops. As a result, the old sales tags are replaced by new ones bearing higher figures. The higher sales tags do not, of course, represent merely a higher retail mark-on; mark-on may well remain the same or increase only slightly although maintained mark-on, because of fewer mark-downs, may rise. The higher prices paid are caused by shifts in the emphasis of buying to higher-price lines, to the reflection at the retail stage of higher costs and profits at any or all of the preliminary and final stages of production and distribution, and to decreased mark-downs.

In spite of the limitations on production of consumers' goods and the fact that a high head on the price avalanche had already accumulated in the earlier stages of production, we do not assume that the entire excess effective demand will take the form of increased prices. When demand takes a particularly heavy spurt in some month, we have assumed that, because of the stickiness of prices and resistance to price change in many lines, businessmen will permit their inventories to fall temporarily with the idea of replacing them if they can. They will also turn away customers or lengthen the time required for delivery; in either case, the consumer returns home with the coin still jingling, for the time being at least. We have assumed, on the basis of what seemed reasonable figures each month, that the forced saving amounted to about $225 million during the eight-months period (Table XXIV, lines 8 + 17 + 26). But since four-fifths of the previous month's forced saving is assumed to reënter the market for goods and services the following month, the initial forced saving does not all stay saved. The four-fifths ratio is the one used in our preliminary report and may well be high. It will certainly be high in the light of America's entrance into the war, since patriotic appeals to buy bonds and reduce expenditures will carry new weight and rationing of goods will increase. In judging the reasonableness of the ratio, however, it is important to remember that some part of the four-fifths of the rejected demand which reënters the market the following month will once again be rejected, and that rejected sales which would have been made on installment credit, and which account for the reduced amount of installment credit outstanding, are not thought to be converted in any part into other purchases.

We have not assumed that unplanned reduction in inventories of consumers' goods has played an important part in the adjustment. With inventories of finished goods, except those held by retailers, at low levels and with fear of shortages acute, it seems unlikely that businessmen will be willing to reduce their stocks very considerably. The net change is negligible.

Price changes in consumers' goods, on the other hand, amount to about $355 million (Table XXV, line 22) between July, 1941, and February, 1942, or about 5 percent of July, 1941, sales of consumers' goods. Moreover, on the basis of the tax calculations (Appendix B, p. 223) and some further preliminary calculations, the late spring would witness a rapidly accelerating rise in the cost of living. Moreover, the 5 percent seemed sure to be a bottom rather than a central figure even were defense requirements not to exceed the $25 billion for fiscal 1942 assumed as the basis of the figures, a situation which is now highly improbable.[12] The figure is probably low for two reasons. In the first place, we have assumed that the income received by business enterprise as the result of increased prices will in no part be distributed during the months when it is received and only about one-third of it will be distributed the following month. This means that the "multiplier" for price change is very low. When profits rise, the pressure for dividend distribution and increased wages is likely to cause the true figure to be considerably higher, although it is al-

[12] Actual war outlays for fiscal 1942 were $28 billion (Press Release, Bureau of the Budget, No. OD-4, Oct. 7, 1942).

most impossible to form a good long-distance guess as to what it should be. In the second place, the new data on inventories, which are in process of preparation by the Department of Commerce, suggest that inventory increases were far greater than—perhaps 2½ times—our estimates. This would cause goods ready for sale to be too high and therefore price change too low.

This discussion serves to illustrate the major advantage as well as the major disadvantage of this method of analysis: Assumptions are sufficiently explicit so that they can be critically reviewed and varied as occasion demands; they are, indeed, so explicit that one cannot avoid noting how ill founded they are.

Yet, if the great number of judgments that underlie the figures relate in fact to important determinants of change, do we gain by ignoring them or bulking them together in uncongenial aggregates, aggregates which possess no magic whereby internal disparities cancel out? If there is reason to believe that the effective multiplier for change in profits and in wages differs; if new installment credit is spent on various groups of commodities in different proportions from new wage income; if producers actually do choose, explicitly or automatically, between alternative methods of absorbing redundant buying power and if the nature of that choice has important repercussions on the process of change; if an increase in inventories that is planned and an increase that is the unexpected result of too optimistic sales-expectations cause different decisions concerning future production schedules, then we have no choice but to face these facts in all their uncomfortable complexity when we gauge the change in income and its probable future course. This means that we must either acquire the minimum information necessary to an adequate judgment or refrain from making a judgment. The figures in the chart are, as has been said, little more than arbitrary illustrations of the technique. The job of buttressing the analysis with workmanlike estimates has not been undertaken. Whether or not it can or should be undertaken hinges on whether the necessary information can be obtained.

THE AVAILABILITY OF CRUCIAL INFORMATION

It will be recalled that at the outset two purposes of the procedure were stated—analysis and forecast. The information necessary to analyze the past is not the same as that required to forecast the future. The latter is a far more exacting job; also, it is more difficult at some times than at others. It requires knowledge of the business-cycle patterns of the major variables in order that future change may be set out in quantitative terms. But useful analysis differs less from forecast than might seem to be the case at first glance. The understanding of current developments involves knowledge of their meaning, their implications, their significance. Forecast, on the other hand, must be attached to a statistical record of current data which can also be used to check predictions as the present overtakes the future. Accordingly, we need two sorts of information for both analysis and forecast although their relative importance differs in connection with the two problems: We need time series for the important items in the tables; we need an understanding of their major patterns of change.

STATISTICAL SERIES

The first type of information—time series—is, of course, more readily available for actual production, inventory change, saving, and so forth, than for the corresponding ex ante concepts relating to plans rather than actual occurrences. Accordingly, it will be useful to examine separately the problems of ex post and ex ante measurement.

Ex post measurement.—On the level of actuality, adequate information is probably procurable. Materials out of which to construct monthly over-all measurements of production and sales are constantly increasing. The United States Department of Commerce is preparing data that will greatly enrich the store—quarterly estimates of national income produced by major classes of goods, monthly data for all retail sales and improved information on services, a very weak point in the tables. Greatly improved inventory data are also in preparation at the Department of Commerce; these should yield better estimates of the magnitude of inventories, their monthly changes and the seasonal pattern of change.

It is in the monthly changes in the retained income of business and consumer that the greatest difficulty in getting adequate ex post figures seems to lie. True, data have improved greatly since our estimates were made. The Department of Commerce has completed monthly estimates of total consumer expenditure which, when subtracted from their series on income payments, yields an estimate of saving that conforms closely to our definition of consumer retained income. The Securities and Exchange Commission now compiles quarterly estimates of "liquid consumer saving" by endeavoring to record changes in assets and liabilities of individuals. The consumer income and expenditure studies of 1935–36, 1941 and 1942 are capable of shedding further light. The new quarterly figures of the Department of Commerce provide at once estimates of output of major classes of goods and services and a figure from which, with proper adjustment, income payments can be subtracted to obtain the quarter's retained business income.

But in spite of the progress that has been made, available estimates of saving of business and consumer are subject to errors so large as seriously to impair their usefulness for an analysis of the sort here set forth. It is to be hoped that direct measurement will be extended to cover savings of business and government, that monthly data will be obtained, and that, above all, the accuracy of measurement will improve. It is also important that terms be defined so that the cash flow concepts used, for example, in the income payments series and in this essay can be measured in addition to the concepts based on accrual accounting.

All of these objectives would move within reach were it possible to supplement the sort of data now being compiled by the S.E.C. for consumer saving. These estimates follow the major outlines of the method described by Raymond Goldsmith in *Studies in Income and Wealth*, Vol. III, National Bureau of Economic Research, but changes in bank deposits are estimated with the aid of quarterly reports to the S.E.C. on cash holdings by a large group of companies. Although the construction of figures of this sort is a detailed and technical problem, it seems clear that it will be well nigh impossible to obtain monthly information, or significantly to improve the accuracy of the work, without obtaining the coöperation of some of the chief financial institutions through which funds move when they are newly saved or invested. The net excess of funds currently received by all industrial enterprises over those spent for goods and services will take the form of increased bank accounts, reduced bank debt, or newly acquired financial instruments. A deficiency will take the reverse form. Similarly an excess (or deficiency) of current consumer income over current expenditures for goods will be reflected in current flows to or from the financial markets. Reports from a group of representative banks concerning changes in deposits and loans classified according to whether they involved individuals, industry, governments, or financial markets would make possible both far more accurate estimates and more frequent estimates than are now obtained. Intelligence concerning changes in other sorts of assets, such as stock certificates and real estate, could also probably be obtained more satisfactorily from reports by investment and brokerage houses on total transactions classified on the four-fold basis than from net changes in balance sheets of each of the four groups. But these problems cannot be explored here. Suffice it to point out that in spite of the focal significance of saving of various sorts in the understanding and integration of the economy, its measurement is still far too crude to serve the purposes which, on the basis of the other data available, we are prepared to serve.

Ex ante measurement.—On the ex ante level, the question of sales expectations and desired change in inventories in the consumer-goods industries needs to be evaluated. This is a fascinating question that has unfortunately kept its seals intact. Yet it is hard to imagine a subject that would more richly repay study: How do producers plan their production schedules; what is the sales-forecast component, the inventory component; how does the process change from time to time, from industry to industry, from enterprise to enterprise? How are impulses of change recognized and corrected and what are the time lags involved? What role do prices play? Not only have there been, to my knowledge, practically no basic studies made of this group of problems, but current data are not phrased in terms that throw much light on expectations and their relation to policy. Yet it would seem that the material is not available because the need for it has never been clearly formulated rather than because it is unattainable. The United States Department of Commerce has a large division that appears to be in an excellent position to develop information about expected inventory and production change. In a haphazard way some information of this sort is now gathered and reported in the Industry Survey series. It needs to be organized and standardized.

On the consumer side of the picture, the major source of insight concerning intentions comes from the consumer-expenditure studies mentioned above. A very considerable jump is taken when we assume that consumers whose income is increasing will aim to spend their total income the way that families having had a similar income, during the year in which the survey was made, spent theirs. As a first approximation, however, the assumption will probably do. The divergence between the distribution of consumer expenditure indicated in the 1935–36 study by the National Resources Committee and the distributions suggested by the 1935 or 1936 retail-sales figures suggest that we still have much to learn about how consumers spend new income.[13] Also, we know little or nothing about the divergence between planned and actual saving of consumers. It seems reasonable, however, to suppose that the difference is usually not large. The present time is doubtless unusual in that the rapid price change and the curtailment of certain kinds of consumers' goods may cause the difference to be sizable. It is unlikely that much information on the subject could be obtained without a special survey. However, if adequate data were available on ex post consumer saving, one could get along without the other information. Divergence of consumer saving from the usual patterns could be often interpreted as in part forced saving.

In general, then, we conclude that a critical analysis of month by month change in national income could probably be worked out on the basis of information now available to the public and to confidential Government sources. The two major areas of obscurity relate to

[13] Estimates for sales by all retail stores subdivided into 10 kinds of business and classified as to durable and nondurable goods stores are given in the *Survey of Current Business*, Oct., 1941, pp. 18–25. Table 2 shows that sales of durable goods stores in 1935 were about 23 percent of sales of all retail stores and 25.5 percent in 1936. The National Resources Committee study, made in 1935–36, of *Family Expenditures in the United States*, Statistical Tables and Appendices, Table 100, suggests that 8.8 percent of total family expenditure fell in the durable goods category. There are, of course, many reasons for the discrepancy between the two sets of data—for example, the former figures for total sales exclude services and home-produced food and goods bought from outlets other than retail stores and include sales of building and automobile supply stores which, though doing over 50 percent of their business at retail, also supply contractors and other businessmen. The latter figures do not include expenditures for houses in the durable goods group and include rent and repairs, though not purchased homes or structural improvements or additions. The discrepancy, however, between these two estimates remains troublesome and requires study.

the measurement of retained income of business and consumers on the one hand, and planned inventories and prices on the other hand. There is little doubt that the fog could be lightened if not lifted from both areas.

PATTERNS OF CHANGE

The rpm–grs gap is the hub around which this analysis revolves. The usefulness of the technique in forecasting and analyzing change in national income derives from the value of this concept in illuminating the process of change in the past and in the future.

In this day and age it is obviously foolish to discourse on the pattern of change of quantities that have not been examined as time series. Yet time series are not compiled unless they promise useful information. To escape from the dilemma it is necessary to gamble on a hunch. In order to suggest the appropriate odds, we may excogitate rashly on how the rpm–grs gap could be used as an aid to interpreting and forecasting change. This is a problem in defining patterns of change. In terms of the step-by-step analysis outlined above, the question to be discussed is how, under normal conditions when dollar demand determines not only the price but also the volume of output, to proceed from the corrected figure for output at current prices, developed in Step VI, to the estimates of output the following month at prices of the previous month, required in Step I.

The rpm–grs comparison is calculated to contrast expectations with reality at the finished goods level and the ricocheting effect of that comparison will echo throughout the system. Both the contrast between expectations and reality and the methods used to reconcile the two in the completed sale will influence expectations of the future. Future expectations when translated into a course of action will, in turn, be an important datum bearing on the size of the gap in the future and therefore on whether the expectations will prove to have been optimistic or pessimistic. It will, accordingly, be useful to consider first how the relations between expectations and reality influence the decisions of businessmen concerning future prices and production and then how the nature of those decisions together with other relevant facts determine the size of the rpm–grs gap in the following unit of time.

In determining the selling price (or price range) of output about to be undertaken, the executive has three sorts of information other than costs at his command: 1. There is a history of prices actually received. 2. There is the recollection, whether vague or precise, of the relation of expected to realized prices in the past. 3. There is an assorted body of information and rumor concerning future occurrences. Group 3 has to be analyzed in the light of specific circumstances prevailing at the time. Group 1 provides a knowledge of price trends of the past but does not specify how the trend should be projected into the future. Whether the entrepreneur will be sanguine or fearful in acting on this information will turn significantly on the recent history of the relation between his guesses and experience as given in Group 2.

A similar line of thought applies to estimates of sales-expectations. Here also, both recent history of sales and of the relation of expected to actual sales would bear upon the decision concerning how much could in the future be sold at the expected price. However, in this case, the range of considerations included in Group 3 is probably considerably wider than in the case of price change.

In trying to determine what producers will do, we can, if statistics are adequate, reproduce the history of prices and sales, as required in Group 1. The factors comprehended in Group 3 need to be sketched in freehand with whatever help can be supplied by acute espionage directed towards current and future events.

The grs–rpm comparison yields some guidance in the reconstruction of the considerations included in Group 2. It gives the average relation of expected sales to planned purchases of finished consumers' goods of three main types. The forecaster needs to reconstruct the way in which the suction or backing up of demand for finished goods is experienced at earlier stages of production. He must reconstruct the influence of exaggeration, speculation, fear of scarcity or of getting caught. These comparisons are of greatest help in foretelling sales-expectations in connection with finished consumers' goods and of progressively less help as the early undifferentiated stages and the investment-goods phases of production are approached. Nevertheless, if the history of the relation of expected to actual sales and selling price aids the individual producer and distributor to form estimates of future sales and prices, the rpm-grs comparison should help the forecaster to estimate the sales component of production schedules for the consumers' goods industries.

Estimated sales then need to be converted into estimated production by including inventory change that would be desired or tolerated. A change in sales and therefore in production will in itself involve a change in in-process inventory, and probably in other types of inventory, although our inadequate knowledge of the dynamics of inventory change makes quantitative statement well-nigh impossible. Sanguine or pessimistic expectations concerning price and sales will also influence the size of stocks that it seems wise to hold. Moreover, in so far as planned inventory change diverges from actual change, production schedules for the following month would probably be modified both in the light of the changed expectations and the need to restore inventories to a desired figure.

But we need to know not only how, given a specified relation between plans and actuality, producers lay plans for the future, but also how those future plans when embodied in production schedules will in turn affect the relation between expectations and actuality. Although each businessman may, in accordance with the most classical tenets, plan his output without consideration of how his actions will influence the prices and sales volume which he anticipates, the actions of businessmen as a whole are vital determinants of the size of the market as a whole.

Sanguine expectations of producers of consumers' goods, reflected in enlarged production schedules, will distribute additional income thereby helping to make dreams come true. But unassisted by actions of producers of investment goods, they are most unlikely to provide sufficient income to take the additional product off the market at profitable prices. So long as business and individuals refrain from spending some of their current income on commodities and services, the increased output in the consumers' goods industries will have to be accompanied either by a corresponding increase in planned inventories or by additional production of goods and services which are not bought by domestic consumers—machinery, plant, exports, and so on. The analysis is set up to indicate the extent to which these various elements are present and the contribution of each part to the whole. It should clarify the bearing of such changes as occur on the relation between expected sales and planned purchases, or, ignoring unintended consumer saving, on the relation between expected sales and actual sales of consumers' goods.

The following table summarizes the components of investment and saving that have been isolated by the analysis. The size of the rpm–grs gap is *defined* by adding lines 8, 11, and 15—consumer unintended saving, price change and unplanned inventory change. But the size of the gap is *determined* directly by all of the items listed in the table and indirectly by the size and direction of change in the output of consumers' goods.

In order to thread the strands of an analysis through the guides prescribed by Steps I to VI for period after period, we need to take into account the external factors affecting the items in the table (and the analysis renders little assistance in making these evaluations) as well as their induced reactions. But the particular contribution of the technique which has been described is in focusing attention on changes in the consumers' goods industries, which, under normally prosperous conditions, have accounted for about 80 percent of gross national income. These changes are not merely concomitants of change in ex post investment, but follow patterns of their own, the importance of which does not correspond to the slightness of our knowledge concerning them.

Obviously, the job of projecting into the future the interlocking sequence of cause and effect is more difficult at some times than at others. When a strong inventory or construction boom is pouring its leaven into the income stream, the ramifying sequence of cause and effect is relatively plain, and rough estimates of probable change not out of the question. Answers become more difficult when it is not clear whether a machinery or construction boom will hop an inventory band wagon or the extent to which the depressing influence of low levels of investment-goods output will spread from industry to industry.

Quantitative prediction becomes still more difficult when we wonder not how much faster or slower a prosperous or depressed phase will progress, but whether prosperity will turn into recession or depression

TABLE

SAVING–INVESTMENT FLOWS, JULY, 1941,

	JULY	AUGUST
1. Total retained income (line 2 + 9)	3,186	3,292
2. Consumer retained income (line 3 + 7 + 8)	305	319
3. Consumer withheld income (line 4 + 5 + 6)	369	369
4. Withheld income of prev. m.	372	369
5. Change related to change in income (Table XXII, line 5)	0.1	15.8
6. Change related to change in saving function (Table XXII, line 9)	–3	–16
7. Retained income related to change in consumer credit outstanding (Table XXII, line 18)	–85	–75
8. Unplanned saving (Table XXIV, line 8 + 17 + 26)	21	25
9. Business retained income (line 10 + 11)	2,881	2,973
10. Before price change (Table XXI, line 8)	2,844	2,871
11. Increase due to price change (Table XXV, line 21)	37	102
12. Total government expenditure and capital formation (line 13 + 16 + 17 + 18 + 19)	3,186	3,292
13. Change in business inventories of consumption goods (line 14 + 15)	65	66
14. Planned (Table XXIII, line 3 + 8)	65	74
15. Unplanned (Table XXIV, line 7 + 16)		–8
16. Exports—imports (Table XXIII, line 4)	–40	–40
17. Government services (Table XXI, line 16)	1,186	1,188
18. Consumers' goods purchased by government (Table XXIII, line 5)	100	100
19. Investment goods exclusive of inventories (Table XXV, line 17)	1,875	1,978

into recovery. At these critical periods, the forecasting value of the analysis hinges on whether there is a tendency for changes in the rpm–grs gap to lead in recovery and recession.

The existence of such a lead can neither be proved nor disproved since the answer can only be found in figures and they have not been compiled. Moreover, it is unlikely that they could be compiled for a period covering more than one or two cycles at the present time. The best that we can do, therefore, is to speculate on the probable business-cycle pattern that the rpm–grs comparisons would be likely to have.

XXVII

TO FEBRUARY, 1942 (IN MILLIONS OF DOLLARS)

SEPTEMBER	OCTOBER	NOVEMBER	DECEMBER	JANUARY	FEBRUARY
3,394	3,495	3,583	3,679	3,801	3,907
343	377	379	397	500	588
378	389	387	396	501	584
369	378	389	387	396	501
13.6	13.4	8.4	8.2	9.6	3.8
-5	-2	-10	1	95	79
-65	-55	-45	-40	-30	-25
30	43	37	41	29	29
3,051	3,118	3,204	3,282	3,301	3,319
2,968	3,051	3,130	3,201	3,274	3,304
83	67	74	81	27	15
3,394	3,494	3,581	3,678	3,801	3,908
65	65	50	42	71	65
65	65	58	50	58	45
		-8	-8	13	20
-40	-40	-40	-40	-40	-40
1,190	1,192	1,194	1,196	1,198	1,200
100	100	100	100	100	100
2,079	2,177	2,277	2,380	2,472	2,583

"Adequate" consumer effective demand has been defined as consumer ready purchase money which, for any given interval of time, is equal to or exceeds the aggregate price at which consumers' goods ready for sale were intended to sell; the greater the excess, the greater the suction drawing forth increased output. An excess will be present when government expenditure plus new durable investment goods plus planned inventory change exceeds the sums that consumers choose to save plus the sums that producers aim to retain as a contingent factor on which their production and pricing decisions are based.

During the upward phase of the cycle, many things are likely to occur as prosperity continues which tend to destroy the equality or lessen the excess, causing ex ante saving to approach the investment group of items. Rising incomes usually cause a more than proportionate rise in consumer saving. (The spending of unrealized capital gains may in part counteract this tendency but although this factor could be important at some phase of the upswing, there is no reason why it should grow constantly greater.) It is possible that the purchase of durable consumers' goods does not continue indefinitely to increase at a proportional rate as income increases; in so far as the expansion of this type of expenditure is retarded, consumer credit outstanding (negative saving) tends to increase less rapidly, thus contributing to the tendency for net saving to increase.

Retained receipts of business may also tend to increase: As production nears capacity in some lines, further pressure of buying will bear on prices, and rising prices cause rising profits. The importance of overhead in the cost structure of many industries will also cause profits to rise rapidly as production increases, and the much-heralded curtailment through rising costs is hard to find in practice. The fact that dividends are considerably steadier than earnings means that retained profits increase as profits mount. Depreciation on newly installed plant and equipment tends to swell the retained income aggregate after prosperity has continued for a while. Progressive tax rates on rising profits further tend to increase retained income as we use the term.

The tendency for ex ante saving to rise ever more rapidly as prosperity continues does not seem to be paralleled by a similar tendency in the ex ante investment group. There may, in the first place, be a tendency for innovation-inspired capital formation to cluster pretty heavily at the beginning of a period of improving business. Businessmen are likely to hesitate to undertake plant expansion and major renovation after business prosperity has continued for more than the usual term, and construction and financing costs have risen sharply; presently, the curtailed plans will result in curtailed expenditure. But perhaps most important of all, the planned increase in inventories attributable to the rise in business activity will in all probability taper off. Certainly, the size of stock piles of raw materials required to effect a smooth flow of work does not bear a constant ratio to the volume of output; a minimum number of different items, styles, and sizes is required regardless of the amplitude of the work flow. Similarly, the goods in-process per unit of output may decrease as larger output makes it possible to absorb the unevenesses in the movement of goods and to speed up some operations. Then, too, producers, wary of the current price structure, may grow nervous and wish to cut down on stocks held partly as speculation. Obviously, the increase in inventories resulting from misjudged sales may well cause total inventories to spurt at the peak; but the significance of this sort of ex post capital formation is, of course, very different from that of the ex ante type we have been considering.

If, after prosperity has continued for some months, ex ante saving tends to increase more rapidly than ex ante investment, there would be a fall in consumer ready purchase money *relative to* goods ready for sale. If there had been a considerable margin between the two aggregates this would not necessarily cause a decline in consumers' goods production. It might merely mean that prices would rise less or unplanned decreases in inventory would cease. It would not be until ready purchase money actually fell short of goods ready for sale that the curtailment in consumers' goods production would *necessarily* follow.

However, several reasons make it seem probable that the curtailment would occur sooner. A reduction or cessation in price rise is ordinarily interpreted pessimistically and a softening pressure of demand is similarly interpreted; this pessimism would be of especial importance in connection with speculation in inventories. Moreover, in so far as the acceleration principle is active, the decreasing suction exerted by consumer effective demand may result in an absolute decline in orders for new buildings and new equipment. Finally, it might well be that the equality between aggregate effective demand and supply would be consistent with considerable deficiency of demand for certain products, and that retrenchment in these lines would be enough to turn the tide.

If this is so, it casts doubt on whether the mere equality of even these ex ante conceptions of saving and investment is all that is required to keep the economic system as we know it today operating at prosperity levels or, indeed, at any given level. The analysis suggests that as the excess of rpm over grs starts to lessen and the suction of buying declines, forces are set to work which before long will cause the still flooding tide of output to falter and recede. It suggests, in other words, that prosperity is associated with the production of investment goods and planned inventory change which *exceeds* ex ante saving.

Turning to the downward phase of the cycle, it would seem likely that the deficiency of purchasing power, which is associated with depression, would eventually tend to correct itself. In the first place, several factors would operate to decrease saving: Consumer saving would decline because of the lower level of incomes and the need on the part of many individuals to "eat up savings"; also the reduction of installment debt is likely to cause the net saving related to the repayment of debt to diminish after a point. Retained business income would also tend to decline because of low profits and the tendency to maintain interest and dividend payments. In fact, because of the pressure of overhead costs, a sufficiently reduced volume of business might eventually cause the income retained by business to become a negative figure.

Capital formation, on the other hand, might not decline indefinitely: Repairs become more urgent the longer they are postponed; the ratio of inventories to production may well tend to increase after production approaches basic levels for reasons similar to those that have been given for the decrease in the ratio of inventories to production during prosperous periods. This would cause the decline in investment to slacken.

An increasing decline in saving and a decreasing decline in investment would cause consumer ready purchase money eventually to exceed goods ready for sale *even if both quantities were still declining.* Were this to occur, a reversal in the direction of change in the production of consumers' goods would be expected even if there had been no previous pickup in the producers' goods industries.

Needless to say, if before this point were reached, favorable cost-price relations in construction, or other changes, inspire orders for new buildings and machines by the more optimistic firms, or by those that have experienced a rise in demand somewhat earlier than the rest or are subject to strong secular up-trends, the reversal in the direction of change would occur earlier than it would on the basis of change in the output of the consumption goods alone.

The strands of the argument weave a discernible pattern: One would expect to find the suction of purchasing power diminishing as prosperity ripens. This decreasing gap between goods ready for sale, at the price at which they were intended to sell, and consumer ready purchase money weakens the system's immunity to depression. The lowered vitality results in higher morbidity rates among enterprises first where independent reasons for decreased output exist—adverse cost-price relations, slackening trend-growth rates, random factors of various sorts; second, where continued purchases in one group of enterprises depend on an increasing percentage rate of demand in others; third, in the companies or industries that tag along after their more prosperous neighbors. Each new ailment, by reducing consumer ready purchase money more than it reduces goods ready for sale, squeezes the two aggregates—rpm and grs—together, thus increasing the economy's susceptibility to disease. Because of these diversities within the system, it seems likely that the upward phase of the cycle will come to a close before grs and rpm reach equality, and that the equal point will be an incident of the downward path.

Analogously, the backing up of consumer purchasing power consequent upon goods ready for sale which exceed consumer ready purchase money will tend to lessen as depression continues, thus building a situation in which the hardier members of the system can recover strength. Many depressions of the past have doubtless come to a close long before the differential rate of decline of net ex ante saving and investment has caused rpm to once again exceed grs. In fact, we do not know whether any depression has reached this point. As the margins narrow the mud becomes less sticky, the road hardens and the spirit of enterprise can ride again. Cost-price relations in the construction industries may be favorable, new invention is ready to be exploited. Moreover, since some companies and industries experience lessening demand against a background of strong secular uptrend, considerable relative decline turns readily into an absolute increase in their output. When these sporadic spurts of activity are large enough and occur when the rpm–grs gap has narrowed sufficiently, the cumulative stimulation causes deficiency to turn into excess and revival to grip hold in earnest.

These reflections suggest that the forecasting value of the grs–rpm relation would lie not in its sign but in whether the positive or negative gap was increasing or decreasing. Whether any clear direction of change would be visible in the figures cannot be said without experience with the statistical record, and that experience will be difficult to acquire because of the sort of data required as well as the formidable problem of seasonal adjustment involved. Also, we cannot tell at present whether the series would move with sufficient steadiness to provide an adequate forecasting instrument.

Were it possible to surmount these difficulties, we might still be in the dark concerning the length of the lags or leads to be expected. It seems unlikely that a mechanical rule would work. The line of thought sketched in the last few paragraphs suggests that there might be considerable irregularity in the lengths to which the narrowing of either excess or deficiency of purchasing power might be expected to proceed before the turns were reached. It suggests, also, that one would expect the answer to this question to differ with the vitality of the expansive forces within an economy—when they were strong an upturn would occur well before rpm exceeded grs; when they were weak, it seems likely that even vast amounts of government spending might fail to cause a spontaneous rise until after extensive liquidation had taken place.

These observations suggest that the technique which has been described could hardly be expected to perform immediate feats of forecasting, even were the base figures computed with reasonable adequacy. Since it is an implement devoid of magic, the investigator utilizing it would have to learn a craft. And it is a difficult craft requiring clever mechanical assistance. It is not easy to devise instruments sensitive to changes in expectations and plans as well as to actual occurrences. Yet so long as actions are preceded by calculations, such tools must be devised if we wish to understand and certainly to predict the action. The instruments, moreover, will at first be blunt; only after considerable sharpening in use would the edges be keen enough to employ on the more ambitious forecasting jobs—those extended in time or related to periods when expansion or contraction seemed hesitant. In the meantime, although the forecasting aims must be modest, the current history of change which the figures yield would provide information essential to the determination of wise public policy.

Appendix A

NOTES ON THE BASE FIGURES FOR JUNE, 1941

TABLE XXI, LINE 3

Income produced by the durable producers' goods industries is the sum of durable producers' goods other than construction and construction currently produced (at the prices of the previous month) whether sold to the private or government sector of the economy or held as an increase in inventories.

Durable producers' goods other than construction: To the flow of finished producers' goods other than construction, as estimated by Simon Kuznets of the National Bureau of Economic Research, was added an estimate of change in inventories of producers' goods. (Inventory change in producers' goods industries was assumed to bear the same relation to total inventory change as producers' goods bore to total commodity flow—Kuznets figures. This assumption was predicated on an examination of ratios of inventory change to flow of producers' and consumers' goods for 1920–1935, from the National Bureau of Economic Research publications, *Commodity Flow and Capital Formation* and *National Income and Capital Formation.*) This figure was extrapolated to June 1941 by using the index of production of durable goods published by the Board of Governors of the Federal Reserve Board.

The figure for production of producers' goods at 1939 prices was corrected for price change. An index of prices was constructed by using the Bureau of Labor Statistics wholesale price indexes for iron and steel, chemicals, farm machinery, and motor vehicles with weights of 6, 2, 1, 1, respectively.

Comment: The Federal Reserve Board index is a poor one to use not only because of its inclusion of consumers' as well as producers' durable goods but also because of the importance of earlier stages of manufacture in the aggregate covered by the index. As explained in the discussion of Step III in the text, our measures ought to concentrate on changing output at the later stages of production. For these reasons, the index of production of durable producers' goods constructed by the Federal Reserve Bank of New York, corrected for its trend adjustment, would have been preferable. Its advantages were counteracted, however, by the fact that it includes housing and has not been revised to take account of the added weight which should be given to defense production.

TABLE XXI, LINE 3 (*Continued*)

The volume of construction was estimated by extrapolating the Kuznets estimate for construction in 1939 by means of indexes of value of construction compiled in the following way: The Federal Reserve Board's seasonally adjusted index of total construction, based on contracts let, was adjusted for the difference between the time when the contract is let and the time when payment is made to factors of production. The National Resources Planning Board's study of *Economic Effects of the Federal Public Works Expenditures: 1933–1938*, by J. K. Galbraith provided the basis for the adjustment. In the summer months (after February) the lag between letting the contract and beginning work was found to be about 21 days; in the winter (November through February) it was about 45 days. Therefore, from November to February the index was lagged two months, and from March to November, one month, with adjustments between October and November, and February and March. Payments are made by contractors as work is done and the Galbraith analysis of the number of man hours of work on the project was taken as a measure of work currently performed. Galbraith breaks down the data into 22 categories. All of them are not of equal importance but the percentages of total work in each category completed in any one month were added and the sum divided by 22 to get the average volume of construction in that month. Therefore, the percentage of work completed in the first month of actual work, as revealed by the above calculation, multiplied by the index of contracts let the preceding month (or for the month before the last during the winter) is the index of construction performed in the current month on contracts let during the previous month (or during the month before the last). In the same way, the percentage of work completed in each month from the second to the fifteenth (99.5 percent of all construction had been completed by the end of the 15th month), multiplied respectively by the index of contracts let in the second to fifteenth preceding month, will give an index of work completed in the current month on contracts let in each of the preceding ones. The sum of all such indexes is the index of total construction performed in the current month.

Comment: At a time when the volume of construction is changing considerably, some sort of adjustment ought to be made for the difference between the time when contracts are let and payments made. The technique here used, however, is probably too elaborate and the period of 15 months too long in view of the fact that public works doubtless typically take longer to complete than the average contract for commercial construction.

TABLE XXI, LINE 5

Income currently produced by consumers' nondurable goods industries: Kuznets' estimate of perishable and semidurable commodities flowing to

TABLE XXI, LINE 5 (*Continued*)

consumers in 1939, plus an estimate of related inventory change, gave an estimate of the dollar aggregate for 1939. (Inventory change in this category was assumed to bear the same relation to total inventory change as total nondurable commodities did to total commodity flow.)

This figure was extrapolated by the Federal Reserve Bank of New York index of production of consumers' nondurable goods. The index is composed of series which are seasonally adjusted; they are also adjusted for long-term trend. The compilers of the index estimate that the trend in 1939–40 was 1.6 percent per year. The same figure was assumed to apply to 1940–41. It was, therefore, divided by 12 and added cumulatively for each month beginning with January, 1939. This gave a series of ratios by which later months increased over January, 1939, because of the long-term trend. The ratios for each month, plus 100, were multiplied by the index number for the month to give the index with the trend adjustment removed.

The dollar aggregate for 1939 was divided by the sum of the monthly indexes for 1939 to give the volume of production per index point at 1939 prices. This figure, multiplied by the index number for June, 1941, derived as described above, gave production at 1939 prices during June, 1941.

An index of price change was constructed by using the B.L.S. Cost of Living Indexes for Food and Clothing weighted 3 and 1, respectively. (These indexes were issued quarterly until October, 1940, and monthly thereafter.) The figure for June, 1941, was then converted to current prices.

TABLE XXI, LINE 6

Income currently produced by consumers' durable goods industries: These figures were constructed by following a similar procedure to that used for nondurable commodities. The Kuznets figure for 1939, plus inventory change, was projected to June, 1941, by the Federal Reserve Bank of New York index of production of consumers' durable goods. A trend of 2 percent per annum was reintroduced. Prices were adjusted by an index composed of Fairchild's retail price index for home furnishings, and the B.L.S. wholesale price indexes for motor vehicles and automobile tires and tubes, weighted 2, 1, and 1, respectively.

TABLE XXI, LINE 7

Income currently produced by the service industries: The dollar figure for services in 1939 was the difference between U.S. Department of Commerce figure for National Income Produced in 1939 and the National Bureau figure for consumers' commodities plus net capital formation. The Federal Reserve Bank of New York index for Miscellaneous Services was used to project the base figure to June, 1941.

TABLE XXI, LINE 7 (*Continued*)

Comment: The reason for the procedure lies in a subsequent problem—the calculation of retained business income. This figure is the difference between income produced and income payments. Total income produced must of course equal total national product. The Department of Commerce figures have to be used for monthly calculations of income payments and the projected National Bureau figures have to be used for national product classified as consumers' durable and nondurable commodities and services and capital formation. (The Department of Commerce is developing their own series on a quarterly basis.) But if we ignore the difference due to faulty estimation and differences in procedure (it would of course be possible to make some allowances for this element but we have not undertaken to do so), the Department of Commerce income produced should equal N.B.E.R. national product. Therefore Department of Commerce income payments plus retained income equals N.B.E.R. consumers' outlay for commodities, capital formation, and consumers' services. But since the Department of Commerce and N.B.E.R. estimates of national income are not the same, and since income payments, consumers' commodities and capital formation are estimated directly, a reconciliation of the two series ought to appear either in services (calculated by the Bureau as the difference between commodity flow to individuals plus capital formation and total national income) or in retained income. When the reconciliation was made in the service group, the estimated services seemed to yield a very sensible figure. Harold Barger, at the National Bureau of Economic Research, made independent calculations of services (*Outlay and Income in the United States, 1921–1938,* 1942) which yield an estimate for services in 1938 of $22,365 million. The figure obtained for 1939 by the process described above was $22,300 million.

The Federal Reserve Bank of New York's index for miscellaneous services is a poor projecting index for our purposes; it does not include important consumer services such as purchased electricity, theater and moving picture tickets, education; whereas it does include newspaper and radio advertising which are not consumer services. There is a confidential series at the Department of Commerce which would probably be a better index to use.

TABLE XXI, LINE 8

Retained income of business enterprises: This figure is obtained by adding to total income produced by business enterprises (Table XXI, line 2) the income directly distributed by Governments (Table XXI, line 16), and subtracting therefrom income payments to individuals (Table XXI, line 23). This figure should theoretically include retained profits of business, losses charged to income account, credits to reserve accounts charged to income account in excess of expenditures charged to the same reserves, and the income charge for taxes.

Comment: The difference between the U.S. Department of Commerce figure for income produced and income paid out does not conform precisely to our theoretical requirements for retained income even after direct payments of gov-

TABLE XXI, LINE 8 (*Continued*)

ernments are included in income produced in order to make a rough adjustment for the inclusion in retained income of taxes paid by business enterprises. In addition, errors of estimate necessarily present in both the output and income figures are, unless they cancel out, present in the difference. On the basis of a rough calculation of taxes, business retained reserves, profits, etc., the retained income figures seem somewhat high. Consumer retained income, on the other hand, seems correspondingly low. Both of these figures urgently require reëxamination. (See discussion in text, pp 190–91.

It is well to bear in mind that the base figures for June or their current extentions derive the retained income figure from production and income-payments data. Unless direct information on retained income of the sort suggested in the text were available, no independent calculation of monthly changes in retained income would be possible. The forecasts, however, work from the opposite direction—changes in retained income and production are estimated and changes in income payments deduced therefrom.

TABLE XXI, LINE 13

Income distributed to individuals by business enterprises: The U.S. Department of Commerce estimate of income payments in 1940 was projected to June, 1941, by applying their adjusted index for total income payments. Income distributed directly by Governments (Table XXI, line 16) was subtracted.

TABLE XXI, LINES 14 AND 15

Labor and ownership income: Total income distributed to individuals by business enterprise (Table XXI, line 13) is divided into ownership and labor income. The U.S. Department of Commerce adjusted index for salaries and wages is applied to the corresponding dollar aggregate for 1940. To the dollar figures for January through June, obtained in this way, the monthly amounts of direct and work relief, and social-security benefits and other labor income are added, and labor income distributed directly by governments (Table XXI, line 20) subtracted, to get the total for labor income distributed by business enterprises. This total is subtracted from total income payments minus income distributed directly by governments (Table XXI, line 16), to get the ownership income figure for business enterprises. From January to June, ownership income represented approximately 32 percent of total income payments by business enterprises and this figure is used for June.

Comment: The division of income into two categories recognizes the fact that incomes of various sorts are spent or saved in accordance with varying patterns. It would be preferable to divide income payments into income received in families having more and having less than $3,000 current income, or into additional income-level groups. But since data on which to base the assignment of current

TABLE XXI, LINES 14 AND 15 (*Continued*)

income to these categories are not available, the ownership and labor income categories have been used. It is assumed that they represent income that would be spent in accordance with a high and low income spending pattern, respectively. Further study of the schedules obtained in the 1935–36 National Resources Committee's study of consumer income and expenditure would provide a sounder basis for accepting or rejecting this assumption.

TABLE XXI, LINE 18

Ownership income distributed directly by governments: Ownership income distributed by the Federal Government includes interest payments as reported in the Treasury statements. A rough seasonal adjustment was made.

TABLE XXI, LINE 19

Ownership income distributed by state and local governments is little more than a guess. For 1932 an estimate has been made of expenditures for interest and redemption and is reported in Finances of States and Local Subdivisions for that year. Taking into account the probable change in debt, etc., between 1932 and 1940, $50 million was taken as a reasonable figure for ownership payments from state and local governments in June, 1941.

TABLE XXI, LINE 21

Labor income and benefits distributed directly by governments: For the Federal Government, this category includes salaries, social-security and railroad-retirement benefits, agricultural aid, and W.P.A. payments. According to an analysis of "Occupations and Salaries in Federal Employment" by Malcolm L. Smith in the *Monthly Labor Review,* January, 1941, Federal payrolls may be estimated to have amounted to about $242 million in December, 1940; this suggests that state and local payrolls amounted to $393 million, since total government payrolls other than work relief were reported in the U.S. Department of Commerce Income Payments series as $635 million in December, 1940. The assumption was made that the state and local payrolls did not change between December and June, 1941; the June figure for federal payrolls was, therefore, total government payrolls for June as reported in the *Survey of Current Business* minus $393 million. Social-security and railroad-retirement payments were taken from the *Treasury Bulletin* and roughly corrected for seasonal irregularities. Agricultural aid is the Treasury figure adjusted for seasonal change. W.P.A. payments were adjusted for seasonal variation by assuming that payments in 1940 varied from month to month according to the true seasonal pattern; June, 1941, payments were, accordingly, divided by June, 1940, payments and the resulting relative multiplied by the 1940 average monthly payment.

TABLE XXI, LINE 22

State and local labor income and benefits included wages and salaries of $393 million (see previous paragraph) plus relief wages and direct relief minus federal relief as reported in the *Survey of Current Business.*

TABLE XXI, LINE 23

Total income distributed to individuals: The United States Department of Commerce estimate of income payments in 1940 was projected to June, 1941 by applying their adjusted index for total income payments.

TABLE XXII, LINE 2

Rpm for previous month: Rpm for May was assumed to be identical with the dollar volume of flow of commodities and services to consumers in May.

TABLE XXII, LINE 6

Portion of income increment withheld by consumers: Change in ownership income between May and June is multiplied by 35 percent to obtain an estimate of the portion of new income saved. The figure of 35 percent is based on a computation using data in Table 24A, *Consumer Expenditure in the United States* (National Resources Committee). We assume that ownership income is received by families with total incomes of over $3,000. When the aggregate savings for families in income levels above $3,000 are summated, they amount to 39 percent of the total income. The figure was reduced to 35 percent.

Comment: In view of the fact that the figure of 39 percent refers to total income in 1935–36 and that the appropriate percentage for the table should refer to marginal income, in view of the fact also that a large proportion of ownership income is received by families having an income of considerably over $3,000, the figure selected may well be considerably too low.

TABLE XXII, LINE 7

The figure for labor income retained was based on analogous procedure and reasoning. In this case, the consumer-expenditure study indicated that average saving of families with incomes of under $3,000 was 2.5 percent; and a figure of 5 percent was selected as applicable to marginal income. This figure may well be low.

TABLE XXII, LINES 8–17

Change in the proportion of total income spent: This section attempts to estimate changes in saving related to change in the income-saving function as opposed to change in income. For June, 1941, all of the items were given an arbitrary value of zero.

TABLE XXII, LINE 18

Change in installment credit outstanding: The total consumer short-term credit outstanding in December, 1940, was estimated as about $5,000 million dollars. (*Survey of Current Business,* September, 1941, p. 9.) Monthly data sampled by the U.S. Department of Commerce on Installment Loans to Consumers totaled $982 million outstanding in December, 1940. The ratio between these two figures was applied to the Department of Commerce sample of installment loans outstanding in May and in June, 1941. The difference between these estimates for May–June is the change in installment credit outstanding.

TABLE XXII, LINE 19

In order to obtain the figure for the change in the change in installment credit outstanding, it was necessary to repeat this procedure for April and May. Since the increase in installment credit outstanding between April and May was $85 million, and, between May and June, $100 million, ready purchase money for June will, other things being unchanged, be greater by $15 million than it was in May.

TABLE XXII, LINES 21, 28 AND 35

Rpm of previous month applicable to the purchase of nondurable commodities, durable commodities and services, respectively: For each of these three classes of consumer expenditures, rpm of the previous month was taken as sales for the previous month, that is, sales for May. It was assumed that sales in each category were equal to production minus whatever inventory increase was indicated by the Department of Commerce figures on inventory change for selected durable and nondurable goods between April–May.

Comment: It will be noted that the concept measured was consumers' expenditures, not rpm. It would have been preferable to attempt to go behind the expenditures to an estimate of ready purchase money. But in order to do this it is necessary to have either some direct evidence as to planned inventory change and consumer saving or the support of the numerical relations developed in our analysis. Since the evidence is not available and the analysis had to start somewhere, it was necessary to use the ex post rather than the ex ante concept.

TABLE XXII, LINES 22, 29 AND 36

Change related to change in income increment after taxes: The ratios applied to the change related to change in income increment after taxes are the characteristic ratios for January to June, 1941, of consumers' goods produced in each of the three categories to total consumers' goods produced.

Comment: These figures diverge considerably from the ratios characteristic of the consumer expenditure study made by the National Resources Committe in 1935–36. The figures were 57 percent, 9 percent and 34 percent for nondurable,

TABLE XXII, LINES 22, 29 AND 36 (*Continued*)

durable, and service goods, respectively. The major difference lies in the division between durable and nondurable commodities, and a good part of this difference might actually reflect the difference between the 1935–36 and the 1941 consumption patterns.

A more refined treatment might make a distinction between the way in which increments of labor and of ownership income are spent in the various categories. Calculations based on Table 101 of *Family Expenditures in the United States*, Statistical Tables and Appendixes, suggest that when the data are summarized for families with incomes of under $3,000 and over $3,000, the pairs of ratios are as follows: nondurable commodities, 60 and 47 percent; durable commodities, 8 and 12 percent; services, 32 and 41 percent. The analysis is still too crude to make distinctions of this sort useful. This is particularly so since the distinction between ownership and labor income is only the crudest approximation to a distinction between incomes above and below $3,000.

TABLE XXII, LINES 25 AND 32

Change related to change in installment credit outstanding: The change in the change in installment credit is allocated to nondurable and durable commodities on the basis of an informed guess. Clothing would probably be the chief item in the nondurable goods group likely to be purchased, to any extent, on installment credit, therefore the large majority of the additional purchasing power resulting from the accelerated rate of borrowing was assigned to ready purchase money for durable commodities.

TABLE XXIII, LINES 3 AND 8

Planned inventory change: For June, 1941, no distinction was made between planned and involuntary inventory change. On the basis of a comparison of inventory data in the National Bureau of Economic Research publications, *Commodity Flow and Capital Formation* (Vol. I, Table VII–6), with commodity flow data in *National Income and Capital Formation 1919–1935* (Appendix Table VII) a reasonable ratio, for prosperous years, of inventory to commodity flow was selected for nondurable commodities and durable commodities and applied to the 1939 figure for commodity flow of durable and nondurable consumers' goods. These figures were projected to June, 1941, on the basis of appropriate monthly inventory data published in the *Survey of Current Business*.

Comment: This is a totally inadequate procedure. In the first place, the base figure is absurdly inadequate. The ratios of inventories to sales vary a great deal for different years and therefore the selection of an average ratio as appropriate to a given year involves indeterminate error. Moreover, although the type of index used to project the production data is pertinent to the selection of the appropriate inventory data, the inventory material does not permit the isolation of the appropriate stock piles In the second place, the Department of Commerce

TABLE XXIII, LINES 3 AND 8 (*Continued*)

data on inventory change published in the *Survey of Current Business* is for manufacturing inventories only and is a new series for which seasonal adjustment had not been worked out. For nondurable goods, the nondurable subdivision of inventory change was used; for durable commodities only the indexes for automobiles and equipment and other durable goods were used with respective weights of 4 and 1. Obviously, these data, even if they were accurate reflections of the area which they represent, are totally inadequate for our purposes.

The U.S. Department of Commerce has almost completed an improved inventory series which develops seasonally adjusted estimates of total manufacturers', wholesalers', and retailers', inventories. More careful work on the production index in conjunction with the richer inventory data ought to permit the development of vastly improved estimates. Moreover, the new data on retail sales might make it possible to obtain a direct check on the calculations of retail sales arrived at, as in these computations, by starting with an estimate of production and adjusting for goods produced that were not sold to domestic consumers.

The new Department of Commerce data on manufacturing inventories suggests that seasonally adjusted inventories increased $391 million from May to June, 1941. The data on inventory change of distributors are not yet available. But it is apparent that our figures grossly underestimate change. This means that sales to consumers are overstated and consumer retained income understated.

TABLE XXIII, LINE 4

Exports minus imports: Exports including reëxports of foods were subtracted from the imports of food as reported for June in the *Survey of Current Business* to obtain net exports and a very rough adjustment for seasonal irregularity was made.

Comment: Needless to say, this, too, is a sadly inadequate procedure. In addition to the obvious inadequacies of the coverage and the seasonal adjustment, there is no estimate of tourists' expenditures abroad nor of expenditure of foreign nationals in this country. At the present time the former item is too small to worry about although the latter one may well be substantial. Were more adequate material constructed, it would probably be preferable not to treat the item in connection with exports and imports but as a factor which modifies ready purchase money.

The absence of appropriate information made it necessary to omit exports minus imports of consumer durable commodities.

TABLE XXIII, LINE 5

Consumers' goods purchased by the government: An effort was made to include in this category food and clothing for the army and maintenance for government employees. On the basis of *Defense—One Year,* published by the Office of Emergency Management, the Federal Government was esti-

TABLE XXIII, LINE 5 (*Continued*)

mated to have purchased about $69 million of consumers' nondurable commodities in January, 1941. An additional $6 million a month was included to allow for expanded army requirements between January and June, thus raising the $69 million by $30 million.

Appendix B

NOTES ON THE FORECASTS

TABLE XXI, LINES 3 TO 7

Production at prices of the previous month: See discussion of Step VI, and Table XXVI.

TABLE XXI, LINES 9 TO 12

Retained income of business: June to July and July to August: Changes in retained income associated with change in the volume of production at constant prices and with changes in prices and taxes was taken as $5 million and $-10 million respectively. Since no change in prices of output was taken into account for June to July, line 9 for July—retained income of previous month at prices of previous month—is the same as line 8 for June—current retained income at prices of previous month. During July, prices were estimated to have increased by $37 million (Table XXV, line 21). Line 9 for August—$2,881 million—is therefore obtained by adding $37 million to $2,844 million—line 8 for July, since it is assumed that all the increase in income due to increased prices is retained for one month.

August to September: Change in production at constant prices was $103 million. (Production at previous month's prices for September, Table XXI, line 2, minus production at current prices for August, Table XXV, line 18.) This, in other words, is the amount by which the physical production schedules of producers were increased. If the amount of retained business income related to the production schedules of the previous month remained the same, and if marginal retained income on the increase in production was 30 percent, there would be an increase of $31 million in business retained profits, unspent reserve accruals, taxes, and so on. Since we assume that the total increase in prices swells retained business income in the first instance, the price increase in August amounting to $102 million (Table XXV, line 21) meant that retained business income in August was increased by this amount. By September, however, we can assume that at least a part of this sum found its way into increased wages, dividends, profits withdrawn by entrepreneurs, and the like. If we assume that 35 percent was thus recirculated, retained income in September before price change would be reduced, relative to the August figure after price change, by $36 million.

Retained income of business enterprises in September, in terms of August prices, was, therefore: $2,973 million (retained income after price

TABLE XXI, LINES 9 TO 12 (*Continued*)

change in August) plus $31 million minus $36 million or $2,968 million before price change in September.

September to October: Production at constant prices (Table XXI, line 2, for October minus Table XXV, line 18 for September) increased by $93 million and we assume that 30 percent, or $28 million, was retained. Change in prices during September had aggregated $83 million and we assume that one-third was recirculated by October and that retained income was thereby reduced by $28 million. Retained income for September was $3,051 million after price change; adding $28 million and subtracting $28 million yields $3,051 million—the retained income before price change in October.

October to November: Change in production at constant prices: $82 million. The increase in retained income is 30 percent of $82 million or $25 million. The change in prices during October was $67 million, but because of the new excise taxes, we assume that only 20 percent was recirculated in November. The excise taxes were paid out of the remainder and amounted to somewhat over $30 million in November. Twenty percent of $67 million is $13 million. October retained income was $3,118 million after price change; add $25 million and subtract $13 million and November retained income before price change is found to be $3,130 million. (If we assume that, had it not been for the new taxes, one-third of $67 million would have been recirculated and that, therefore, retained income would have been reduced by $22 million rather than $13 million, then the increase in retained income related to the excise taxes in November was $22 minus $13 or $9 million. The rest of the $30 million of increase in excise taxes would presumably have been paid out of income which would have been retained had the taxes not been increased.)

November to December: Change in production at constant prices was $70 million; assuming that 28 percent was retained, the retained income on the new increment to production was $20 million. The figure of 28 percent is substituted for the previous ratio of 30 percent on the assumption that increasing costs will start to be felt as production continues to rise. Change in income due to changes in prices during November was $74 million. We assume that the system starts to adjust to the new excise taxes and that therefore 25 percent of the price increase of the previous month will be recirculated this month. Twenty-five percent of $74 million is $18 million. We also assume that Christmas bonuses will be greater than usual and cause a decrease of $5 million in retained income. Retained income in November of $3,204 plus $20 million minus $5 million minus $18 million equals $3,201 million—retained income in December before price change. (If one-third of the total price increase in November would have been distributed in December had it not been for the excise taxes, then the increase in retained income resulting from the tax would be $24 million minus $18 million, or $6 million.)

TABLE XXI, LINES 9 TO 12 (*Continued*)

December to January, 1942: Change in production at constant prices was $55 million, times 28 percent equals $15 million. Change in prices was $81 million. As the system adjusts to the new excise taxes, 28 percent or $23 million is recirculated. Retained income for December, after price change, was $3,282 million, plus $15 million minus $23 million equals $3,274 million.

January to February: We assume that by now a further increase in marginal costs cause 27 percent of the $47 million increase in production, or $12 million, to be retained. Thirty-three percent of the price rise of $27 million, or $9 million, is now being recirculated. Retained income for January after price change was $3,301 million, plus $12 million minus $9 million equals $3,304 million—retained income for February before price change. (It will be noted that we make no adjustment in retained income resulting from changed income taxes in 1942. There seems to be no reason to assume that the higher taxes have not already been anticipated in the retained income totals for 1941 since tax reserves are typically set aside during the year in which they accrue. Moreover, we assume that the accruals for 1942 income will be at about the same rates as for 1941. As a matter of fact, there may even have been excess tax reserves set aside which might now be distributed as dividends, but we assume that this tendency would be compensated for by the cases where reserves for taxes were not set up.)

TABLE XXI, LINE 13

Income distributed to individuals by business enterprises: The retained income of business (Table XXI, line 8) is subtracted from the income currently produced by business enterprises at the prices of the previous month (Table XXI, line 2) to give the estimates of total income distributed to individuals by business enterprises.

TABLE XXI, LINES 14 AND 15

Ownership and labor income distributed to individuals by business enterprises: The increasing impact of priorities causing losses to small business enterprises and of rising wages and employment suggests that there may be a shift in the distribution of income from ownership to labor income in the course of fiscal 1942. We have assumed that somewhat over $1 billion, annual rate, will be so shifted. This is considerably less than the amount estimated in the preliminary report since there the figure also contemplated the transfer that would be effected by changed taxes. Of the total income distributed to individuals by business enterprises, ownership income is, in accordance with this line of thought, reduced from 32 percent in June, 1941, to 30.7 percent in June, 1942. Accordingly, to obtain the figure for ownership income (Table XXI, line 14) the figure for Income distributed

TABLE XXI, LINES 14 AND 15 (*Continued*)

to individuals by business enterprises (Table XXI, line 13) was multiplied by the following percentages: July, 31.2; August, 31.2; September, 31.1; October, 31.1; November, 31.0; December, 30.9; January, 30.9; and February, 30.8. Labor income (Table XXI, line 15) is the difference between the resulting figures and total income distributed to individuals by business.

TABLE XXI, LINES 17 TO 22

Income distributed directly by governments: We have assumed that there is no change in any of the subgroups in this category except in the amount of wages, salaries, etc., distributed by the Federal Government which is assumed to increase by $2 million per month.

TABLE XXII, LINES 5 TO 7

Portion of income increment withheld by consumers: The 35 percent ratio for ownership income and 5 percent for labor income, discussed in Appendix A, was maintained throughout the twelve-month period.

Comment: Perhaps the figures should ordinarily be raised as the level of income rises, on the assumption that the amount of saving at the margin is not independent of the location of the margin. In view of the paucity of relevant information, however, no attempt was made to make the necessary allowances. Moreover, the unusual complexion of the period under consideration may well have caused very considerable increases in the proportion of the income increment saved. (For an interesting insight into the problems involved in anticipating changes in income distribution when total income changes, see a recently circulated study by the Office of Price Administration, Division of Research, Consumer Income and Demand Branch, entitled "Estimates of Distribution of Consumer Income in the United States," June 27, 1942. See also *Survey of Current Business,* April, 1942, "The Changing Relation of Consumer Income and Expenditures," by R. B. Bangs.)

TABLE XXII, LINE 10

Rpm increment related to change in taxes: In order to calculate the change in the proportion of total income spent that is related to changes in taxes, we do not need to know the total amount of taxes paid but the extent to which they have changed. In December, 1941, a given amount of current income was being paid to the government and therefore did not enter the market for consumers' goods as ready purchase money. If income were the same in January, 1942, taxes would have to remain the same (other things being unchanged) in order for rpm to be maintained at the December level. Only a *change* in taxes would cause rpm in January to differ from rpm in December (other things being unchanged). If taxes had risen in January, rpm in January would be reduced. The following month, only a *still further rise* from the December level would cause rpm in February to be decreased

TABLE XXII, LINE 10 (*Continued*)

relative to rpm in January (other things being unchanged). When, therefore, we measure change in taxes, against some fixed base such as last years' taxes (Table XXII, line 10), it is the change in the change (Table XXII, line 11), that is, the change from the previous month, which is relevant to our calculation of the rpm increment related to change in the proportion of total income spent.

But what we really need to know is not the total change in taxes paid, but the change in taxes paid out of money which would otherwise have been spent for consumers' goods. An increase in tax payments will not effect rpm if it merely involves writing out a check to the government rather than to the broker. In order to estimate the change in the amount of taxes which would effect rpm we therefore need to estimate not only the change in total taxes paid by individuals but the amount paid out of money which would otherwise be spent on consumers' goods.

This calculation involves two problems: (1) the determination of the change in taxes arising from change in income and in tax rates; and (2) the determination of the proportion of the increased tax burden that will be paid out of money which would otherwise have been spent. Our only guide to this second question is a judgment concerning the income levels of the families by whom various proportions of the new taxes will be paid.

We assume that between June and December, 1941, there were no significant changes in income taxes paid by private individuals. Accordingly, our problem focuses on the 1941 Revenue Act.

The Senate Committee considering the 1941 Revenue bill estimated that individual income taxes would yield about $3,420 million on estimated 1941 incomes, an increase of $1,197 million over what the previous law would have yielded on the same income.

Using the figures on income levels and the number of individuals and families in each level as developed by the Consumer Expenditure study of the National Resources Committee, and using the tax figures given by the Senate Finance Committee, we can estimate very roughly that the 1941 Revenue Act would, because of the changes in rates and exemptions alone, cause individuals and families with incomes of $3,000 or under to increase their tax payments by about $496 million during calendar 1942.

Dividing $496 million by $1,197 million, we may estimate that about 40 percent of the increase in taxes, resulting from a change in the rates alone, will be paid by those having an income of $3,000 per year or under.

But the figure that we require relates to the total increase in tax payments over the previous year or months; we therefore need to evaluate the increase related to changed incomes as well as tax rates. In the summer of 1941, George Lent estimated the probable quarterly individual income-tax payments. He arrived at a figure of $300 million for the last quarter of 1941

	Jan.	Feb.	March	April	May	June
1. Change in income taxes of individuals paid during the current quarter compared with the 4th quarter of 1941 (in millions of dollars)	$1,000	$1,000	$1,000	$1,000	$1,000	$1,000
Family incomes of $3,000 and under						
2. Percent of change in taxes paid by this group	40	40	40	40	40	40
3. Percent of change in taxes paid out of money that would otherwise have been spent	66.6	66.6	66.6	66.6	66.6	66.6
4. Percent of purchasing restriction for the quarter felt during the current month	20	35	45	33.3	33.3	33.3
5. Total change in spending, current month compared with Dec., 1941 (lines $1 \times 2 \times 3 \times 4$), in millions of dollars	$-53	$-93	$-120	$-89	$-89	$-89
Family incomes of $3,000 and over						
6. Percent of change in taxes paid by this group	60	60	60	60	60	60
7. Percent of change in taxes paid out of money that would otherwise have been spent	33.3	33.3	33.3	33.3	33.3	33.3
8. Percent of purchasing restriction for the quarter felt during the current month	20	35	45	33.3	33.3	33.3
9. Change in spending, current month compared with Dec., 1941 (lines $1 \times 6 \times 7 \times 8$), in millions of dollars	$-40	$-70	$-90	$-67	$-67	$-67
10. Change in spending for all income levels, current month compared with Dec., 1941 (lines $5 + 9$), in millions of dollars	$-93	$-163	$-210	$-156	$-156	$-156
11. Change since previous month, in millions of dollars	$-93	$-70	$-47	$+54	0	0

TABLE XXII, LINE 10 (*Continued*)

and $1,200 million for the first quarter of 1942. The October Treasury estimates suggest that Lent's 1942 figures should be raised by about 10 percent. Accordingly, the difference in tax payments related to both changed rates and incomes between the last quarter of 1941 and the first quarter of 1942 is $1,320 million minus $300 million or about $1,000 million.

Although it is likely that the increase in taxes related to increasing incomes would fall somewhat more heavily on the higher income levels than the increase related to the change in rate, we will use the 40 percent figure for both purposes and assume that $400 million of the increase during the first quarter of 1942 was paid by individuals or families having incomes of under $3,000. Let us also assume that these people paid two-thirds of their taxes out of money that would otherwise have been spent for goods and services and the other third out of capital or income that would have been retained. We may assume that the reverse proportions would apply to the over $3,000 income group.

We need to make one further set of judgments: We shall assume that the March 15th tax payments do not exert a restrictive effect on March expenditure only, but on those of January, February and March (20 percent of the total in January, 35 percent in February and 45 percent in March).

Were we to carry the estimates past the February figure required for the tables, and it will be instructive to do so, we would assume that there would be no further intensification of decreased spending over the March level. There might well be a relaxation of the tax-imposed restriction, but it seems reasonable to suppose that, in so far as the March payments exceed the other quarterly payments, saving rather than spending is reduced.

We may now estimate, for the period January to June, 1942, the decrease in spending related to taxes; the table on p. 223 summarizes the procedure.

TABLE XXII, LINE 12

Rpm increment related to advance buying: An average for three months centered in the middle month was made for June and for July, for the new Department of Commerce seasonally adjusted index of all retail sales. The index numbers are 140.6 in June and 142.5 in July, an increase of 1.9 points or 1.35 percent. A similar adjustment of the Department of Commerce seasonally corrected index of income payments yields index numbers of 131.0 in June and 132.6 in July, an increase of 1.6 points or 1.22 percent. Sales therefore increased .13 percent more than income and since all retail sales in June were $4,576 million, the corresponding dollar figure was $.13 \times \$4,576$ or $5.9 million. This figure reflects the change in the portion of new income saved as well as changes in other factors affecting the savings-income function. Since saving related to items other than advance buying

TABLE XXII, LINE 12 (*Continued*)

tended to use a slightly larger proportion of consumer income in July than in June, we can assume that somewhat over the $5.9 million related to advance buying. However, some considerable portion of the total would reflect a very short-term anticipation of wants which would be immediately followed by changes in the opposite direction; in other series we attempt to eliminate this sort of movement by seasonal adjustment. Perhaps a half of the over $5.9 million total might represent articles purchased in July rather than in August or even September; these anticipations we exclude. The rest involve a longer period of anticipation of wants and are therefore regarded as significant dishoarding resulting in an increase in ready purchase money of $3 million.

The figures for other months are no more than guesses keyed to the same general order of magnitude. They relate to total advance buying during the month, that is, to change from June, advance buying having been assumed to have been zero in that month.

TABLE XXII, LINE 14

Rpm increment related to dishoarding of last month's forced saving: We assume that four-fifths of the forced saving of last month reappears on the market for goods and services this month. The four-fifths ratio is the one used in our preliminary report. It is important to note that it applies to cash sales only. In other words, when sales that would have been made on installment credit are not made because of unavailability of goods, we assume that the borrowing capacity remains completely unutilized.

TABLE XXII, LINE 16

Rpm increment related to causes other than those already enumerated: We have assumed that there will be a greater than seasonal increase in dishoarding in December, 1941. A figure of $3 million was pulled out of a hat to express the extent to which people were willing to spend more than the usual amount of money, which had been or would be saved, for Christmas gifts.

Comment: The factors enumerated as significant to the July to February forecasts might differ very considerably from those appearing most important at some other time. When a depression is in its early stages, the fear of unemployment might cause a greater than usual amount of saving. When recovery is just starting, the repayment of debt might cause an unusually small proportion of marginal income to be spent on consumption goods. A rise in prices which consumers believe to be excessive may cause a "buyers strike" and related increases in saving. The introduction of comprehensive social insurance might cause a decrease in the saving-income function. The list could be expanded indefinitely.

TABLE XXII, LINE 16 (*Continued*)

Assuming that other things remain the same, any influence which it seems important to recognize may be fitted into the quantitative formulation. Starting with current income, current rpm may be computed by subtracting current saving. Starting with rpm for the previous interval, current rpm may be calculated by subtracting the increase in saving between the current and previous interval; this is the procedure used in Table XXII: remembering that t applies to an *interval* of time, $rpm_{t_2} = rpm_{t_1} - (S_{t_2} - S_{t_1})$

For some sorts of items such as installment credit, data are available in balance sheet form. For these items the calculation of the related change in rpm from one interval to the next requires a preliminary step—S_{t_1} must be obtained by subtracting the observation at the beginning of the previous period from the observation at the end of the previous period. Similarly S_{t_2} must be obtained by subtracting the observation at the beginning of the current period from the observation at the end of the current period.

For other items, data for current saving are available in the form of change measured from some base period (December, 1941, for taxes, Table XXII, line 10; and June, 1941, for the items in Table XXII, lines 12, 14, and 16; in all cases saving in the base period is assumed to have been zero). Change from the previous to the current interval must be obtained by subtracting the figure for the previous month from that for the current month.

For still other items, such as Table XXII, line 5—the portion of the income increment withheld by consumers—the data are available directly in the form of the change between the current and previous month. An increase in saving stated in this form may therefore be subtracted without further ado from the rpm of the previous month.

TABLE XXII, LINE 18

Rpm related to change in installment credit: The monthly estimates of change in installment credit were in part the result of keeping assumptions consistent with those of the preliminary report and in part related to the monthly decreases in durable consumers' goods.

TABLE XXIII, LINES 3 AND 8

Planned inventory change: The estimates of the amounts that producers would aim to increase inventories were made after considering price trends, the difficulty of obtaining goods, probable changes in the output of certain commodities and other effects of priorities. Needless to say, the figures set down are little more than guesses.

Comment: There is a brief discussion in the text, p. 192, of the possibility of obtaining information on which to base sounder estimates of planned changes in inventories. It seems likely, however, that estimates of these quantities would always be far better for the near than for the far future.

TABLE XXIII, LINE 4

Exports minus imports: In accordance with the assumptions in the preliminary report, no allowance was made for a change in net exports between July, 1941, and June, 1942.

TABLE XXIII, LINE 5

Consumers' goods purchased by the government: At the time when the estimates were made, it was thought that there would be little increase in the size of the armed forces above the current level. Therefore no change was made from month to month in the estimate of food, clothing, and the like, purchased by the government.

TABLE XXIV, LINES 1 TO 27

Comparison of rpm and grs: Two sorts of judgments need to be made in connection with the reconciliation of rpm and grs.

In the first place, the changing emphasis in the production totals and the fixed ratio used for the allocation of rpm to each of the three major subdivisions of consumers' goods means that there is bound to be a growing excess of purchasing power in the lines the production of which is being curtailed and a possible deficiency in the other groups. But it seems likely that consumers, realizing that they will not be able to buy autos, refrigerators, and so on, tend to plan to spend somewhat more than they otherwise would on such goods as are available. The shifts in rpm from the durable to the nondurable commodities is made with these considerations in mind (see lines 4, 13 and 22). Since it seems likely that a fairly continuous change in expenditure patterns would be involved, the month-to-month shifts bear a fairly stable relation to each other.

The shift of rpm from services to nondurable commodities is predicated on the thought that the short-term inflexibility of consumption of rent, light, and heat would cause a somewhat smaller proportion of the consumer's dollar to be spent on services as prices and incomes rise. Accordingly, particularly for the first six months of the period, these transfers are assumed to occur in considerable quantity.

For the period under consideration, a considerable portion of the excess rpm for services was assumed to have been allocated by consumers to nondurable commodities. The remainder was absorbed by a price rise in services which was, on the whole, more moderate than for commodities.

Having once decided how ready purchase money will be finally allocated to the various major categories of expenditures, we then need to come to some conclusion as to how an excess or deficiency of rpm over grs in each of the three major groups will be adjusted. It has been assumed that there

TABLE XXIV, LINES 1 TO 27 (*Continued*)

would be considerable resistance to unplanned inventory change because of the fact that stocks of finished goods are low and producers are under pressure to hold rather than to dispose of them. We have also assumed that consumers wishing to purchase nondurable goods or services are loath not to do so and that therefore forced saving associated with rpm allocated to these groups of goods has to overcome considerable resistance. In the case of durable commodities, however, we assume that consumers are reconciled to the fact that goods will be hard to get and that therefore forced saving occurs fairly readily. Price change in all three groups is thought of as easily touched off. The rise that has already occurred in basic prices creates a tendency for retail prices to rise. Excess purchasing power, therefore, needs merely to support rather than to provoke the rising retail price level.

In connection with services, however, a special problem enters. We have said that the concept of goods ready for sale does not apply to services which are for the most part produced to order and for which no inventory accumulation is possible. Demand may therefore be readily met, regardless of whether preparations to do so have been made in advance. (This statement has obvious qualifications, but will serve as a rough approximation.) If then rpm for services seems so much greater than services produced, that the difference can neither be accounted for by price change nor forced consumer saving, it is likely that the supply of services would increase. A situation of this sort did not arise during the months covered by the tables but some preliminary calculations for the spring months suggest that the excess rpm might well have given rise to a larger physical supply of services than that incorporated in Table XXVI.

Comment: It may be useful to run through the procedure which would be followed if, for example, in May, 1942, the excess rpm for services (when the output of services conforms to the figures used in the preliminary report plus allowance for change in price) were to reach proportions suggesting that a larger supply would be forthcoming. The output of services, Table XXI, line 7, would be taken from Table XXVI after correction for change in price for the previous month as indicated in Table XXV, line 13. When the analysis is carried through Step IV, a large excess rpm for services would appear. In view of this extra buying power, it would seem reasonable to suppose that the output of services would have been increased and the amount of the increase would, presumably, bear some relation to the excess rpm; it would be recorded in Table XXIV, line 25, and the analysis would be worked through again, beginning in Step I with the new figure for services. Of course, the provision of additional services would provide additional income and the application of this income to various sorts of goods and services might suggest a third approximation to the amount of services produced. But where estimation is of necessity rough, it is possible, on the basis of the figures for the immediately preceding few months to guess at the order of magnitude of the excess rpm for services in May and incorporate the second approxi-

TABLE XXIV, LINES 1 TO 27 (*Continued*)

mation of the output of services into the first set of computations for May, starting with Step I.

TABLE XXV

Sales and production at current prices: For the most part, the figures in this table follow mechanically from those in the previous steps of the procedure.

The estimate of price change in the producers' goods industries (line 15) is based in part on the amount of price change suggested in the consumers' goods lines, since it is assumed that there will be a general parallelism of movement. In part, other considerations, such as special government pressures, and differences in relative strength of demand, are taken in consideration.

Comment: Theoretically, consumers' goods purchased by the government, exports minus imports and perhaps inventories should have been converted to current prices before making the calculation of production at current prices in lines 5 and 10. It did not, however, seem sensible to bother about these adjustments for figures as crude as those presented in the tables.

TABLE XXVI

Production at June, 1941, prices: Table XXVI presents one phase of the procedure involved in Step VI. It converts the assumptions made in our preliminary report concerning changes in production at constant prices between June, 1941, and June, 1942, to a series of monthly estimates of production at June prices.

The slight differences in the categories used in the preliminary report and in this monograph are reconciled in the following way: all figures are for differences in the annual rate of output in June, 1941, and June, 1942, and are summarized in the right-hand column of the table: The increase in durable producers' goods construction of $11.7 billion (line 1) is composed of an increase in government order of $14.7 billion and a decrease of $3.0 billion in privately financed production goods including inventories in the producers' goods industries. The increase of $14.7 billion on government orders plus the increase in direct government expenditures of $.3 billion (line 11) gives the total increase in defense expenditure of $15 billion. We assume that production can expand by somewhat over $12 billion, therefore no net reduction in the consumers' goods industries is required—government expenditure, direct and indirect, will increase by $15 billion and privately financed producers' goods will decrease by $3 billion. However, diversion of certain resources to defense from consumption industries will be required, most of which will come from the durable goods group (line 6) which decreases by $5.5 billion. Consumers' perishable commodities and services can therefore increase by about the same amount—$6 billion (lines

TABLE XXVI (*Continued*)

4 and 8). Since it seems likely that services will increase relatively more than perishable commodities, we assume that half of the increase will fall in the service and half in the commodity field; this involves a 7 percent increase in consumers' perishable commodities and an 11 percent increase in services.

The month-to-month changes are with one exception calculated by making a straight line progression from the rate in June, 1941, to the assumed rate of June, 1942. The exception is consumers' durable commodities.

TABLE XXVI, LINE 6

Consumers' durable commodities: Total output of consumers' durable commodities in June, 1941, was divided into two groups—automobiles and other durable commodities. It was assumed that the June rate of output would, by November, 1941, be reduced by 15 percent for autos and 5 percent for other commodities; by January, 1942, a reduction of 40 percent for autos and 15 percent for other durable commodities would be in effect; and by June, 1942, current output would have dropped relative to a year ago by 67 percent for autos and 25 percent for other durable consumers' commodities. Weighted by the approximate value of output in each of the two categories, the monthly reductions relative to June, 1941, would be $100 million in November, $275 million in January, and $335 million in June, 1942. A curve was drawn free hand approximately through these four points and monthly increments of cumulative change read from the chart. These figures were subtracted from the base figure for June, 1941, to get the monthly estimates of output of durable consumers' goods at June, 1941 prices.

TABLE XXI, LINES 2 TO 7

Income produced by business enterprise: August estimates of change in output at constant prices in Table XXVI were, for each of the major categories of goods, expressed as a percentage of the previous month (Table XXVI, lines 2, 5, 7, and 9). These ratios were then multiplied by the estimates for each type of good of output for July at current prices given in Table XXV (lines 5, 10, 12, and 17). The procedure was repeated for each subsequent month. (The July figure was taken directly from Table XXVI since this gives output at June prices which is, of course the figure required for output at previous months' prices for July in Table XXI.)

LIST OF REFERENCES

Analysis of the Sources of War Finance and an Estimate of the National Income and Expenditure in 1938 and 1940. British White Paper, London, 1941. Cmd. 6261.

Analysis of the Sources of War Finance and an Estimate of the National Income and Expenditure in 1938, 1940 and 1941. British White Paper, London, 1942. Cmd. 6347.

Angell, James W. Investment and Business Cycles. New York, 1941.

—— "Taxation, Inflation, and the Defense Program." *Review of Economic Statistics,* May, 1941.

Bangs, R. B. "The Changing Relation of Consumer Income and Expenditures." *Survey of Current Business,* April, 1942.

Barger, Harold. Outlay and Income in the United States, 1921–1938. National Bureau of Economic Research, New York, 1942.

Blakey, Roy G., and Violet Johnson. State Income Taxes. Chicago, 1942.

Bräuer, Karl. "Die Besteuerung der Kriegsgewinne in den Europäischen Staaten." *Finanz und Volkswirtschaftliche Zeitfragen.* Stuttgart, 1921.

Burr, Susan S., and William Vickrey. "Estimating Income and Estate Tax Yields." *Studies in Current Tax Problems.* New York, 1937.

Canadian Government. "Table of Tax Deductions." *Canada Gazette,* Vol. LXXVI, No. 89, Aug. 26, 1942.

Flier, M. J. van der. War Finances in the Netherlands up to 1918. Oxford, 1923.

Gilbert, Milton, and Robert Bangs. "National Income and the War Effort —First Half of 1942." *Survey of Current Business,* Aug., 1942.

Gilbert, Richard V., and Victor Perlo. "The Investment-Factor Method of Forecasting Business Activity." *Econometrica,* July-October, 1942.

Green, R. W. "An Excess Income Tax." *Economic Journal,* Dec., 1920.

Haberler, Gottfried. Consumer Installment Credit and Economic Fluctuations. National Bureau of Economic Research, New York, 1942.

Hansen, A. H. Fiscal Policy and Business Cycles. New York, 1941.

Hart, A. G., E. D. Allen, and others. Paying for Defense. Philadelphia, 1941.

Hicks, J. R., U. K. Hicks, and L. Rostas. The Taxation of War Wealth. Oxford, 1941.

Holthausen, Duncan M., Malcolm M. Merriam, and Rolf Nugent. The Volume of Consumer Installment Credit. National Bureau of Economic Research, New York, 1940.

Hughes, W. J. "An Alternative to the Last Two Budgets." *Economic Journal,* Dec., 1941.

Institute of Statistics (Oxford). "The Black Market." *Bulletin.* March 14, 1942.

Institut Solvay. "L'Impôt sur les bénéfices de guerre." Brussels, 1919.

Kuznets, Simon. Commodity Flow and Capital Formation. National Bureau of Economic Research, New York, 1938.

—— National Income and Capital Formation, 1919–1935. National Bureau of Economic Research, New York, 1937.

—— National Income and Its Composition, 1919–1938. National Bureau of Economic Research, New York, 1941.

Mack, R. P. Flow of Business Funds and Consumer Purchasing Power. New York, 1940.

Myers, J. H. "Excess Profits Tax on Individuals." *Taxes,* Dec., 1941.

National Resources Committee. Consumer Expenditure in the United States. Washington, D.C., 1939.

—— Consumer Incomes in the United States. Washington, D.C., 1938.

—— Family Expenditures in the United States. Washington, D.C., 1941.

Paish, F. W. "The Budget and the White Paper." *London and Cambridge Economic Service's Report on Current Economic Conditions,* May, 1941.

Pigou, A. C. "Types of War Inflation." *Economic Journal,* Dec., 1941.

Singer, H. W. "The German War Economy in the Light of Economic Periodicals." *Economic Journal,* April, 1941 (II); June–Sept., 1941 (III); April, 1942 (V).

Smith, Malcolm L. "Occupations and Salaries in Federal Employment." *Monthly Labor Review,* Jan., 1941.

U.S. Bureau of the Budget. "Revision of Federal Budget Estimates." Press release, Oct. 7, 1942.

U.S. Congress. House of Representatives Ways and Means Committee. Hearings, 1942 Revenue Revision.

U.S. Dept. of Commerce. State and Local Government Debt: 1940. Special Study No. 13, April, 1941.

U.S. Office of Emergency Management. Defense—One Year. Washington, D.C., 1941.

U.S. Treasury Dept. Annual Report of the Secretary of the Treasury, for the Fiscal Year Ended June 30, 1941. Washington, D.C., 1941.

U.S. Treasury Dept. Statistics of Income.

Wells, F. A. "Voluntary Absenteeism in the Cutlery Trade." *Review of Economic Studies,* Summer, 1942.

INDEX

Bei Fragen zur Produktsicherheit wenden Sie sich bitte an:
If you have any questions regarding product safety,
please contact:

Walter de Gruyter GmbH
Genthiner Straße 13
10785 Berlin
productsafety@degruyterbrill.com